A Kyros Collection

The Kyrian Letters
Transformative Messages For Higher Vision

By Sandra J. Radhoff

Heritage Publications

For inquiries, information or placing orders, please call or write:
Heritage Publications
P.O. Box 71
Virginia Beach, VA 23458
804-428-0400

ISBN 1-882545-00-1

Printed in the United States of America

Cover Illustration and Design by Denton Lund

CONTENTS

i

INTRODUCTION

The Kyrian Letters is a collection of channeled writings from an energy called Kyros, received over a span of eight years. Let's discuss the nature and focus of the material, in order to understand it.

Channeling has become widespread in the New Age community, but there are diverse opinions about what channeling is, and about the truth and validity of channeled material. To me, channeling is simply opening myself up and allowing information to flow without attempting to intellectualize or analyze the information. For years, like many others, I believed in separation and contact with separate entities outside of myself. However, recently I had the impacting awareness that there is nothing outside the human channel, only One Mind, Universal Mind, and we all have access to information within that One Mind. For me, there is nothing outside myself—no separate beings or entities. Kyros is not an entity separate from me, but rather an energy, a vibration, a consciousness with which I connect in the process called channeling. I am Kyros; Kyros is me—a higher consciousness of me, whatever me happens to be in its totality. I have concluded that whatever Man is, he is far more than he recognizes himself to be in present consciousness. We all operate on many levels of consciousness simultaneously, even though we express through what I call present consciousness. What occurs during channeling is that we tap into a higher level of consciousness and allow ourselves to bring it through present consciousness.

Channeling is not phenomenal; it is natural. It is something we all do whether we use the term channeling or not. This connection with higher levels of consciousness can be expressed in many ways—speech, writing, art, music, cooking, and everything we do. I am a conscious channel, which means that I am aware at all times of what is happening during the process of receiving information. I am aware when I am channeling simply by the way in which the information flows and by the nature of the information which is transmitted and received.

You may wonder, then: if there is nothing outside the channel, why has the name Kyros been offered? As I said, when I began channeling I believed in separate entities, and Kyros was the name I was given.

Through the channeling of the Kyros consciousness, I learned that names are not really important except to us. Humans have a need to be able to separate, organize and sometimes to personalize. Since I channel other energies, the name Kyros was given to assist me in separating and organizing the information received. It also helped me to feel more personal about that connection. I have learned that the importance lies not in the messenger, but in the message.

The information from the Kyros energy was not originally intended to become a book, at least not on the conscious level. I began channeling the Kyros material in 1982 in a study group called Universalia. Among other activities, the study group involved weekly assignments for members. One of those assignments was to channel during the week and present results to the others at the following meetings. Every week I channeled and presented one or more messages from Kyros.

The Kyrian Letters represents the work I did within Universalia. The writings consist of messages on all aspects of Life. The beautiful messages from Kyros were always first for me, the human channel. They were answers to my questions in times of confusion, unhappiness, anger, and so forth. I quickly discovered from members of the group and from readers of "The Universalian," our bi-monthly newsletter, that the messages helped others, too. Essentially, Kyros' messages are generic.

Kyros offers a very gentle, beautiful, and comforting philosophy of living. The messages offer understanding and hope and provide a higher way of looking at life's situations and experiences. Kyros is never critical, demanding, or commanding. The Kyros material offers a new and a higher perception of life wherein the human is elevated to see the beauty of his own beingness and the truth of his own essence. He is guided into understanding his connection with the All of Creation and his unique and vital part in it. The thread which weaves through the Kyros material is that when we want change, we must begin with our individual selves. Because the material is non-critical and non-judgmental, it can provide a bridge between all systems which separate us—religious, educational and governmental.

As for the truth and validity of the Kyros material, that is up to you, the reader to decide. According to Kyros, everything is truth at some level of awareness. Truth is relative to each human being and is based on level of awareness and perception. Truth changes as an individual grows and unfolds in consciousness. What was truth yesterday may not be so today, but it was still truth yesterday. Kyros insists that when you read or hear something, go within and test it against your own sense of truth. If it doesn't feel right, reject it because it may not be your truth.

The Kyrian Letters was brought forth in written form. Simple and easily understood, it is diverse in subject and covers almost every life situation. The Kyros material is a gentle and loving guide to living a higher life here on Earth and understanding life's experiences from a higher level. The material assists us in learning to love ourselves and others and in removing fears that block us from higher living. Basically, it moves us to see with higher vision. In the Bible Jesus said, "Do not judge by appearances, but judge with right judgment." This is what Kyros seems to say—that nothing we see on our mundane level of experience is what it appears to be, and we are guided, if willing, into a higher Light of seeing and into the understanding that our sole purpose for being here is to learn, to teach and to love.

DEDICATION

This book is dedicated to Bob and Jan Martin, who worked with me on this project for many years and supported and encouraged me with their love. It is also dedicated to the Universalia organization, especially to the original members—the first to be introduced to the Kyros messages. Finally, it is dedicated to the Kyros in each one of us—that higher part of our beingness.

PART I

IS ANYBODY OUT THERE?

The messages in this section discuss the process of channeling, and what to be aware of when reading channeled material, seeking advice from channels, or when learning to channel. The primary message is to learn to be discerning and trust your own inner guidance. No human entity is ever alone—he always has access to the God part of his being. Channeling is simply a form of communication with one's Higher Self, Universal Mind, God, or whatever one chooses to call it. When we feel alone and cry, "Is anybody out there?" it is because we have separated ourselves from that higher connection. When we are connected to Spirit, we become our own best channels and have no need to seek counsel elsewhere.

CHANNELING

Because each entity is individually connected to Universal Mind, channeling is occurring all the time at some level. Universal Thought flows into individualized mind, which is composed of the seven levels of consciousness. It passes through the various veils of consciousness until it reaches the present conscious state. If the individual brain computer and its programming can decipher and interpret the input, it becomes an individualized thought able to be verbalized in a comprehensible way. To the entity, it is perceived as a new and unique idea, and if the entity empowers the idea, he will bring it into manifested form. Individualized God Expression is then the co-creator with Absolute God Essence.

A question occurred regarding the channeled concept, the "infinity game." All that pours forth from Universal Mind is pure and designed for the highest good of All Creation. A Universal Thought, however, loses some of its purity as it moves through the levels of consciousness. In the state of present consciousness it can be totally reversed from its original nature. Remember that Universal Thought is an energy which can never be accurately deciphered and interpreted by the human brain. You must also remember that what is verbalized by the human channel is influenced

1

to a degree by the channel's own programming, his ego, his level of awareness, his ability to interpret, his vernacular, his current belief system, and even by collective consciousness. There is no pure human channeling. Probably the purest thoughts one has are those which cannot be verbalized. You all have many of those. As a human channel grows and expands in awareness and as he becomes more consciously aligned to Universal Mind, the channeling is less influenced by those things mentioned earlier.

What I want you to understand is that that which is termed channeling is not a unique phenomenon. Everyone channels whether they call it that or not. So when someone says "this or that was channeled," it does not necessarily mean that it is to be your truth. All you have on planet Earth is relative truth, and what is truth for one may not be so for another. You must test all input from your external world against your own sense of truth. This is why there is division over that which is called the infinity game. Some view it as good, others as non-good. It lost its purity as it came into collective consciousness, and once an idea ceases to focus on serving the highest good of All Creation, division naturally follows. If all those involved were entities of high integrity and were selfless, the present problems would not have been encountered. You must remember that upon the human plane the levels of awareness among entities are myriad in nature and number. This so called game became impregnated by much negative energy of your man-made laws. Many who became involved were having financial difficulties in their lives. Fear within their particular circumstances was the driving force to enter the game. When fear rather than faith and love is the motivator, a positive outcome is not assured. All will learn from this lesson, and the greatest lesson they will learn is that they have not yet reached the understanding of what abundance consciousness really is.

Another aspect of channeling I wish to address has to do with the dependence that so many entities have on human channels. A good channel is one who attempts to guide others into the awareness of their own abilities to connect with their own higher guidance. But many entities move from channel to channel like groupies following rock stars. Ramtha, Lazaris, Mafu, and the others have all offered great wisdom and knowledge from which to glean, but the human entity should still learn to test another's truth against his own and to become connected to his own higher guidance. Some entities depend on channels to tell them what to do in their lives or to tell them what will happen in the future. Some channels do have the awareness to give you the answers, and sometimes they predict a future with great accuracy. Most, however, are adept at reading probabilities based on an awareness of a present state of consciousness. No one can, with great accuracy, tell you what lies ahead because the future is not set. And no one can tell you what is going to happen to you with any degree of certainty because you are ever changing, and with a mere shift of consciousness you can alter your life course. Psychics have a great awareness of human patterns, and they predict probabilities based on present consciousness. Each one of you can do this for yourselves by simply becoming aware and attuned to your own present consciousness. Some psychics and readers are also able to inject ideas into an open, nondiscerning mind. If a psychic tells you something and you believe it, you can empower it, bring it into manifested form, and thus prove the psychic correct. But it was you who created the reality; it was not a reality which was pre-set.

With channels, I would advise gleaning the wisdom and knowledge you can from them, testing it against your own sense of truth, and learning to trust your own higher guidance. Your higher guidance is uniquely for you, and it is the only guidance you should trust completely. You have all your own answers. Even though your answers may help others, they are still yours. Do not be awed by the channeling abilities of others and blindly follow, for this is how cults are born and where you surrender your own power. Most of all be discerning, for therein is the path to wisdom.

CHANNELS SHOULD RELEASE
FROM EXPECTATIONS

I wish to address the confusion which one entity had regarding not being able to feel the love of Sananda as she could feel the love of Jesus. In developing and unfolding as channels, it is wise to learn to move beyond feelings. Physical feelings are ego-based and are untrustworthy. Feelings must be replaced by inner knowing. For example, it is preferable to move to a point of knowing Sananda's love rather than feeling Sananda's love. Too many potentially good channels become blocked by their own expectations of having to feel something. The best channels have moved beyond the need for physical phenomena, into the realm of knowing. Expectations and preconceived ideas of what you think you should experience can block the flow from higher dimensions as well as create doubt and confusion. A good channel will simply open his or her mind and allow the information to flow without expectations and without setting conditions.

It is also advantageous to a channel's development if he seeks to release himself from his definitions of what God is or is not, for this limits

3

and restricts the infinite nature of God and all His expressions. This is oftentimes difficult for channels who have had a strong religious background. They have been programmed to believe God does this or that, God thinks this or that, God feels this way or that. The ways and nature of the Creator are as diverse as the atoms in the Cosmos. It was written that if one sees God and conceives something in his mind, then he is not seeing God but one of God's effects. It is best not to attempt to form images of the imageless.

You already know of the things which influence a channel and prevent total accuracy, such things as an inability to translate universal symbols into human symbols, prior programming, belief system, and so forth. You cannot change all of the things which have an influence on you, but there are things a channel can do to become clearer and more accurate. Aside from releasing yourself from learned definitions about the nature of the Creator, one should also release and refrain from assigning personalities and qualities to the entities and energies he channels. If an entity wishes to express personality aspects or qualities, he will do so. But do not assign qualities or personalities to higher entities, for in doing this you will create illusions and block the information. I am a good example. I have not offered you personality or quality distinctions (although some of you have assigned me the quality of being long-winded), and I have never been assigned an image. I have offered you a name for your own need to be able to separate the energies and entities that you channel, and I have explained my mission within your particular life experience—to be your master guide. Beyond that nothing else is needed. You do not feel my presence—you know my presence. And you have an understanding of the vibrational connection.

I would like to conclude by saying that if a human entity channels Jesus, he may be channeling from the astral plane or he may be channeling Sananda or Christ and labeling the energy Jesus. One can discern who is being channeled by the nature of the information given. Sananda is the spiritual energy of the man known as Jesus. At the Baptism of the man Jesus, the Christ energy and consciousness entered and completed the earthly mission.

Remember that if you base your channeling on what you feel, there is a chance of greater inaccuracy. Knowing, as opposed to feeling, insures greater accuracy. Those who are lightworkers need never fear that they will channel lower realms if they believe them to exist. Trusting leads to knowing, and knowing leads to clear guidance and information.

THE IMPORTANCE OF INTEGRITY
IN CHANNELING

Many times when human entities enter into periods of confusion, indecision, frustration, and so forth, they feel they need or want answers. Those conditions oftentimes block them from receiving answers from their own guidance centers. They will seek answers or take counsel from another human channel. This message is directed to those who seek answers from human channels because of a blockage or because of a lack of confidence in their own guidance. It is also directed to those who channel to others, and it concerns integrity.

When you seek another for answers to your questions, you must always remember that for each question asked there are many answers available. Each human channel vibrates upon a particular level of awareness and will bring forth answers from energies corresponding to that level of awareness. This is one reason why answers will vary from channel to channel. The receiver of the answers must always test the answer against his own inner guidance. Many do not do this and blindly accept anything. It does not mean that answers given to you are false; it means that answers may not be the best ones for you at your particular level of awareness.

On your human plane there are two primary types of channels: Alpha and Theta. Alpha channels give more specific details but can oftentimes be inaccurate because they channel primarily from the astral plane. Those who channel from the astral plane or the Alpha level are also more prone to bring forth a lot of their own intellect, ego, and Earth programming into their channeling. An Alpha channel will oftentimes give you dates, places, and a lot of specific commands as to how to live your life. This can sometimes prove in error in your physical world. Theta channels communicate with dimensions far beyond the astral plane, and because there is less interest in time and space, do not offer a lot of specific personal detail. A Theta channel can channel at the Alpha level, but an Alpha channel will seldom channel at the Theta level. Theta channels really prefer to channel at the upper dimensional levels as opposed to the astral level.

You can tell the difference between Theta and Alpha channeling by the information given. If a channel tells you that you will die in six months or that you are going to go to Egypt in November or that your planet will be hit by a comet on a particular day, or if the information *commands* you to do something, this is Alpha channeling. A Theta channel offers answers from dimensions which allow the receiver to choose whether to accept or reject the answers. Sometimes answers coming through a Theta channel are frustrating if you want specifics. Theta answers force you to think and test the answers against your own guidance, and you will manifest your own answers based on your own level of awareness. Theta information offers you a wide range of answers from which to choose and thus to manifest, whereas Alpha information offers you specific answers. Theta information really appears more cosmic and generic than Alpha information, but it is the information which encourages the greater unfoldment of your being.

Those who channel may be asked to assist another who is blocked. If you, the channel, are too close to the situation and have already formed a lot of intellectual opinions, it is probably best not to channel unless you are adept at separating yourself from your opinions. A good channel must work very hard to separate from his intellectual, emotional, moral, ethical, and religious programming when in the process of channeling. One must be as open as possible to incoming information so that it is not laced with personal beliefs. A good channel must always realize that his own truth may not be appropriate for another entity. In one sense a channel has a lot of power, but he must not abuse or misuse this power. It can be dangerous if it is abused and is used to direct entities who do not test the information for themselves. There are many entities who are vulnerable and believe that what issues forth from a human channel is Absolute Truth. If a channel renders information from his own programming and sense of truth, this can be dangerous. If it is deliberately and knowingly done, this is a misuse of power.

Channels should present their information with integrity and never misuse their power. Seekers should be taught that truth is relative, no matter what energy it is coming from. They should be taught that human channels are imperfect, impaired by Earth programming, and that universal symbols cannot be accurately translated and interpreted by the human brain. They should be taught that they can inwardly challenge and dismiss any truth which does not align with their own level of truth. The whole purpose in learning to channel is to achieve a greater freedom to connect with one's own guidance and to learn to trust it.

From our point of view, we offer you information which you are free to accept or reject. We offer guidance and direction on how to walk your paths with greater comfort, ease, joy, and courage. We try to create the awareness that you are far more than you realize. We try to comfort and sustain you in periods of blockage, but we will not command you to do anything. You always have free choice in what you accept or reject as your truth.

6

DISCREPANCIES AMONG
HUMAN CHANNELS

There seems to be a problem with some regarding perceived discrepancies between various channels of higher knowledge. I will do my best to try to explain why this occurs as well as why you should not be troubled by discrepancies.

First, consider the human channel, an entity with an organic brain computer which is continually processing not only external data from your third dimensional world, but also internal data coming in from the seven inner levels of consciousness. Everything external and internal is processed and stored. The human channel also stores in his total mind all data gathered from all his expressions on the planet and elsewhere plus all the lessons and influences gathered in his present expression. Due to training in his present expression, he interprets all information within the framework of his own vernacular and understanding. The human channel is also influenced to a degree by the vibrations and thoughts contained within the mass consciousness of planet Earth, as well as the vibrations of Cosmic consciousness. It is, I believe, beyond your comprehension to understand the intricate and complex work going on, not only within your brain computers, but your minds as well. Information being channeled from higher dimensions is given in the form of universal symbols which is then translated and interpreted by the brain, and in this process, purity and total accuracy are lost.

Then consider the concept of truth. In a physical dimension you do not have Absolute Truth. You have fragments of Absolute Truth, called relative truth. Now when you perceive discrepancies among human channels, it does not mean that one is sharing truth and the others are sharing non-truths. It means they are sharing truth or information from different levels of growth and awareness.

Do not judge who is right and who is wrong, for this creates problems for you. What I would advise when varied information is shared with you is to study all the information given and then seek your own inner guidance as to what information is true for you. Your own inner guidance will not fail you in leading you on the pathway of your own truth for your unique level of understanding and awareness. Remember that levels of growth and awareness are ascending and dynamic, not static. When perceived discrepancies occur, go within and accept whatever information is more aligned with your own level of awareness and understanding, knowing that as you grow, this also might change.

7

Do not be perplexed and upset by perceived discrepancies. Accept what you are led to accept, disregard what you are not guided to believe, and trust in your own inner guidance on your path of unfoldment and enlightenment. Don't allow yourselves to be blocked by perceived discrepancies, for this is a waste of energy which could be better spent in going within and seeking the truth of your own unique and individual beingness and becoming.

WHY DO ENTITIES COMMUNICATE DIFFERENTLY TO VARIED CHANNELS?

The reason that there is a seeming difference and sometimes a discrepancy between the information emerging from a singular spiritual or ET entity to varied human channels has to do primarily with four things: (1) the human channel's brain computer, (2) the level of awareness of the human channel, (3) the amount of intellectual and ego input by the human channel, and (4) the type of artificial Earth programming the human channel has received throughout his present life experience. Let us take these four areas one by one.

1. Each human channel has an individual and unique brain which receives, processes, analyzes, interprets, and transmits uniquely. As Universal symbols are received from higher dimensions and translated into symbols comprehensible to the channel, some purity of the message is lost.
2. Information from higher dimensions is transmitted relative to the channel's level of awareness.
3. Information transmitted from higher dimensions is less pure because of the intellectual and ego input of the human channel. Rarely, if ever, is information received from higher dimensions in pure form. Of the two—ego and intellect—the intellect input has less effect on the purity of the information being transmitted. The best channels are more mental, because they tend to have greater sensitivity and awareness to all of Creation. Ego input emerges from human emotions and survival programming and has a greater effect on the purity of the transmitted information. If a human channel is experiencing emotional stress, it is better for the channel to try to become clear before attempting to receive and interpret Universal symbols. The more a channel is able to detach from intellectual and ego input, the purer the channeling will be.
4. The type of Earth programming a human channel has received determines what kind of information he will be given, namely the

8

education he has received, his patterns of thought and logic, his openness, and his belief system. All transmissions from higher dimensions are Universal symbols. They are not transmitted in King James English, modern English, or any of your Earth's language symbols. When a human channel allows the spirit or his guide to direct the translation of Universal symbols, the guide will always try to align the Universal symbol as closely as is possible to your Earth symbol in order to bring about as clear a comprehension as is possible. Some ET entities have learned your Earth's many language symbols and can transmit directly.

Channeling is a one-to-one connection between an energy of a higher dimension and the human channel. A channel does not receive purely nor does he translate and interpret perfectly, but a channel does not have to defend what he has received or attempt to prove its authenticity in any way. A channel is an open vessel receiving the flow of information. In the sharing of it he should never have as his concern whether others believe or do not believe. Each entity will accept the truth which is best aligned to his own level of awareness.

WHY DOES THERE SEEM TO BE A SEPARATION BETWEEN UNIVERSAL MIND AND OTHER ENTITIES THAT ARE CHANNELED?

The primary reason there appears to be a separateness between the entities you channel and Universal Mind is simply because your individual mind creates the condition. Universal Mind contains Total Knowledge and Absolute Truth. It is Creative Energy and Complete Intelligence and Knowing in Motion. It is energy, it is vibration—the highest vibration. As it moves forth from its core or center, its vibration slows and connects with other aspects of Creation. When a vibration moving outward from Universal Mind slows to the point where a vibrational connection can be made with an aspect of creation, the aspect receives knowledge from Universal Mind on the level where the perception of the knowledge can be comprehended and understood by the individual aspect. This is how knowledge is transmitted through the dimensions and planes of life. Your guides and spirit teachers vibrate higher than you do in your conscious state, so that their vibrational contact with the Universal mind creates knowledge that is purer.

It is rare that a human can connect directly with Universal Mind. Usually what occurs is that a human entity will raise his vibrations to connect with a spiritual entity of similar vibrations so that the knowledge can be transmitted in a relay fashion. With the exception of your guides and Masters, entities of higher vibrational patterns will not lower their vibrations to meet yours. You must raise yours to connect with them. The higher you are able to raise your vibrational energy and your level of awareness, the purer the knowledge will be in your channeling and the more diversified your contacts will be.

All knowledge is transmitted from Universal Mind, but it comes from many levels. Remember that your upper four levels of consciousness receive purer knowledge than your lower three. In fact, your omni-conscious level is always in direct alignment to Universal Mind. As a human, however, you are primarily concerned with what you receive in your conscious state.

PART II

DOES ANYBODY LOVE ME?

Relationships with other humans and even with other life forms provide us with our greatest lessons. Every relationship, whether it brings us joy or sorrow, teaches us about others and, more importantly, about ourselves. Each relationship in our life assists in our learning and encourages our growth and unfoldment. Love is a word with many definitions and many expressions within our relationships. Kyros speaks of relationships, on loving and being loved, on maintaining relationships, and on why relationships must sometimes end.

SPIRIT GUIDES AND TEACHERS
ARE GARDENERS

With respect to those who are termed spirit guides and teachers, it is important to remember that nothing is beyond your own being. By this I mean that nothing is, in truth, external to yourself. It appears this way only because human entities have a tendency to separate and fragment Life. As a subject in your world, you perceive everything you observe as external to that subject called *you*. When you perceive things external to yourself, you are separate from them; you are not in oneness with that which you perceive. Externalizing beyond your own being is how you create your illusions. One of the lessons upon your journey is to understand your Oneness with All that Is. Yet, the path seems to go through illusionary separation.

Nothing is outside of the subject or the perceiver. I, Kyros, am not a spiritual energy existing in a space or a time external to you. This truth is difficult to explain to entities who live in a space/time dimension of form and who create illusionary realities of separateness. You see, all there really is is the One Mind, Life Force, God, or whatever you choose to call it. Let's use a simple example—a balloon. If you blow up a balloon, that which is in the balloon is the same as that which is outside of it. That sameness is separated by the balloon itself. Release the air from the balloon and that which was within becomes one with that which was outside of the separation line of the balloon. During communication or in channeling, the separation line dissolves and oneness occurs. That which you term individualized mind is the One Mind when the subjective line of separation is dissolved. There are seven levels of consciousness in mind, and the human entity is operating on all of them including Omniconsciousness. Omniconsciousness *is* the One Mind and *cannot* be individualized.

That which you term your mind is the One Mind and recognizes no separation. However, present consciousness within your mind does recognize and create the illusion of separation, within a space/time dimension, which is also illusion. This creates the appearance of higher guidance coming from some place beyond you, which you fragment, separate, and compartmentalize into those who you call spirit guides and teachers.

No human entity is ever without guidance or direction on his walk. You may say the direction is coming from God, Kyros, intuition or a gut feeling. It is all true, for regardless of who you give credit to, it is still issuing from your own oneness with Universal Intelligence or Cosmic Consciousness. For the human, the choice is always whether to follow the guidance or not. Other beings of Nature tend to be more attuned to Oneness and thus are more obedient to inner direction. Do not think that something as natural as a tree upon your planet receives no inner direction.

Let's make things more simple and begin to follow the human entity's belief that spirit guides and teachers are separate from you, for it's really alright to believe this also. When you exit third dimensional life, you will understand what I have tried to explain about One Mind and Oneness with All, and you will understand that separation was your vehicle for expressing on planet Earth, as well as the ego programming of your brain computer. You will come to understand that what you really are is spiritual energy with Absolute Consciousness.

Why are we part of a human entity's life? Our purpose is not to protect the material form except in the very highest sense of the word, because the survival programming of the ego has been magnificently created for the maintenance and protection of the physical vehicle. Part of our purpose is to create the awareness that you have reached the evolutionary point where you don't need to rely so heavily on survival programming. This involves teaching you higher truths so that you will change your own programming. A change in programming results in a shift in individual consciousness which feeds into the collective consciousness. In time this will produce a higher order of life upon planet Earth. Collective consciousness will not shift until individual consciousness has shifted, and so the work must be done first with the individual. This is why I always say that everything begins with *you*, the individualized God expression. All human entities receive guidance or direction whether they are aware of it or not. The greater one's awareness level is, the easier expansion of awareness becomes. Our purpose is to guide those who are willing through the process of soul evolution which is essentially movement into higher consciousness. I do not use the term spiritual evolution because the spirit and the soul are not the same and because the spirit is already in a state of perfection.

Part of our work is to assist you in making your Earth journey happier and more fulfilling, which is how it really should be. When you release from old programming and see things with expanded awareness, your consciousness shifts and you begin to think differently. As you know, empowered thoughts are what you bring into your manifested illusionary reality. In your movement through the process toward higher awareness, your thoughts are aligned to your awareness level, and your outer world of reality reflects what you are. Therefore, the more highly aware you become and the more attuned you are to higher guidance, the higher your thoughts will be. And the more aligned you are to Universal Mind, the greater will be your ability to empower these thoughts with the greatest power: Love. This then fills your journey with joy, thus making your particular mission much easier to achieve. If your inner world is rich in joy, this will be reflected in your self-created outer world.

Essentially our work involves teaching you higher truths. We offer a lot of knowledge, and some of it oftentimes seems a bit mundane. Knowledge is given only to be converted into wisdom. Wisdom is knowledge used for the highest good, and without wisdom knowledge is of little value. What matters is not what you know, but rather how you utilize what you know on your journey.

In closing, then, our primary purpose is simply to assist you in your unfoldment. Those whom you term spirit guides and teachers are like gardeners carefully tending to beautiful, growing flowers. They are weeding, fertilizing, providing light and warmth, removing dead petals and leaves—all for the purpose of allowing those flowers to unfold to their greatest potential and beauty in Earth's garden of Life.

MAN'S DOMINION HAS CREATED IMBALANCE

"Then God said, 'Let the water teem with an abundance of living creatures and on the earth let birds fly beneath the dome of the sky.' And so it happened ... God saw how good it was and God blessed them, saying, 'Be fertile and multiply, and fill the water of the seas; and let the birds multiply on earth.'

"Then God said, 'Let the earth bring forth all kinds of living creatures: cattle, creeping things, and wild animals, all kinds of cattle, and all kinds of creeping things of the earth.' God saw how good it was. Then God said, 'Let us make man in our image, after our likeness. Let them have dominion over the fish of the sea, the birds of the air, and the cattle, and over the wild animals and all the creatures that crawl on the ground.'"

Once upon a time a long time ago Man was given sovereign authority over the creatures of the air, land, and water. This authority conferred on mankind brought with it great responsibility.

In the beginning, perhaps, Man worried less about his responsibility because he had to focus upon his own survival. There was probably a bit more equality between Man and animals then because Man had not yet developed weapons against which no animal could compete. There was a time when Man took only what he needed from the animals for his own survival and Man was both prey and predator. Perhaps it was the prey/predator nature of Man which kept nature in balance. As time passed Man became smarter but not necessarily wiser. He developed weaponry which gave him a superior advantage over the animals, and he became primarily a predator. With this new sophistication came greed and the desire for wealth. The great slaughter began and is still continuing on your planet.

Man kills for more than his needs. He kills for money, and this blood money provides man with leopard and ermine coats; polar bear rugs for his den; ivory for his pianos; alligator hides for his shoes; and so on. The big game hunter is able to sit calmly while hundreds of glass eyes stare blankly at him from the mounted heads of animals he has killed. In this he often takes pride. Man found no wrong in wiping out the great buffalo herds to near extinction. Why should he? Didn't God give him dominion over the animals?

Nature has become unbalanced to the point that some species became overpopulated and were forced to starve to death because of food shortages. He killed the hawks to protect his chickens and the wolves to protect his sheep, never realizing that these predators kept certain species in balance. He killed snakes of all kinds, never realizing that they controlled the rodent population. With his newfound sophistication, he built factories and great cities and polluted the air and the waters. He

14

leveled mountains and tore down forests, pushing the animals farther and farther back, limiting their space for survival. Where do animals go when they have no place or space to go? This is what Man has done with his sovereign authority, his dominion over the animals. Even with your domesticated animals, there is abuse and cruelty. Even these pets are not kept in control, since there are thousands of dogs and cats who end up being put to death yearly because no one wants them.

Man needs to begin viewing animals as dissimilar life forms which contain a spirit and a God essence. He needs to see them as God expressing through various forms, created in the same way as himself. He needs to see himself in the role of caretaker and guardian of his world. He needs to begin to understand that animals are at his mercy and that they rely on him to provide them with a space to live with clean air and water. He needs to begin to understand the nature of dissimilar life forms and their roles in maintaining the delicate balance within nature. He needs to start striving toward restoring the balance. He needs to realize that everything created has a right to live. Most of all, he needs to start respecting the animals as God-created life forms and begin loving them as his brothers. Remember that what you do for the animals of your planet, you also do for yourselves. Man, too, is a part of the Animal Kingdom.

THE ANIMAL KINGDOM

Within the framework of Earth's scientific classification, Man or Homo sapiens is a member of the Animal Kingdom. Members of the Earth include Insects, Fish, Birds, Reptiles, Amphibians, and Mammals. Man, a mammal, considers himself to be the highest life form within the Animal Kingdom with all other forms subject unto him. Although dolphins and whales are, as a group, of a higher vibration than Man, Man retains his position as the highest life form on Earth primarily because his spirit works with and through his intelligence on a conscious level. Because of the evolution of his brain, Man thinks and uses logic in solving problems and is aided by other levels of consciousness. Other animal life forms rely primarily on their pre-consciousness or instinctual level for survival on the third dimension. The brain computers of whales and dolphins are more complex than Man's and are, as a group, more in tune with the Cosmic Mind, and thus the vibrations of this group are higher than any found on your planet within a single group.

Man and what you term lower animal forms all contain a spirit within and are guided either consciously or unconsciously by the spirit. All were created by the Source and therefore are expressions of the Source. And all, regardless of their present level, are on a progressive journey, toward oneness and mergence with the Creator. With the exception of some alien transplants, all are going through physical evolution.

Each individual animal is an aspect of his group oversoul or singular spirit. He enters various dimensions to grow and progress, to learn and teach, just as Man does. When an animal dies, his spirit enters the fourth dimension, just as yours does. Because there is greater innocence among lower animal forms because of the reliability on instinct with no intellectual knowledge, they enter the fourth dimension with higher vibrations. They then journey to higher vibrational dimensions. Therefore, it is true that there are planets where the animal and plant forms are higher than Man on Earth.

The primary purpose of lower life forms has been to serve Man. Animals have fed you, clothed you, and labored for you. Animals have also served one another in providing a balance within your world. Unfortunately, it has been Man who has undone the natural balance. Intelligence is not always a good thing if it is not wedded in harmony with wisdom.

If you become attuned to your animal brothers, they can show you the baser qualities within yourselves which you, hopefully, have subjected in your evolved natures. They can show you the instinctual nature which still resides within your pre-consciousness. Most of mankind should have transcended beyond animal instinct. When Man negatively resorts to animalistic behavior, he incurs Karma, whereas an animal does not. This has to do with innocence.

Animals are more in harmony with nature than is Man. This is because of the acuteness of their physical senses, and also because they have not surrendered their sixth psychic sense or cosmic sense. Man, as a whole, has this sense, but generally lets it lie dormant. Because of the evolution of the brain, Man relies more on his ability to rationalize than he does on increasing his intuitional or psychic abilities. Because they have no egos, animals can more easily accept life as it comes to them. They do not concern themselves with whether they are pretty or rich or smart. They simply are. They concern themselves with survival, and on some higher level they strive to fulfill their purpose. They do not concern themselves with aging or death. They simply live.

The greatest thing Man can teach animals is love, for most animals are responsive to this vibration. In fact, love is really as inherent in lower animal forms as it is in Man and all of Creation. Man has been responsible for creating vibrations of aggression and fear in lower animal forms and for continuing to maintain them on your planet. If you can teach an animal to love, your loving can assist him on his journey, as well as adding to your own progression and growth.

Animals enter your lives just as people do—to teach and to be taught. They exit from your life experience when their mission is fulfilled. They are manifestations of God expressing, just as people are. If you hurt or kill an animal brother, never do so with aggression, joy, or hate in your heart, for this incurs Karma. If you hunt or fish to provide food for your table, bless the spirit of that which you have killed, for he has served you. Yes, Man was given dominion over the animals, but let your dominion be of love and not of greed and a lack of respect for other life forms. Learn to be wise and careful guardians of your planet and of those forms which live upon it.

THE PURPOSE OF PETS

The most wondrous lesson a human entity can learn from a pet is unconditional love, and this is particularly true of dogs. If you are blessed with the gift of this particular life form, you are aware of how he always accepts you no matter how you act or how you look. There is within his nature a loyalty that is seldom surpassed by any other life form, including Man. Other lessons you can learn from this particular life form are the qualities of patience and trust. Even though I have singled out this special life form, all life forms have these qualities within them. The human entity must remember that lower forms are influenced to a degree by the collective consciousness of your planet. Not all human entities should be allowed to care for pets. Some simply have not evolved highly enough in consciousness or wisdom to take care of dissimilar life forms properly. Thus, many pets are abused and mistreated, and great Karma is incurred.

Pets are like any other relationship you may have. Entities should be caretakers and guardians of dissimilar life forms if they truly understand that all creations are God expressing and that all Creation is connected and woven in Oneness. Thus, one who mistreats an animal does so not only to God, but to himself as well. There truly is no separation.

Animals have as much right to live upon your planet as you do. Before accepting guardianship of a pet, I would advise the entity to think about his own nature and his attitude toward dissimilar life forms. If you feel that you are superior to all other life forms and if you feel that dissimilar life forms are of little value, then it truly is best for you and the life form that you do not become a pet owner. If you discover that you are aggressive and hostile within your human relationships, it is probable that this same pattern will exist in a relationship with another life form. If you discover that you have neither time nor energy to offer the pet, I would advise against assuming any responsibility within this special relationship.

If you are loving and respectful and wise and you choose to assume the responsibility of caring for a dissimilar life form, you will benefit in so many ways, and your life will be enriched through your learning and loving together. As I said, you will learn great lessons on a level which transcends verbal communication, and you will both be vibrationally lifted. Most of all, that which you offer the pet will be returned to you in many ways. This special connection between you and another form can bring you joy, delight, and a wondrous understanding of love. Oftentimes a pet can be your greatest teacher in your life walk.

YOUR CHILDREN ARE NOT YOURS

Your wise Earth entity, Kahlil Gibran, wrote: "Your children are not your children. They are the sons and daughters of Life's longing for itself." This is a great and simple truth if one but listens and hears it in the stillness of his heart.

Human entities sometimes attempt to possess one another or feel that others belong to them or that they belong to another. No one belongs to anyone. We all belong to the One Life. When you say "these are 'my' children," the words should declare only that you have been the physical vehicle which allowed their passage onto the Earth plane (birth) and that they share the same physical bloodline and carry the same physical genes inherent within a particular Earth family lineage. In truth, regardless of how a child comes to you, whether by birth, adoption, or other ways, it really involves a higher spiritual agreement whereby you have been chosen and have agreed to become the guardian, way shower, and protector of a developing human vehicle for a period of time. Although the child will receive programming from others in his external world, it is the parent who is the initial and primary programmer. Because the child is a spiritual entity, you can never, in truth, own or possess that child, just as you can never be possessed by another, except as you allow it. Although the ego of another can be placed in servitude, suppressed under the domination of another, and broken, the spirit is ever free and cannot be possessed.

The parent is never solely responsible for the programming a child receives. Like you, he receives programming from the culture or society in which he is raised, from all those entities who share his life, from

18

religious institutions and educational systems, from the collective mind, and from his own inner guidance system.

There is much emphasis at present on the term "dysfunctional family." The truth is that there is probably some dysfunction in all family units. The whole point of becoming aware of dysfunction is to be able to transform the results of it in your own life. The purpose of the awareness is not to lay blame on others or make excuses for yourself. It is a tool to be used for change and transformation. It is important to realize that all Earth entities are in a process of learning, growing, unfolding, and becoming. This does not stop when one becomes a parent. The process continues and the parent and the child experience it together. Parents are usually young in Earth years and are at varying stages of maturation and levels of awareness. With first children in particular, parents oftentimes don't know much more about being a parent than the child knows about being a child. You enter the experience together and learn and teach each other. Things always become easier through experience so that by the time other children arrive, you have accumulated more knowledge about parenting. One's initial parenting knowledge comes primarily from how one was raised by his own parents.

The responsibility of raising children is great, and it is one of the most important Earth roles one will have if taken seriously. When you become a parent you essentially become the Earth guide for another human entity for a period of time, and for that period of time you become the model in the child's world. Doing this well requires great love, patience, discipline, and sometimes seeming sacrifice. I might add that a sense of humor is very helpful in this shared experience. It's a beautiful and wonderful and fulfilling experience if you, with higher vision, see and understand that what you are doing is preparing the way for another spiritual entity to express the best of himself on his Earth walk.

Your relationship with your children will be better and more fulfilling if you can see them as spiritual entities expressing through a physical vehicle for their own unique mission. At higher levels, they are your spiritual equals, and you are joined in that oneness. As parents you relate better if you accept their uniqueness of expression. You will relate better if you will guide rather than control.

If you have loved and have done the best that you were able according to your own level of wisdom and awareness, they will always hold you in their hearts. The mother robin feeds her young and teaches them to fly and then releases them to the sky. Feel joy when your children have wings strong enough to fly. Know that in their minds and hearts they carry you forward into the future. Another truth was given you from the wise Gibran about your children: "They come through you but not from you, and though they are with you yet they belong not to you." You will never be separated if you know that we are All One.

DEEP RELATIONSHIPS

Relationships are extremely important because they provide the conditions for one's greatest learning. Relating always involves a communication on some level of consciousness. One is contained within this process at all times whether he is aware of it or not, and it is not necessary that verbalization occur.

A relationship with another is really an exchange of communication. How deep the relationship is actually determines the amount of feedback and the kind of insights which are shared. Relationships are important to your learning because they provide you with the opportunity to see both yourself and life from the perspective of another. Granted, another's perspective may be just as limited as your own at times, but it can be a way to glean more knowledge about yourself and your world.

Relationships can be compared to a cake. Some relationships are like the frosting: they never go beneath the surface level to the cake itself. You experience only what is shown to the external world, and you never know what lies beneath the frosting. In others you slice down into the cake itself, deeper and deeper, and experience the inner world beneath the outer frosting level. The deeper you go, the more knowledge and insights you gain about yourself and the other person.

Although some relationships are definitely Karmic-based, most deeper relationships occur for the purpose of learning and teaching. In deep level relationships, it is not accidental when two entities come together. At higher levels it has been agreed and conditions are set up to bring the human entities together to do their work. When the work is finished, the entities oftentimes drift apart. Thus some relationships last an entire life walk, while others are more brief. Time is really of no consequence; what is learned and taught is where the value lies. This is where individual growth and unfoldment occur.

Cultivate and nurture deep relationships, but release from them when their time has passed. No matter how many relationships one has, it is still a solo flight and essentially a solitary walk. Relationships are simply another tool to be utilized in the process of growth and unfoldment.

Many humans do not allow others to cut beneath their frosting or surface level. Out of fear they will not risk being vulnerable. It is always true that when you allow your deeper feelings and thoughts to be

20

expressed, you move into a space of seeming vulnerability. I say seeming because, in truth, you are never vulnerable. This is an illusion produced by an ego born of fear. If there is a fear of vulnerability, it simply indicates that you are unsure of your own power and that you really have no trust in your own God expression. When you will not allow yourself to go beneath the surface level of another, it really means that you fear the unknown God which expresses through the other.

The true seeker will always opt for deeper relationships because he knows that this is where his greatest learning can occur. And he will encourage others to go deeper. Oftentimes a human entity will actually block another from exposing his inner depths out of fear. He is afraid of knowing what the other thinks or feels because it might threaten to unmask him in some way or expose to him that what he presents to the external world might not be what he really is.

Each has many surface relationships in his walk. This is alright, for in many of these encounters there is no real need to go any deeper. However, when the potential for a deeper level relationship exists and it continues to remain on the surface because of one person's fear, the relationship will most probably end because it will produce no growth or unfoldment. A true seeker sees his purpose as that of continuing to grow and unfold, and he will always search out those conditions, people, and experiences which will enable him to do this. One who lives on the surface blocks not only his own growth but also the growth of those he relates to. He is neither student nor teacher, and out of fear he does not take the inner journey into self.

LOVE IS A KNOWING IN YOUR SOUL

All love and its expressions are fragments of unconditional love. In other words, all love has within it elements of the purest love of all, the God-love, the unconditional love. So all love is of value and holds the potential of leading one into unconditional love. If you can truly love another, you hold the potential of loving all.

In your world there are many entities who desperately seek to fall in love. Many are lonely and are seeking primarily a feeling. When one falls in love, there is a wonderful excitement, a magical appeal, a heightened sensuality, and a desire to physically express the feelings of love. There is no wrong in this as long as one realizes that if this love fails to deepen and become more substantial, then the love relationship will most likely end. It must move into a higher love if it is to continue.

21

Many entities fall in and out of love frequently, and this oftentimes occurs because there is a type of addiction to that feeling. Once the feeling passes, they go in search of it once again. They tend to seek the thrill of new love and new physical experiences. But in their hearts, they continue to be lonely seekers for something which seems as elusive as a butterfly in springtime's sun.

One should not seek love. One wise Earth entity said that you should concentrate on being love givers rather than love seekers. How much happier you would be if you could understand that if you focus on offering love without thought of receiving, love will come to you and embrace your life in ways you have not dreamed of. A butterfly will not land upon a person in motion, but if you sit quietly, it will come to you and softly sit upon your hand. If you've ever experienced this in your life, you can recall the joy of having something so fragile and so beautiful come to you and softly, without fear, rest upon your hand. Yet if you try to capture the butterfly, it will fly from you. If you do capture it and try to contain it, it will die. Often entities spend their lives chasing the butterflies of love, never realizing that all they have to do is remain still. They chase the dream and it continues to be elusive and they never truly find that which they seem to seek.

Many who are more focused upon the physical and emotional expressions of love have a tendency to try to direct or control the course of the relationship, usually through expectations and demands. This only brings about the dissolution of love. Remember that the capture of the butterfly means death. To express, a butterfly must be ever free. Perhaps your Earth entity, Kahlil Gibran, said it best: "And think not you can direct the course of love, for love, if it finds you worthy, directs your course."

Another problem which love-seeking entities seem to have is that of failing to see love when it is present. Focused too intently upon the chase or a particular feeling, an entity may be blind to a butterfly which may be fluttering nearby. Sometimes one is so busy looking outward for something else that he fails to see the gift which may have been placed before him. Or if he does notice the gift, he may decide he doesn't like the wrappings and ribbon and, hence, never takes the time to open the gift to see what wonders might be contained within. How many gifts in your life remain unopened? How many butterflies have you been blind to?

Many seek the elusive ideal person. They seldom, if ever, find this. This is because the ideal changes as an entity grows, so that what was envisioned as ideal yesterday, is no longer so today. All entities have a mind image of what they think the ideal would be for them. To have it, you'd have to construct a robot because human entities are changing, flowing, and multi-faceted. Your ideal cannot remain unchanged.

So, in loving, what should you seek? Seek only to give your own love and its expressions. You are worthy of love only if you are open to receive it and allow it to come gently to you in whatever form it chooses. And it does come, like sunshine warming you, like a soft breeze on your brow, like the touch of a butterfly. Your beloved, if that is what you yearn for, will come to you, but you must be wise enough to know when the beloved is standing before you offering the gifts which can give you peace and wholeness. Yes, love on your plane is a feeling, but it is also a knowing. If you are a love-seeker, you will not know the real from the transitory. In your relationships, do not be too quick to judge them and place limitations upon them if they do not measure up to your present ideal. Allow things to unfold, for you never know what you may miss by giving up too soon.

You are so restless, entities, and you need not be. It is your restlessness, fear, impatience, and loneliness which keep love from coming to you. That which you so yearn for does not come with an explosion in your heart; it comes subtly and softly as a knowing in your soul.

UNCONDITIONAL LOVING
AND THE PROCESS OF ALLOWING

I wish to discuss unconditional love and unconditional loving. Loving is the action which produces love. Unconditional love gives birth to the action of loving. Unconditional love must be present before the action can take place. The action of unconditional loving cannot precede the state of unconditional love being present in the being offering it, and the result of unconditional love cannot be experienced by the one who is to receive it without the action of unconditional loving. Love gives birth to loving which gives birth again to love.

What is unconditional love and loving but a willingness to allow without judgment or resistance? To allow something means to simply permit it to be. Sometimes resistance enters if you believe you must condone or bless it. Yet in either blessing or cursing, condoning or condemning, you enter the process of judgment. Unconditional love and its process of loving must be void of judgment. Your only responsibility is to allow. You are not required in your allowing to condone or bless— only to permit whatever is, to be.

I think human entities have difficulty with this process because of their limited definition of the word allowing. If a child comes to you and

23

asks your permission to do something, you will either say "yes" or "no"—you will either allow or not allow. If you allow, you are essentially giving your blessing to what the child wishes to do. If the child receives what he has asked for, then he views the action as a loving one. This, however, is not unconditional love in the purest sense, for the action required a decision which was the result of judgment.

I used the preceding example only to show you that your perception of the term *allowing* is limited. Because of your limited attitude you feel that you must bless all that you are asked to allow, and because of this you oftentimes feel resistant. The concept that you must give permission with a blessing to everything which comes into your life experience can be burdensome.

If you can grow to understand that you do not have to give permission and that you are not required to offer judgment, the process of allowing will become much easier. Giving permission and permitting to be are not quite the same thing. To give permission requires a decision on your part and seems to insist on a positive blessing. It seems as if you are required to say, "It's okay" even if the ego part of you is resistant. Permitting to be is simply allowing what is without judgment of any kind. It does not mean that from your ego you have to like what may be happening.

Unconditional love is present in the higher self, not in the ego self. It is the higher self which does the allowing when you are aligned to its guidance. The ego self knows nothing of unconditional love or loving. Unconditional love has no basis in emotion; it is not feeling. It is action. You may say "I love this" or "I love that" or "I love him" or "I love her," but all this is connected with feeling and with selection. Selection and feeling are the result of judgments by the ego self. On the human plane, it is good that you are able to feel love, but do not delude yourselves into thinking that it is unconditional love. Most of your loving is not unconditional. Unconditional love with its action of loving is impersonal, non-selective, and without judgment. This is because it originates in the higher self or the God self of one's being. You cannot be unconditionally loving to one without being unconditionally loving to all.

Human entities have a difficult time in the area of love and of loving, and this is simply because they do not practice unconditional love and loving. Each entity has his own perception of what it means to love and what it means to be loved, and these differing perceptions oftentimes cause great chaos. Most love is based in ego, feeling, and emotion. Much is based in sexual expression, possession, demands, and expectations. Human love oftentimes begets as much pain, self-sacrifice, disappointment, sadness, unfulfillment, emptiness, and longing as it does joy and beauty and richness. It will be this way until human entities evolve to the point where they are completely aligned to the God self of their beings.

If you were able to make this connection, how would you live in the world as it is? What would it be like? First of all, it would be much easier because you would not be controlled by the wants and needs of the ego self. Connection would mean pure allowing without judgment. Without judgment there would be no pain, no self-sacrifice, no resistance. Without resistance you would be in the true flow of Life. But it would also mean being impersonal and non-selective because God is both, and this type of loving emerges from your God self. Most human entities could not handle this because the egos of entities like to be selected, like to be number one, like to be the most special. The God self sees all as the most special and as number one. So this impersonal nature of the God self could create great pain for those who do not understand.

It will be awhile in the evolutionary process before unconditional love enters the collective consciousness, but it is something which one can work on individually. When something happens in your life experience where your ego begins to feel resistant, try to move into alignment with your higher self. Allow whatever is occurring simply to be without attaching any judgment to it. If you attach no judgment, there will be no pain. Pain only comes when the ego comes into play and, indeed, it is a great teacher. You may say, "Well, what if what is happening is an action of non-love designed to hurt me? Am I supposed to sit there and simply allow it?" I say, "Yes." As I said, you can only be hurt when the ego comes into play because the higher self recognizes no pain. In actions of non-love against you, you need not worry, for all actions of non-love will be balanced accordingly by the great law of Cause and Effect. It is not your mission to create the balancing unless Life utilizes you as an impersonal instrument.

You are never responsible for the actions of non-love by others; you are only responsible for your own actions. If you intend to cause pain to another or if you consciously know that your actions will cause pain for another, you do incur Karma, and the actions will be balanced in some way. Be concerned only about your own actions. Human entities do experience transitory moments of unconditional love and loving, so they do have a subtle awareness of the immense and intense joy and freedom which it brings. If they had not experienced this, they would not try so hard to achieve it. Most human entities, however, do not unconditionally love themselves, and this is really the starting point. Not only do they not allow others to be without judgment, they do not allow themselves to be without judgment. As I stated earlier, you cannot unconditionally love one without unconditionally loving all. Once you can unconditionally love that beauteous creation called you, you will unconditionally love all.

GENDER CONSCIOUSNESS IN RELATIONSHIPS

The basic reason for conflict within any human relationship, regardless of gender, is simply that most human entities neither see nor relate to others as spiritual beings. If this awareness were present upon your planet, there would be no battles, no wars, no conflict. This awareness would bring only respect and honor among human entities. Only honor would be given to the connecting thread of the God Essence which binds the beautiful tapestry of humankind together. Problems exist within human relationships because more focus is placed upon perceived differences, such as gender, personality, roles, ego and societal programming, and varied thought processes, than on connections.

With respect to the male/female conflict, you have only to examine your written history of the evolutionary processes of the two genders to understand why there is such a large gap in understanding. Women have undergone and still undergo in certain areas being treated as inferior to the male. This was due in part to the influence of patriarchal societies. Man feared the powerful energy of the female, which was really equal to his own. Initially all was balanced. Because the female form was seemingly less powerful physically, man attempted to suppress female energy. Female consciousness was oppressed, and she became submissive to her male counterpart. It became part of her Earth programming. The positive effect of this suppression of the female and her energy was that it actually refined her qualities of nurturing, gentleness, patience, understanding, and love.

It is feminine energy which is leading the world into the New Age of Aquarius. It will increase for a time and then will move to restore balance, which is a perfect blending of masculine and feminine energies.

The only reason I have brought up the evolutionary process of the female on planet Earth (for, indeed, males have undergone their own process) is to bring you to the subject of gender consciousness. Gender consciousness has an influence, though sometimes subtle and unconscious, on the interactions between males and females. All entities are affected by mass consciousness and its varying vibrations, but an individual entity is also influenced by a collective gender consciousness. Mass consciousness is really a combination of vibrations of individuals and does not specifically divide itself into masculine and feminine energies. However, because of the dominance of the male, mass consciousness leans toward being more masculine. Gender consciousness refers to the collective energies, vibrations, and thoughts of a specific gender from the time of separation of the human into two distinct genders. For example, you, as a female expressing, are influenced by both mass consciousness and by the collective female gender consciousness. This will have some effect on how you interact with male counterparts. Conflicts occur between men and women because they do not understand one another and cannot always adequately communicate with one another. One of the reasons why the two genders have difficulty understanding each other is because gender consciousness has a great bearing on how one literally thinks or approaches his life experience. Essentially, men and women do not think alike and approach a common problem or situation differently.

Another reason for conflict between men and women has to do with individual ego and societal programming. If, as a female expression, you have been programmed to believe that you are inferior to the male energy, this will color your approach to your interaction with males and how you will relate in a conflict situation. This type of Earth programming may even trigger more confrontations with males. Females may, at some level, resent the dominance and authority of the male. This could be unconscious because of the collective gender consciousness of the female. She cannot trust the male because at some level she perceives him as the aggressive suppressor and oppressor of the Female Energy.

The male, on the other hand, is under the collective gender consciousness of Male Energy and has also been programmed. His programming might have included beliefs that he is strong, dominant and superior to the female. As feminine energy continues to challenge masculine energy, which it must do to restore balance and harmony for the New Age, males will feel more threatened and may fight even harder.

On a denser, more physical level of interpretation, women are struggling for what they perceive they've never had, and men are struggling to hold onto it out of fear of losing it. So from one vantage point, it seems as if that which is termed the battle of the sexes goes on and on. On a higher level the conflict which exists and which is increasing between men and women is seen only as a movement to restore harmony to Earth by instilling a perfect balance of masculine and feminine energies.

In past communications a statement of prophecy was offered which said: "The Eagle will not soar until the Phoenix rises." Although there are many levels of interpretation, one of them sees the Eagle as representing the masculine polarity or energy and the Phoenix as representing the feminine polarity or energy. It has to do with the restoration of feminine energy to planet Earth. If you look at how the natures of both males and females are changing, you can see that the phoenix is in the process of re-creation. You must also be aware that what is occurring in your physical manifested world of form is also occurring in the inner worlds of each individual entity. An individual human entity contains both feminine and masculine energy with its resulting qualities. Internally, men are having to deal with the emergence of their own feminine energy, and women are having to deal with the emergence of the masculine energy. The battle is an inner one as well as an outer one. Men who do not resist their inner feminine energy will allow themselves to become more nurturing, more sensitive, and more caring. Women who do not block their inner masculine energy will be stronger, more confident, and more assertive.

As this natural and necessary balancing is occurring, there might be fewer conflicts between men and women and between entities of the same gender as well, if human entities raised their awareness. They would view others first and foremost as spiritual entities; then, as persons, human brothers and sisters with equal rights to express on the planet; and thirdly, as male and female energies. Reaching this level of awareness assists you in seeing that what you are truly seeking in all of your conflicts is oneness and unity and not separation and division.

RELATIONSHIPS ARE GARDENS

Relationships are like gardens which two people decide to plant and maintain together. Think of the gardens you may soon be planting. The first thing you will do is examine the soil. Is it still frozen? Is it filled with rocks? Is it rich and fertile?

In human relationships the soil represents the potential of a beautiful interaction. Sometimes there are too many obstacles to form a relationship or to plant a garden. If the ground is still frozen you may have to wait for it to thaw. In human terms it could mean that the time is not right for a particular relationship. If the soil is filled with rocks it may mean you will have to remove the rocks before you can prepare the garden for planting. With some potential relationships it may mean you will have to remove psychological, emotional, or mental obstacles before you can form a good relationship with another. Before examining the soil of another, examine your own soil first. You cannot form a beautiful relationship with another until you have cleared and tilled your own inner soil.

After the soil is prepared you will both plant the seeds of love, caring, sharing, understanding, consideration, compassion, loyalty, and joy. You will both go out and work in the garden you have created together. You will remove any rocks or obstacles which come into your garden, and you will quickly pull out weeds of discord and disharmony which seek to prevent the seeds you have planted from growing. You will water it with your love and fertilize it with positive thoughts of one another. You will destroy the insects of negativity as quickly as they land upon the young plants.

The gardens of beautiful human relationships are often laid to waste when one entity comes to believe that he no longer has to work in the garden. Sometimes the other will try very hard to maintain the garden by himself. Soon he discovers that there are too many weeds strangling the life of the young plants, and too many insects of negativity sucking their life juices. Soon he becomes overwhelmed and tired from the work and sadly, perhaps, watches the garden die. In the garden of a human relationship, two gardeners must work to maintain it. One person alone is not a relationship.

In your life experiences you all are involved in many relationships of varying levels of growth, and there is the potential for many more on your Earthly walk. You have relationships with parents, spouses, friends, children, pets, those of us who come to help you, the Source, and even with your Higher Self. In some gardens, you are just preparing the soil; in others you are clearing away obstacles or waiting for the right time to plant. In some the plants are growing strong and beautiful in the Light and are being maintained with care and love; in others the plants are dying from lack of care. In every relationship which you decide to enter into, you have a responsibility to work in that garden. If you want the beautiful flowers to grow strong and healthy, both entities must give their very best to the maintenance and care of that garden.

ACCEPTANCE: THE KEY
TO UNCONDITIONAL LOVE

It is important to understand all aspects of love in order to reach the point of unconditional love. One of the vital things you must do is to remove the boxes you place around other people. The only way to achieve this is to remove the box which you have placed around yourself. A box consists of those things that you think *you* should be and those things that others think *you* should be. It is the expectations, not only that you have set for yourself, but also the expectations that your external world has placed upon you. You place boxes around others when you expect people and situations to be a certain way. Unfortunately, the thickest box is usually around yourself.

There is little chance of reaching the point of unconditional love if one has expectations, because the basic ingredient in unconditional love is total acceptance. There can be no unconditional love even if there is limited acceptance. It's all or nothing. You might love but you are not unconditionally loving if your love for another is based on how well your own expectations are being met by the other.

I wish I could help you understand the joy you will have when the boxes of human expectations—which are really prisons—are removed so that the individual entity is able to totally express his God self. To totally accept another is sometimes difficult primarily because of one's established belief system and/or because of programming received throughout the time of one's life experience. An individual will set certain standards for himself based on the above. This is bad enough, but it's worse when he places his own standards on another.

Doing this leads to a lot of disappointment and disenchantment within one's life experience. If one has a lot of pride in his own set of standards, he will find great fault in others whose standards he perceives to be less than his own. This will cause the individual to become highly critical of others. What you must realize is that you are a unique expression of God. Your feelings and thoughts are unique to you; your standards of behavior and your perception of the world are unique to you; your programming and belief system are unique to you. You are a unique piece of work created by the Master Sculptor. You are not a mold. If you, an individual entity, are so totally unique, then so are all the other entities around you. You have no Cosmic right to place others into the molds which you have created. You cannot place an original piece of sculpture into a mold because it will not fit. It's already been formed by a Master Hand and instilled with the Lifeforce of the Creator, and it will only shatter the mold you have created. This shattering can sometimes be quite devastating to a person who creates a mold for another.

The original piece of sculpture (the human entity) is very pliable and will oftentimes try very hard to squeeze into another's mold. But the spirit containing the Lifeforce of the Creator is very powerful and will struggle until he breaks free from the confines of the man-created mold. The reason the spirit struggles to the point of release is because the spirit knows that the purpose of the life journey is to express the uniqueness of the original piece of sculpture. Whether known on the conscious level or

30

not, an entity has, as part of Cosmic programming, the awareness that he must express his being in order to grow and unfold and become all that his Creator intended him to be.

This is why it is so wrong to try to create molds or build boxes for either yourself or others. You must learn to accept yourself and others if you are ever going to unconditionally love. You must learn to see the beauty and the good in each original piece of sculpture, and you cannot do this if you are always looking for cracks or chips with your imperfect vision or if you are always desiring to change the original form. Remember that imperfect vision can only see imperfection. Perfect vision, which is inner vision, sees perfection unfolding.

If you learn to accept yourself and others, your life will be filled with joy as you unfold and as you observe the unfoldment of others. There can be no pain or disappointment or disenchantment when you release yourself and others from your expectations and when you tear down the boxes and allow the fresh air of freedom of expression to flow. Once you allow yourself and others the freedom to be and to become, you are flowing into unconditional love. It will be like watching a garden of flowers growing, and each day will be filled with joy and expectancy as the petals unfold.

Although you might influence and assist others in their unfoldment, the only one you will ever change is yourself. This is your responsibility. True change or complete unfoldment will come to the planet when unconditional love is present in all men. So start working on yourself. You are responsible for your own individual world. Instill it with unconditional love, remembering always that what is sent out from you is returned back to you.

BETRAYAL WITHIN RELATIONSHIPS

Many human entities experience betrayal by another within the framework of a relationship. On the human level, this is perhaps one of the most painful of the Earth experiences because it can be likened to rape on the emotional level of one's being, and it tends to rob one of his richest illusions: the belief in the integrity of another human entity. The acknowledgment of the betrayal by the one who is betrayed forces him into sifting through the ashes of seeming destruction in order to find something to rebuild with. However, to heal oneself after a betrayal or a broken commitment involves a process, and within that process one is offered the potential to grow and unfold.

Your great teacher and example, the Christ, experienced a betrayal by a friend which led Him to the cross of Golgatha. Although He was aware of the betrayal beforehand and knew that it was a necessary element in the Earth drama which changed your world, he showed through His experience the road which all who are betrayed must walk if they are to be healed. He was the supreme teacher and example.

Betrayal always involves the breaking of a commitment to another or to a cause, and it always involves the surrendering of integrity by the one in the role of the betrayer. One who does not honor his commitments made in Life suffers far more than the one who experiences a broken commitment by another. If all human experiences are lessons for you or another, then why do you think that human entities make commitments in their life situations, since commitments always involve the assuming of responsibility? Commitments are made so that human entities can learn of honor, integrity, and responsibility on the Earth walk. Commitments are broken when there is a failure to learn by an individual entity. For the one betrayed, the lessons become the way of the Christ.

What is the way of the Christ? What is the road to healing and wholeness that He exemplified? The one betrayed experiences a period of inner pain and suffering, although he may not express this to his outer world. In his inner world, the entity who has been betrayed is being forced to release from many illusions and beliefs. As you are very much aware, release from attachments is oftentimes very difficult and painful to the emotional level of one's being. The Christ, after being betrayed, hung upon a cross at Golgatha and experienced great wounding. Is not the act of a betrayal a deep wounding? The Christ had to release—from family, from friends, from spirit, from Life—into that which is called on your plane death.

After a human entity has been wounded in his depths by the act of betrayal and has experienced a period of release, he then will enter the period of death. During this time he will lay to rest all of those illusions and beliefs from which he released. The death period is the balm to his soul. On these deeper levels he has shut down and is resting quietly in the valley of his own being. The outer world may never be aware of this.

What is also occurring on the deeper levels during the death period is regeneration, renewal, and a movement toward a higher vision with respect to Life. The entity is shifting and changing and healing. This death state could be compared to the chrysalis stage of a butterfly.

The Christ experienced the betrayal, the wounding, the release, and the death, and moved into the transformed and resurrected Life. For the human entity who has been betrayed and experienced the process of release and death, the promise is that of renewal and resurrection within his life experience. He can become a transformed entity who sees with new vision. He does, through the process, experience growth on all levels of being. One thing that I must make clear is that the one who is betrayed can remain in any of the periods as long as he needs to or chooses to. He can remain wounded and hurting, he can refuse to release from those things which seemingly cause his suffering, he can remain in the death state and refuse to allow himself the risk of living again, or he can move freely into the resurrected new life which is always available to him. He will remain in a certain state for as long as he chooses to hold it or be held by it.

The Christ process of healing is as follows:

1. Acknowledgment of the betrayal
2. Wounding: the experience of pain on deeper levels
3. Release from attachments to illusions and beliefs
4. Death: laying to rest those attachments which were released and a shifting toward resurrection and regeneration
5. Resurrection: acceptance of a renewed and transformed life and a willingness to risk living.

I know that when one betrays another, when a promise between two is broken, that there is great pain and suffering on the deeper levels. I know the lesson is a hard one. But I also know that if one follows the way of the Christ and allows that process, that it is the road to healing and wholeness and renewed Life.

YOU ATTRACT WHAT YOU ARE

Many human entities upon your planet have been programmed to believe that they must find their one and only, marry, and produce offspring. Under this type of programming, many entities spend a large portion of their time and energy in this search. If they do not find what they are seeking, they feel a sense of failure, lowered self-image, and loneliness.

This is programming which must be changed. Human entities must understand that there is no ideal and no single one and only. A soulmate is simply an entity who is on a similar vibrational level as you. If you grow and your vibrational level changes, that entity will cease to be a soulmate if his vibrational level does not change. It is possible to have many soulmates in a lifetime, because soulmate connections involve similar vibrational patterns. However, whereas you may have many soulmates, you have only one twin flame. At the point of origination of your spirit,

33

it divided into masculine and feminine polarities and began its separate journeys of learning. On higher levels of consciousness you are always connected with your twin flame essence. It's rare to experience incarnated lives together.

You do not have to seek a soulmate in order to be happy in a relationship. It is, of course, a smoother journey if there is a soulmate connection, but it is not necessary. Human entities would be happier in their life walks if they would not spend so much energy in the seeking. Your task is not the seeking of love, but rather one of making yourselves worthy to receive it. How do you prepare yourselves so that you are worthy for that which you seem to so desperately seek? You stop seeking and begin being the God expressions that you are. You learn to love that unique and wonderful creation called you. In learning to love you, you become an open vessel to receive love from others. You will attract to you that which you are. A human entity can be so involved in the seeking that he will not see the beloved which may be standing before him. It's rather like walking down a road and looking only at your feet. You will miss all of the wondrous sights along the way.

Although it is wonderful to share your life journey with one whom you love and are compatible with, you must always remember that whether single or paired, your journey is a solo one. You walk your own singular path. Though the wingtips of others may touch yours, you soar alone in the skies of your own being.

Entities seek to attract love because that is what they are in the truth of their own beings—Love. Many entities seek another out of need or a sense that their happiness can only be found in another. Learn, Beloved Ones, that if you seek another out of your own neediness, your needs will never be met. Do not seek another to provide you with your happiness, for the purpose of another is not to provide for your happiness. Seek your own happiness within your own being. Do not seek another for the purpose of security because, in truth, there is no security in the manifested world. Security is to be found within yourself. Share your life with another because you desire to share and not because you have need or the belief that another will make you happy and secure. Happiness and security may be the gifts within a relationship, but do not make happiness and security the goal of the relationship. Beyond learning to love the beauteous creation that you are, part of preparing oneself to be a vessel to receive love is that of becoming strong, self-reliant, secure, and happy within your own self.

Before seeking a good and positive relationship with another, seek first to establish a good relationship between you and You. One who is comfortable with himself will be comfortable with another. One who is comfortable with himself will never be lonely, even when he is solitary and alone. There is a great and vast difference between aloneness and loneliness. Many human entities do not know how to enjoy being just with themselves, and aloneness then becomes loneliness. Loneliness then leads one into depression, frustration, and self-pity. It might be helpful if you could come to the understanding that even in those times when there are no others around you and even though your path is singular and your own, you are never truly alone. You are so much more than you are in your present consciousness and in your limited thinking. You are divine beings, divine in your spiritual inheritance and individualized expressions of God. Would God—could God—be lonely? Use your alone times not to be lonely, but to better know you and express more of the totality of your own beingness.

Beloved Ones, let your hearts be filled with the light and love of who you are, remembering always that you will attract to you what you are in essence. As divine beings, enter into that sacred communion with yourself and love that which you are. Make perfect that relationship between you and You, and then it is this that will be manifested in your outer world.

THE RESPONSIBILITIES OF LOVE

You are responsible only for your own loving; you are not responsible for how another receives it or accepts it. If you love others and you express it according to your own capacity, you are only responsible for offering the gift; they are responsible for accepting it in the spirit in which it is offered or for rejecting it by saying it does not meet their standards or expectations. If your gift is thrown back at your feet because the receiver did not like your choice of wrappings or ribbon, this is not your problem. Your responsibility is, like a gardener, to continue to tend to the garden of your own being so that those seeds of love which have been sown within you are nurtured. In this way your own capacity for love increases and produces an abundance of lovingness.

There is no earthly way to define unconditional love, although many have sought to devise an absolute definition or description. All that humans define as love are fragments of the state of unconditional love. The closest I can come to defining it for your human comprehension is to say that it exists when you are in Oneness with All that is, with the Essence itself, and when you are the Essence itself. It is important to strive toward the state of unconditional love. Every time you release yourself from

35

limiting definitions of love and from your own expectations of love, you increase your own capacity for loving and being loved. When you do this you move closer to Oneness and closer to the state of unconditional loving.

How can you release yourself from some of the limitations and expectations you have placed on your own loving and on your capacity to receive love from others? First, analyze how you believe you should express love to another in the way that is natural and right for your own capacity at the time. Your ego will enter in and try to discern the expectations of the other. So your expression of love will be based on the definitions and standards of the other, rather than on your own natural expression. For example, your natural expression might be to give a flower as a way of expressing love. Yet, you know, according to the other person's definition of love, that he will only believe he is loved if you offer a diamond. So your own ego, in wanting to make the other know he is loved, will offer a diamond. What I'm saying here is that when you give the diamond, when your inner guidance was to offer the flower, you are more concerned with the gift being accepted than in the offering of the gift. The ego is concerned with whether the gift is accepted; the spirit is concerned only with the offering of the gift of love.

You must also analyze how you expect love to be expressed to you. How many flowers have you thrown back at others because you wanted diamonds? Your ego says, "I will not accept flowers. I deserve diamonds." When you set conditions about how you want love expressed to you, you oftentimes will toss back a flower with a diamond hidden in its bloom.

In the garden of your individual being, seeds of love have been planted. This is the only garden you are responsible for. You are responsible for tending the seeds and nurturing them and helping them to grow and produce an abundance of fruit. You are responsible for offering the fruit of your garden to others so that more fruit may grow in your garden. Remember that fruit not shared with others will rot in your garden, and as more and more piles up, new fruit will die on the vine. Only by giving it away freely will your capacity to grow more increase.

If you give a man an apple, give it freely, expecting nothing in return, and do not concern yourself with whether he eats it or not or whether he thanks you or whether he tosses it away. Concern yourself only in the giving, in the offering of the gift. And when an apple is given to you, do not look on it and say, "It is too small," or "The color is not red enough," or "I prefer oranges." Accept the gift as freely as it was given to you.

TRUE INTIMACY IS A SPIRITUAL CONNECTION

Oftentimes when one hears the phrase intimate relationship, it is thought of in terms of a physical/sexual relationship. Although a physical/sexual relationship can be an expression of an intimate relationship, there are many physical/sexual relationships totally void of intimacy, and likewise there are many intimate relationships which are without physical/sexual expressions. There are many human entities who are bonded in the marital experience, for example, who have never enjoyed an intimate connection. And there are many Earth relationships in which intimacy is present, but where physical/sexual expression would be inappropriate.

True intimacy between entities is a spiritual connection which is expressed in a lovingness on the material plane of life. True intimacy involves feeling open and safe with another and allowing the other person to feel open and safe with you. It is a mutual allowing of each other to be who and where you are without fear of judgment or adverse criticism. It is a mutual respect and acknowledgment of the other's beingness: a mutual trust and love and caring between entities. Therefore, intimacy can exist in any relationship which you may have—with your parents, children, friends, mates or lovers, co-workers, and even, to a degree, with dissimilar life forms such as pets. Various intimate relationships will have different forms of expressions in the external world depending on the roles being played within the relationships, but all involve mutual trust and allowing the other to be without judgment—in other words, the mutual creation and maintenance of safe space.

An intimate connection involves the participation of more than one individual entity within the relationship, because the experience of intimacy is a shared experience, it is a spiritual bonding. To form this bond, however, the individual entities must begin their work at the individual level. Each must be willing to risk, and it is because of this that the majority of relationships are not intimate, no matter how close they may appear to be. To risk means letting down one's defenses, removing the protective shields, and becoming, in a sense, vulnerable to another. This is frightening to some because vulnerability is oftentimes associated with weakness. The truth is, Beloved Ones, it shows greater strength to trust and become vulnerable to another. You are not giving your power to another by declaring who you really are, but rather you are using that power to open the door to an intimate connection.

There are many reasons why human entities resist forming intimate relationships and prefer to keep them more casual. The greatest reason is fear of rejection by another. Many simply do not trust that the other will accept them if they reveal who they are. Most human entities have things about their lives that they feel might be unacceptable to others. So rather than risking finding out, they will resist an intimate connection. Most human entities have been in relationships where they have experienced rejection and this is, as you know, very painful, primarily to one's ego. After suffering one or more rejections, many human entities cease to trust or trust only to a certain point and no further. Having tried, perhaps, to form an intimate bond and been rejected enhances the idea that you are unacceptable, and your defenses become stronger. You say to yourself, "I will not share the totality of myself because I am unacceptable." Essentially you are saying, "If one has found me unacceptable, all will. I will close that part of me off so that no one can ever hurt or reject me again."

In addition to fear of rejection, prior programming, and not being able to trust, another reason many entities resist intimate connections is simply that they do not want the responsibility which might be attached to it. They simply do not want to be placed in the position of having to deal with another's exposed vulnerability because they don't want to be the guardian of another's trust. Many human entities prefer to create and maintain a certain but safe image of others, and to enter an intimate relationship could mean the shattering of that image, of seeing something they do not wish to see, of possibly becoming the rejector of another. You see, rejecting another can oftentimes be just as painful as being rejected by another. So the safe space for many entities is to keep others at a distance and avoid any responsibility of having to reject or accept.

Still another reason many human entities resist intimate bonds with others is because they do not have intimate connections with their God self. They have not taken the inner journey into self to see who they really are, and they have not faced those things which make them feel bad or unworthy about themselves. To protect themselves they create a false image, a mask, to show to the outer world and they say, "This is who I am." But these things in the shadows do not die, Beloved Ones, and they, in a sense, become your jailkeepers and maintain your sense of unworthiness, no matter what image you have created for the external world. You cannot be free until you enter the shadows of yourself and acknowledge and release from them. There can be no shadows without light, and light is your true essence. Shadows are your illusions, misperceptions, and your own judgments about self.

You cannot truly be intimate with another until you have reached a place of intimacy with yourself. You cannot truly trust another until you become true to yourself. You cannot truly accept another if you do not accept yourself. You cannot truly allow another to be until you allow yourself to be. You cannot truly love another until you truly love that wondrous creation called you. You cannot truly create a safe space with another until you create it within yourself.

Once safe space is created within you, all your walls and boundaries come tumbling down, and you have no fear of risking entering into intimate relationships. Once you know who you are, you have no fear. The gift of intimacy offered by individual entities, one to the other, creates a wonderful garden for growth and unfoldment. Being in a truly intimate relationship with another, regardless of the external roles being played out, brings with it the closest you will come to unconditional love on the Earth plane. Because a true intimate relationship is more accepting, supportive, and nurturing than other relationships, growth of those participating is accelerated. Know that the gift of intimacy is one of the nicer gifts human entities can offer each other.

PART III

WHAT DO I DO?

One's life journey can be considered a composite of a multitude of singular experiences. Some of these life experiences can be confusing, perplexing, painful, and filled with many emotions and states of consciousness. This section contains the guidance messages of Kyros. They relate to the emotions and life situations which we all experience, and assist in helping us raise our eyes and perceive our mundane experiences with higher vision and greater understanding.

HOW TO DEAL WITH CONFRONTATION

There has been much talk of late regarding the conflict which is increasing between those who have been labeled as fundamentalists and those who are participants in the New Age Movement. This is going to continue to increase over the next few Earth years, and those of you who are proponents of a new age must prepare yourselves for confrontation. There are ways in which to do this and remain aligned to the philosophy of the New Age Movement. The primary way is to become aware of what is really occurring beyond the external happenings in your plane of experience.

First of all, the New Age is only new to you because you live in a time dimension and you create illusions of beginnings and endings. This new age is a natural, cyclic, and evolutionary transition from one level of planetary consciousness to another. The planet and those creations which live upon it have been flowing and gradually ascending in vibration for years. It's just that, as time passed, the awareness of this very natural shift reached the conscious awareness of man. Some have greeted it with eagerness, joy, and understanding; others have viewed it as a threat. Many human entities, as you well know, have a great fear of change, and many will resist and battle against it. But since change is natural and evolutionary and Cosmic in nature, fighting against it will be to no avail.

41

Another awareness you should have is that those who are adversaries of the New Age are expressions of God, just as you are. What they speak is truth, just as yours is. What they believe is just as valid to them as what you believe. The difference lies in the level of awareness and understanding. You understand that truth is relative and unfolding. Some entities close off to new input and block new truth, or rather unfolding truth, and become imprisoned by their belief systems rather than freed by them. But all is truth at some level of awareness, so the truth of the fundamentalist Christian is just as valid as that of the New Age proponent. Knowing this should allow you to be generous in your reaction to and understanding of those who hold opposing beliefs.

Another awareness you should strive to attain is that of realizing that those who oppose you are reacting, at least the greater part of the time, out of intense fear. Many religions in their interpretations of holy writings have created a fearful world for the adherents of those religions. For some, Satan, Hell, demons, Armageddon, and so forth, are very real—so real, in fact, that they could bring manifestations of these into their illusionary reality. Fortunately for them, they counter their fear with a faith in a God who will save them and forgive them. With some of the present confrontations, these entities have become more influenced by their programmed fear consciousness than by their faith consciousness.

On another level, these people with set beliefs are having their beliefs challenged. As many of you can attest, when your beliefs are challenged and tested, you can feel very confused and uncomfortable. Have you never thought, "What if the fundamentalists are right?" Do you think those flashes of doubt never enter a fundamentalist's mind and he might think, "What if the New Agers are right?" For you who are trying to understand what is occurring both on your level and on the higher levels, I would simply say that it is not a question of being right or wrong. It is simply a question of a natural and necessary shift in planetary consciousness. New Agers are merely on a higher rung on the ladder of their understanding of what is occurring.

True proponents of New Age thought do not attempt to force their beliefs onto others. They share with those who are seeking. Do not be one who forcefully attempts to push your beliefs onto others by saying that you are right and they are wrong. Remember that it is never a question of right and wrong, but rather a question of differing levels of awareness of truth. As for the question of defending your own truth against those who will confront and oppose you, I would say that if you truly believe in what you say you believe, it needs no defense. Those who feel they must argue and defend their truth or belief are, somewhere in their being, unsure of

42

it. In your world, entities have either attempted to force their beliefs on others or have been forced to defend their beliefs to others to the point that millions have died in the name of God. This is sad, but it, too, was part of the evolution of consciousness.

With respect to the New Age Movement, the division is widening between the proponents and the opponents, and you, as proponents, will be attacked and confronted both individually and collectively. Do not become angry and enter into confrontation and begin wildly arguing. You know your truth; act on it. It needs no defense. Meet your adversaries with love and understanding and then you become the example. Remember that they come to you from fear consciousness; you remain steadfast in faith consciousness. Know your truth in your heart, for then when it is attacked it does not create confusion and doubt within you, and when you share your truth you will do so with clarity, understanding, and sureness. A New Ager who is unsure of this truth will be easily unbalanced by opposing opinions. Remember that your critics have studied their own truth well. To be an able spokesperson for the New Age Movement, one would do well to study both sides of the coin. Opponents are more easily overcome if you take the time and expend the energy in studying the nature of your critics. Yet the whole purpose of a spokesperson for the New Age is not to defend it or to counter the beliefs of others, but to merely bridge the gap of misunderstanding which exists. Those who wish to listen will hear; but there are so many who do not want your message and who fear it, and there is more important work for you to do than using your energy to try to convince those who cover their ears and raise up their swords.

The War of Consciousness has begun. It will rage for quite some time. For you I would simply say to practice what you say you believe, and that is basically love and trust. This is the only defense you will need in the world arena. No matter how much you disagree with others, allow others their own truth. Most of all, stand firm in your own truth. Things are accelerating and you must be prepared for increased criticism. What has been set in motion cannot be stopped. There are too many fires burning now for them all to be extinguished.

Walk your walk in love, light, and confidence, knowing that all is as it should be.

REALITY IS WHAT YOU PERCEIVE IT TO BE

You've been told many times that one creates his own reality, and this is essentially true. Your reality on the external plane of experience is based on your present consciousness. What you are in consciousness is what is manifested into form.

There are times, however, when you may look at your life situation and think, "I did not create this reality. I did not choose this situation." And oftentimes, at least on the physical plane, this may appear to be true. Sometimes an entity is pulled into or becomes caught up in the drama of another entity and feels as if he doesn't know his lines or as if someone else is writing his script for him. Sometimes one can feel as though he is but a marionette with someone else pulling his strings and dancing him on and off the stage at will. One can, at these times, feel both manipulated and powerless, as well as frightened and confused. It's rather like being asked to play a game and not being told the rules. Obviously you can't play the game well if you don't know how to play at all. This becomes an extremely uncomfortable position to be in.

There are, of course, entities upon your planet who are manipulative and who seek to seize the power of others. This occurs simply because of the myriad of levels of awareness upon your planet. An entity does have a choice as to whether he will allow himself to be manipulated or whether he will surrender his power to another. If one does allow this to occur, he has chosen to enter the reality or life situation of another and so, in a sense, he is in agreement with the created reality. He may not have personally written the play, but he, by this choice, has agreed to enter the stage. He may not have created the particular life situation he finds himself in, but his entrance means that he has agreed to it. Sometimes the dramas one is pulled into or becomes caught up in are not really the result of his own actions or thoughts, but are the result of the actions or thoughts of others, which he has (sometimes unknowingly on the conscious level, at least) agreed to. This agreement prevents one from being a victim, because at the higher levels there are no victims on the life walk. Entities either create their own realities or they agree to enter the realities of others.

If one is involved in a situation he does not care for which has been created by another entity, he has the same options available to him that he had when he agreed, consciously or unconsciously, to enter. He can take back the power he surrendered and begin writing his own script, thus refusing to read the lines written by another. If he doesn't understand the rules of the game, he can create his own rules, and in so doing he changes the nature of the game plan. Writing your own script and changing the rules are but simple analogies to the shifting of your consciousness. The shifting of consciousness changes that which you perceive as reality in your world.

44

Reality is *what is* at any now moment of time in your life experience, and *what is* is exactly what you perceive it to be. A shift in consciousness shifts your perception and creates a different reality.

Entities who image spirit direction or higher self guidance as something beyond themselves pulling strings and pushing buttons as if they were no more than controllable robots are usually ego-directed. This usually results in the human entity becoming manipulative in the creation of reality for both himself and others who surrender their power and agree to the created reality.

In the creation of reality nothing is outside of yourself—not spirit, not the higher self, not the God essence, and not the ego. When you say "Not my will, but thy will be done" you must remember that "my" and "thy" are the same if you believe that you are God expressing. However, whatever you choose to be directed by, whether it be spirit or ego, does have to do with your will. It would better read, "Not my ego's will, but my spirit's will be done." When an entity truly knows who he is and trusts in this, "my" and "thy" are in alignment, and power is increased, not surrendered.

You can change any reality, move from any situation, create something more preferable to you by a mere shift in consciousness. This does require your will, and if you align with your own God essence and trust in the knowing of who you are, "my" and "thy" are aligned in Oneness. This is when you can be completely certain of where your direction is coming from.

On the external level, when a shift of consciousness occurs which is based on spiritual direction, then an entity takes back his own power and is able to move away from the created realities of others. An entity is then able to create or perceive the reality he chooses. Always a human entity has choice—the freedom of will. The freedom of will is no more than choosing between spirit and ego direction—the choice of holding your own power or surrendering it—of being in control of *what is* (reality) or being controlled by it.

Allow the spirit to direct your present consciousness, and this is what you will create in form. It has always been this way and it always shall be. The more aware you become, the more aligned you are to spirit, the fewer negative perceptions you will have in which to create and color your reality. Then you will be in charge of your own *what is*!

SUFFERING

Your friend who believes that man must suffer in order to transcend suffering is, of course, creating his own reality of suffering on all levels of his life. What one is in consciousness is what is brought into form. This is the path he has chosen based on his own belief system, and in accordance with his particular level of awareness, it is truth. But it is relative truth. And until his consciousness shifts, he will continue to create the reality of suffering.

The majority of human entities suffer in some way, but most do so because they believe in suffering and collectively and individually empower the concept of suffering and thus bring it into form. Many suffer because they believe they are victims and that there truly is a God who plays favorites. Some suffer because this is the only way they feel they can learn the lessons in life. Once humans can remember the sweetness of honey better than the bitterness of gall, then perhaps they will not have to learn lessons through suffering.

Human suffering can be transcended, but only when you realize that you don't have to suffer and you stop creating it for yourselves. If your belief system is that you must suffer, then you surely will do so. Many who choose a path of suffering are a little sadistic and gain a certain pleasure out of saying to others: "See how I am suffering. See what the world is doing to me. It's your duty to alleviate my suffering." The compassionate, loving ones will go to his aid and assume something not their own, only to discover that no matter what they do, the suffering continues. This is because there has not been a shift in consciousness.

Man will not transcend suffering by suffering. He will transcend it when he *knows* he does not have to suffer. When all men know who they are—who they *truly* are—they will release from suffering because suffering is not of God. You all have suffered or will suffer within your lives because you have not yet released from the belief that suffering is a part of the human walk. What you suffer and how much you suffer is dependent on your level of awareness and on your perception. If you could learn that all experience is neutral until you charge it with your perception, you might be more accepting of your experiences, which are illusions anyway. When a life situation comes to you, usually for learning, instead of suffering, try viewing it as simply a situation from which you can learn. You will be amazed at how quickly you will learn and release from it. When you focus upon how much perceived pain is involved or what you have lost or are losing or how you are struggling, you can actually bring more intensity into the situation. You will remain a victim in life until you realize that there are no victims. You choose your path, you create your reality, and you can change your reality with a shift in consciousness.

Now granted, your own choice to suffer or to witness another's suffering can teach you empathy and compassion—two things necessary in a world which collectively believes in suffering. These are needed because there are many in your world who are simply ignorant of the fact that suffering is a man-created illusion. These are the ones who need your compassion, love, caring, and giving. Those entities who believe in suffering and who continue to empower it with their thinking, you really will not be able to help much.

To break the pattern of suffering requires a new perception, a new way of thinking, and a shift in consciousness. What you are in consciousness is what you create in form. Do not look upon another and say that he is suffering because he is experiencing some condition you would not choose for your learning. It is possible that he may not be perceiving that he is suffering. You will always know, if you are aware, who you can or should help and who you will be unable to help. The greatest help you can give to another after tending to whatever outer suffering is present, is to assist in redirecting his consciousness.

SEPARATION OF THE DREAM
FROM THE DREAMER

When you are experiencing deep inner turmoil and confusion within your life experience and you are uncertain about what to do next, the best thing you can do is to work to move back to your own center and view your life with more objectivity. Try to pull away from yourself and become the observer of the dream you are walking through. I know this is difficult because human entities generally operate from the subjective mode, and the dream and the dreamer seem to be one in reality.

Turmoil and confusion are subjective and are created by the ego, which is also subjective. Becoming the observer of the dream separates the dream from the dreamer, and this splitting apart allows one to be able to see the total picture with more clarity and with greater vision as to what will come next. The future is never pre-set as you well know, but one's choices in the moment have a great bearing on future moments. So momentary choices made with clarity and vision offer a greater assurance of a future filled with opportunities more to one's liking. It offers one greater control over future moments than do choices made from turmoil and confusion.

When turmoil and confusion are present within one's life experience, it generally has to do with the space he is in—not so much the external environmental space, but rather the mental space. If the mental space is filled with anger, resentment, fear, and so forth, then this affects your thinking, and acting on these emotions takes your power from you and gives it to others. It also begins affecting the physical form in various manifestations, and it prevents you from focusing on your particular mission within this life.

When the dreamer separates from the dream; when the creator separates from his creation, he sees them for what they truly are—illusions. This done, they lose their impact, and turmoil and confusion are released. In truth, you are your only reality and all else is your illusionary reality, void of substance. A dream cannot hurt you because it is not real; you, the dreamer, can hurt yourself because you are real. Only when the dream and the dreamer become one can the dream hurt you.

For those who experience pain and turmoil and confusion, I would say, look at the dream for what it is. Is it a dream you want? If it is not, then create a new one. This is what makes you co-creators with God. Because God expresses His essence through that dreamer called you, you have the power and the creativity to create new dreams. It's always available for your use. In the subjective state you become one with the dream and oftentimes become entrapped by the dream.

Pain is self-chosen by the ego subjective self, for the ego is forever trying to protect the varied levels of the vehicle (physical, mental, and emotional). To a degree, this is necessary simply because form is necessary for that part of the journey. So, frequently the intense emotions of the ego cause more damage to that form that it tries so desperately to defend and protect. This is one reason for suicides (physical destruction of the form), mental illness (mental destruction of the form), and physical diseases (emotional destruction of the form). The ego, in trying to protect the form (which is its purpose through emotion), can actually destroy what it strives so hard to save.

When the ego is creating intense emotions of pain, turmoil, and confusion, spirit enters and tries to bring you into balance by making you aware of the destruction which is occurring on various levels of beingness and by trying to help you understand that the dream is not real and to help you, the dreamer, to separate from the dream which might be entrapping you.

The spirit, being void of ego attachments and emotions, when listened to, will try to guide you from those things which are destructive as a result of ego emotions. Because it is knowingness and trust and love, it will attempt to bring you to the awareness of the true unreality of the dream. Your own spirit is working for your own highest good, growth, and unfoldment. That balance and harmony between spirit and ego will always work for your highest good, growth, and abundance on your Earth walk.

You see, you are your only reality. You are the dreamer dreaming the dream through your emotions, your attitudes, your thoughts, your choices, and your decisions. A new choice, a new decision, a new thought, a new attitude, or a new emotion changes the dream. Only the dreamer can change the dream, just as only the artist can add a new stroke and change the composition, and only the sculptor can add new clay to what he is molding.

Because you are a creator, begin creating a new dream for your learning and your growth. If you allow balance between your spirit and your ego, those dreams you create will bring you wondrous joy and lessons void of pain. You, the true reality, God expressing, the dreamer, the creator of dreams, can with one empowered thought in a now moment reshape the composition of your next dream. The power is yours and so is the choice as to what the dream will be.

STRUGGLE GIVES BIRTH TO STRENGTH

Struggle gives birth to strength if you don't give up the struggle too soon. With human entities, the primary struggle goes on within, and the main purpose of inner struggle is to emerge into a new creation.

Do not think that inner struggle is resistant to that which is termed the flow of Life. The flow is an acceptance of what is without wanting it to be other than what it is in a now moment. Acceptance of one's own inner struggle is non-resistant and in the flow of Life. The new creature trying to be born, like the butterfly, must be strong enough to survive, and this can only be so if struggle precedes the birth. If a butterfly did not struggle, his wings would not be strong enough to carry him aloft into his new world.

It is true that with struggle there is also stress. In Nature this stress is a positive energy or force which is necessary to give birth to new life. With human entities this is not always the case, simply because humans tend to have an aversion to struggle and stress. Many seem to desire to grow and unfold without having to, in any way, work for it. Growth and unfoldment is a natural process for all of Nature, including man. In other words, you will, whether you like it or not, grow and unfold. The God energy within each aspect of creation simply will not be blocked from moving toward its fullest expression through each aspect.

49

The human entity truly desires peace and joy and a sense of well-being. Oftentimes when struggle occurs for the purpose of growth and the unfoldment of his being, instead of flowing with it he creates negative stress energy. If anything creates temporary blockages to growth, it is negative stress energy. You all know what happens when the self-created negative stress levels become too high. You begin manifesting negative conditions within your external world and onto your vehicle. So instead of having to deal with simply the natural inner struggle needed for growth, you must also deal with the self-created illusionary struggle within your outer world.

Why do human entities create negative stress energy when they are experiencing natural inner struggles designed to give birth to a greater, more wondrous being? Primarily because most entities do not realize or will not accept that growth is the purpose. That in itself causes them to view struggle far too seriously.

Stress comes to the human entity in the form of fear and worry which are based on ignorance of what the outcome of the struggle experience will be. The caterpillar which spins the cocoon has no idea that he will become a beauteous butterfly. For all he knows, he could be building his own tomb. Perhaps if he knew his future, he would not struggle so hard to break free from the cocoon. Having only crawled upon the ground and not having the faintest idea of what flying was all about, he might opt not to risk himself to that experience.

During an experience of struggle, the human entity will frequently begin to fear the future or worry about the outcome of his experience. The more he does this, the more prolonged the experience becomes and the greater the possibility that what you fear most will come upon you. This has to do with the empowering and the energizing of thoughts and bringing them into manifestation. An individual's future is not preset. One's future is like a large bouquet of mixed flowers laced with weeds. What you empower in your thoughts oftentimes determines what flower or weed will be given you. If you truly knew exactly what lay stretched out before you, you would not grow.

You will always enter periods of struggle within your life. These periods will be followed by periods of peace and joy and the realization that you have grown and learned and been strengthened. Transformation is an ongoing process into becomingness, and is a natural process of bringing your own God essence into its fullest and truest expression. In these periods of struggle, spin your cocoon with threads of trust, for in this way you can still feel the warmth of the sun (Son) and see the light shining from within your seeming darkness.

Most of all, do not fear the outcome, for those who trust and remain aligned to their true source can always know that their highest good will be served. Do not take the cocoon stages of your life too seriously, for they are but your illusions. All the cocoon stage really means is that your own God essence is desiring to express more fully through you.

RELEASE LEADS TO RESURRECTION

Oftentimes on your life journey you either willingly enter or are pulled into situations which test and challenge the very roots of your belief system. You may find your sense of ethics and morality in disarray, your expectations smashed, your dreams crushed. Life is in chaos and seemingly out of balance. All you have ever believed seems to have gone up in a puff of smoke. In this period you find your perceptions of the outer world have changed. You view all of your relationships in a different light.

In these situations you are like the phoenix consumed by fire and reduced to ashes. You allow yourself the experience of the pain of the fire and then for a time you live in emptiness. Fearing you might drown, you thrash and flounder around in a wild sea of unknown waters, desperately seeking something familiar to grab hold of. There is nothing left which is familiar to you. Everything seems out of focus, hazy.

In time you tire, and in this state you quit thrashing around and begin to allow yourself the experience of drowning. You give up. You release from the world you sought so desperately to hold on to. You are ready to die. And it is at this point that transition and transformation begin to take place.

Resigned, released, relaxed, the entity discovers that he does not slip beneath the waters but floats atop them, bobbing up and down. This restful state allows time for the energy used in thrashing around to return to him. As his energy increases, he begins moving his arms and legs, and he discovers that he is no longer under the control of the sea. He can choose his direction and steer his own course. As he becomes stronger, his vision clears and he no longer fears the unfamiliar open sea. The period of rest I speak of is the healing period or the space of restructuring one's belief system. It is the birthing time of the new phoenix. From out of the ashes of seeming destruction, the beauteous new creature comes forth slowly, in process, until its wings are strong enough to lift to the air and begin its flight. And because the entity had been made empty, he can only now be made full. Total release leads to total resurrection.

51

On the human level it seems that oftentimes resurrection must be born of pain. Resurrection of oneself can also be born of love, but most human entities have not yet comprehended that which is called unconditional love, although they speak of it at great length.

If you would think for a moment of your great master, you will find His own experience to be an example. Even though He was the Christ and knew full well He would be betrayed, do you not think that on one level his heart was not saddened by betrayal by a friend? And do you not think that on one level he momentarily feared the unfamiliar sea stretched out ahead? He did. In one Earth moment he wished for the cup to be taken from Him. Do you not think that on one level he felt the pain of thorns and nails and sword? He did. He allowed Himself the human experience. No great master or avatar has ever walked upon your plane who has not allowed himself the human experience of resurrection born of pain. A master cannot teach with compassion, love, and sensitivity unless he has walked the human path. If you are insensitive to or cannot understand human pain, you cannot lift another up from those feelings. Once you understand the resurrection born of pain, you are then able to teach resurrection born of love. Only if your own heart has been torn asunder can you understand the crying of another's heart. Only if you have wept at the death of a bird can you understand the tears of a child.

Yes, you live in a world of illusion, and pain is one of those created illusions. And, yes, you live in a world of feeling, of sensing, of sensitivity, and these have become your finest tools for learning. To feel upon your plane is to be alive. If you would bathe in the fragrance of a rose and yet would not reach out to touch a velvety petal for fear of the thorn, you will never learn. An entity can never rise above or transcend that which he has no knowledge of. To transcend pain, one must experience it within the human walk. Once transcended, one need never descend to its depths again.

So when you are allowing a resurrection born of pain, do not block the pain, but rather, in your emptiness, face it and think about and consider what the truth of your being really is. If you take this journey into self, I promise you will return a finer vessel. Pain can only create damage if you will not face it or if you pretend that it does not exist. Pain is an illusion which can only touch your essence if you deny its presence. Healing occurs through the process of facing what you are and what you feel.

DEPRESSION: THE INNER REACTION
TO OUTER ACTIONS

As the term implies, depression is a process by which something becomes lowered from what it was. When human entities enter mental or emotional depression, it means that they are in a space which is below what they consider to be normal. Depression emerges from the emotional level of beingness, and coming from there, it is in the realm of the ego which is the survival programming for the human vehicle. The root cause of depression is fear and its offspring are guilt, worry, rejection, insecurity, and so on.

Human entities each respond differently when they enter a depressed state. Some will, as you like to term it, wallow in self pity for awhile. If they do take any time to discern the cause of the depression, they will oftentimes externalize and blame the illusions of the outer world. They will utter such statements as: "I am depressed because my expectations weren't met." "I am depressed because I didn't get what I wanted." "I am depressed because of what so and so said or did." Externalizing or blaming the outer world for one's inner state can sometimes pull the entity out of the state of depression, but it is simply a form of rationalization, and this method is just as much a placebo as are drugs, alcohol, tranquilizers, and so forth. Restored balance is temporary at best, and depression ultimately returns because the cause has not been discerned and dealt with. An unwillingness to seek and address the root cause of depression creates a pattern of depression in one's life. It's rather like putting a bug under a rug. Sooner or later, the bug will crawl out again. The pattern of depression is created when one keeps putting the bug back under the rug. In this way, one's life becomes an emotional rollercoaster filled with highs and lows. This is not balance.

The healthiest way in which to deal with depressed spaces of beingness is to take the journey into self and face up to the real cause of the depression. Usually the cause will be found to be an inner reaction to one's outer actions. For example, if the cause of depression is discovered to be that of guilt, one must realize that that which is termed guilt is an inner response to what one has created in the outer world. So what one must address is not the external action which gave rise to the internal reaction, but rather to the internal reaction itself. You see, the external action which gave rise to the internal reaction which is creating the depression cannot be changed. The action is over and nothing one does or says can change what is past. If the inner reaction is guilt, then this is what you must acknowledge and deal with. One cannot be free of the feeling of guilt unless he first acknowledges that it is guilt which is causing the depression. With guilt or any other depression-producing cause, one should take the lessons from it, forgive himself, and move away from it. When you learn from your inner reactions, the depression lifts and balance is restored. What applies to guilt also applies to the other causes of depression such as fear, worry, and so forth.

Depression is not really a negative experience if one perceives it correctly and understands, not only its purpose, but how to move out of the lowered space. It becomes a negative, damage-producing experience only when it is patterned or long term. To view depression or lowered emotional spaces positively, one must learn to see them for what they are—indicators of imbalance on the emotional level with the potential of affecting the other levels of beingness.

When you view a lowered emotional state as an indicator of imbalance, this is positive in that you become aware that you have some work to do with yourself if you are willing to undertake the inner journey rather than externalize the reason for your depression. On a higher level it is part of your spiritual guidance system. Depression, the entering into a lowered emotional space, an inner reaction to an outer reaction, usually means that your actions in your outer world are not in alignment with your true state, your God essence, the truth of your being. Perceiving the indicator correctly, you will see that what you really need to do is realign with the truth of who you are. It is a spiritual indicator that your outer actions have not reflected your inner truth or knowing. So these things that you label as fear, guilt, worry, rejection, insecurity, and so on are really designed to bring you back to the true path of your being. They were never designed to cause you to feel bad about yourself or to feel unworthy or to wallow in self pity.

The human entity, God expressing in form, was never meant to live his life burdened by guilt, imprisoned by fear, or overcome by worry. He was meant to live freely and abundantly in the joy of his being. This is only possible when the entity is in balance within his beingness and when he is reflecting his inner God essence into the outer world. One's spirit is always working to maintain the alignment so that the truth of the God essence can be expressed in the outer world in order that one's outer actions reflect one's inner truth. Depression, viewed positively, exists to create the awareness that there is a misalignment and an imbalance present.

When you enter depressed spaces, try seeing them as positive spaces created for your growth and unfoldment and as spaces for your learning. See these lowered spaces as a way of bringing you back into an alignment to the truth of your being. Work with these lowered spaces inwardly rather than externalizing the cause for them. Do not blind yourself to the cause through the use of placebos which only produce a temporary release from depression. Learning to take the inward journey when the indicators are present allows you to move out of these spaces quickly so that you do not have to undergo patterned or long term depression periods. Most of all, come to the positive awareness that that which you call human depression can, if you are willing, bring you back into alignment with the truth of your own God expression.

DO YOU FIT IN?

So many human entities are trying so hard to discern where they fit into the Cosmic Plan. They move from one project to another, one relationship to another, one course of study to another, one teacher to another. Frequently they never experience fulfillment or deep inner joy or a true sense of being part of It All and belonging. They hurry and scurry around working against some self-created Cosmic Clock and, in great disharmony, they endure undue stress and pressure. Not knowing where they fit into the Grand Scheme of things, they create missions for themselves in order to experience some sense of purpose, some reason for being. They allow themselves to be driven by the ego to perform, compete, and achieve. They believe that acclaim from the external world will tell them how and where they fit in. But, oh, they miss so much when they walk this chosen path.

The truth is that you would never have been created if you did not fit into the Cosmic Plan. The fact that *you are* means that you already fit in. There is no need to spend energy in an attempt to discover where you fit in. You are just as integral in the Plan as those entities that you have offered fame to and admire for what they have done on your planet. The bag lady is no less important than the leader of a great nation. All have been created and all are important and vital to the Whole of Creation. Once you realize this at your heart level rather than your head level, you will quit your search of where you fit into the Cosmic Plan.

It's alright to move from one course of study to another, one project to another, one relationship to another, one teacher to another, as long as it is not a search to find your place or niche in the world. These movements should merely be for the enhancement of your growth and unfoldment and for the growth and unfoldment of others. Remember that you are both student and teacher and that the focus should never be on the external experience, but rather on the lessons contained within the experience. All

55

created illusionary experiences contain lessons designed to bring you back into the awareness of your connection to and ultimately your Oneness with the Creator. If you are missing this, it might be wise to evaluate the overt external experiences you create for yourself.

With respect to that great Cosmic Clock you work against and which creates such stress and pressure for you—well, there is no Cosmic Clock. Time is your illusion. The true essence of your being is spiritual, and spirit knows no time. Since you have chosen to experience within a framework of time and space, then use it to grow and unfold and learn and teach. Let it be a friend and not your enemy. All those external things which you do that you feel are so important and critical in your life will pass away in the twinkling of an eye. Begin to seek the joy and the beauty contained in all that you do—all those external experiences which you create. In your work, in your play, in your committee meetings, in your alone time, express your love in all these experiences and then time will take on a whole new dimension for you. Pressure and stress and drudgery will be removed from whatever you choose to experience. With the added ingredient of love in all your chosen experiences, you will look forward to whatever you choose to do, and you will have increased energy, and time will never be the enemy. Think about the times you have really looked forward to going somewhere. Didn't you feel a heightened sense of energy, and weren't you ready to go long before the appointed time? The same could apply to going to your jobs or meeting a new person or anything else, if you would only instill everything you do in your lives with the power of your love.

As for creating missions to give you a sense of purpose and of belonging, well, you already have purpose and you already belong. Once you realize this at your deeper level, you will stop trying to discover your mission and purpose. The primary mission of each entity is to reach the point of unconditional love, which is a sense of connectedness leading to Oneness with everything and a willingness to allow whatever is to be and to become. This is the Real Journey—the Great Trip. The mission is an inner one, not an outer one.

You will do many things in your external world of space and time, and some will be of great value and benefit to your individual worlds, but how valuable and beneficial it is will be parallel to how much love you have placed into what you do. The more love you place into whatever you do in your external world, the more success, joy, beauty, and fulfillment you will receive in this, your life journey. If most of your life is spent in unconditional loving, your life will be wondrously exciting, full, and beautiful. You can have it all, and if you don't, you just haven't reached the awareness of who you really are yet. You may say you are God expressing—but do you believe it? Once you believe it, you will begin to act upon it, and then you return to Paradise, and the Kingdom and all the treasures therein are yours.

THE POSITIVE ASPECTS OF DISILLUSIONMENT

Disillusionment can be a positive experience. An experience can be charged in any way that you choose it to be. When your created illusion is not aligned with others, disillusionment may set in, as well as doubt in your own sense of truth.

On an individual level, what is disillusionment? It is simply your own spirit urging you to release or detach from an illusion of your own creation. If you do this, you will be led into a new awareness, or enlightenment. This can be a powerful part of your own unfoldment, but it can also bring much pain and discomfort. Sometimes it's very difficult to release a cherished illusion, and the experience can oftentimes be likened to a death experience in which, for a time, you might mourn and grieve your loss.

In your journey toward Absolute Truth, your relative truth will always be challenged, for this is the process by which you grow and unfold. Since you are not a static being it can be no other way, and every illusion you create will ultimately be challenged. You will constantly be urged to release from whatever illusions you attach to that are not for your highest good. In many ways the spirit is a hard taskmaster.

If this, then, is the case, you may ask: "Am I supposed to experience my life walk in continual disillusionment?" The answer is yes, but this need not be negative if you perceive the process differently. Continual disillusionment (or the release from illusions) is the same thing as continual enlightenment. They are just two sides of the same coin. How much better to ask: "Am I supposed to experience my life walk in continual enlightenment?"

We have noted how human entities experience the process of disillusionment and the suffering they endure in connection with it. Why do they suffer so? Usually it's because they have taken their illusions too seriously and have made them too important, or they have allowed themselves to be imprisoned by them. Consider your own illusions and their importance to you. How seriously do you take them? What is really important to you—your relationships with others, your material possessions, your careers, or your health and well-being? All these are what you have created them to be. What you think and give power to is what you

57

bring into form; what you continue to empower is what you hold in form. Form is the illusion; thought is the essence of the illusion. When energy is no longer empowering thought, the illusion dissipates. This is the release of the illusion and the enlightenment of seeing something new.

Let me offer you the simple example of a balloon. The balloon represents thought. As you begin to blow air into the balloon, it begins to expand into its form. This represents energy or empowering. The more air you expel into the balloon, the larger it becomes and the greater is its form. Now with a balloon you will have two options. You can tie a knot in its end in order to retain its form or you can continue to add air into it. If you've tied a knot in it, you all know that in time (if no more air is added to it) it will eventually become flat. And you know as well that continuing to add air will ultimately cause the balloon to break. In either case, the illusion changes. The point I wish to make is that you cannot hold any of your formed illusions forever.

If you grieve when the balloons of your life flatten or break, you will never find happiness or joy. See the balloons for what they are: illusions you have created and empowered for your own growth. Don't hold onto them so tightly or think they will never change. Allow them to fly free in the ever changing sky. You see, holding on too tightly to any illusion only makes the pain of release from it more difficult. Your created illusions are as vaporous as air and can evaporate as quickly as they were formed. Enjoy them in their own time and release them when their time has passed. Flow with your created illusions, for in this way you will experience the wonder and the majesty of the whole canvas of your life.

HYPOCRISY

Hypocrisy simply means telling others to do what you do not do or will not do, which is not practicing what you preach. Being a hypocrite is not a sin and is certainly not worth beating yourself up over when you look in the mirror and realize that you are perhaps guilty. Sin is nothing more than ignorance of or misuse of universal laws.

When you realize that you are being hypocritical, this is positive because awareness is the first step in its transformation. Let us use an example of love. If you tell others to be loving and you look into the self mirror and see that you are not loving, the human reaction is to feel guilt and to label yourself as a hypocrite. Doing this only makes you feel worse about yourself. It empowers a negative image of self. Yet, if you approach perceived hypocrisy differently, you will be able to transform it with greater ease. If you are encouraging others to be loving and you discover that you are not being loving, you have received a positive awareness, and this is good. What you tell others is generally what you need to hear; what you teach is oftentimes that which you seek to learn. Quite frequently the higher qualities you seek to attain begin first in the head, and as you continue to strive, they move to the heart. You encourage others to be loving because this is what you wish to attain, and the more that you verbalize it and hear yourself saying it, the more it becomes a part of your belief system and the faster it moves toward your heart level. In time, if you don't give up and don't beat yourself up with guilt, you will become that which you seek to be. The attainment of the qualities you seek is, like everything else, a process, an unfoldment, and it is initiated first by a self-awareness, followed by a loving acknowledgment of an imbalance, followed by a transformation.

Do not worry about what others think. Concern yourself with what you think. Speak your word or words because the more you do, the more they become part of you until they come into manifested experience in your life. It is truly a self journey but, oh, how human entities imprison themselves with labels, judgments, and guilts. Speaking something without backing it up with overt actions is not hypocrisy. It is your way of affirming something you desire to move from your head to your heart. And it's okay. Be more gentle with yourselves.

DON'T BLAME GOD OR KARMA
FOR UNHAPPINESS

Within one's life walk, a person will frequently reach places where major decisions need to be made in order to further the growth and unfoldment process. He may be flooded by indecisiveness heightened by fear of the unknown. So he stands rooted, almost paralyzed in his position, split between not being able to stay where he is and fearful of moving on. In your terminology you might say, "you're damned if you do and damned if you don't."

If people remain in a space where they are unhappy and are not growing, they oftentimes comfort themselves with rationalizations, such as, "I'm exactly where God wants me to be in this moment" or "it's my Karma to be here." And so they tolerate and endure and serve out their sentence on planet Earth, and they exit unfulfilled, incomplete, and still imprisoned.

Let's return to that neatly tied statement about "being exactly where God wants me to be." That's true. Except that God is not something external to yourself pulling your strings and, like marionettes, dancing you onto whatever stage serves His whim. God wants you to be wherever you want to be, for He lives inside you; He expresses through you. I would not find too much consolation in believing that you are "exactly where God wants you to be" if you are miserable in that space. That certainly doesn't say much for God, does it? The truth is that you are exactly where you choose to be, happy or unhappy; you choose your place and your space and you can move forward when you choose.

As for Karma—well, you do enter spaces for learning and teaching, for that is what one's life walk is all about, is it not? But do not use Karma as an excuse for all your unhappiness. Quite often human entities enter a space to work out Karmic imbalances and then remain in it long after balancing has occurred because they become complacent and comfortable, though they remain unhappy. One always knows when the balance has occurred, primarily because the spirit begins urging him forward. And sometimes when there is great unhappiness present and this continues to manifest in various ways, more Karma is incurred. Like a merry-go-round at a carnival, you keep putting your quarters in to keep that old wheel turning. All the while, whenever the music stops you can get off. You don't have to keep feeding it unless, of course, you like the ride. But if your spirit keeps saying the ride is over and urging you to get off, and you keep saying, "I'm afraid to get off, so I'll put another quarter in," then so be it. You have a choice. Just don't blame Karma or God if you've elected to be unhappy.

Life was not meant to be experienced in continual unhappiness. There will be some, of course, because you live in an illusionary world of duality and because you choose to work out imbalances within the framework of the Karmic process, which is really a man-made, mini-version of the Universal Law of Cause and Effect. In truth, you do not really even have to accept the Karmic process because the Law of Cause and Effect is the perfect Balancer, and all Creation is under it.

Your path is your own and how you walk upon it is your choice. No one walks with you, and even though another is able to put his own foot into your footprints, he cannot put his foot into the space where yours is resting. It is, however, extremely important to be very honest about your path. Deep within you know what you both need and want to do in order to complete your particular mission and also what would make you feel fulfilled and more complete. The space is within, and this must be where you first begin to serve. Serve your own God essence first; then service flows outward to others.

THINGS AREN'T STUPID

One statement in Leo Buscaglia's book, "Living, Loving and Learning," keeps coming back. It is his statement, "Things are stupid." This is such a simple statement, but yet really so true, at least, in a sense. Of course, things in themselves are not stupid. They are made up of atoms and molecules and thus have atomic and molecular essence. They have energy, are Source created in their basic form, and thus have essence. Atoms and subatomic particles have divine intelligence because they are of the Creator. It is an intelligence beyond your comprehension. Therefore the basic composition of things cannot be stupid.

What is stupid—and what Mr. Buscaglia may be saying—is man's value of things. In societies where there is an abundance of non-essential things and where one's societal position is based on his accumulation of non-essential things, it is possible to be controlled by things, by your illusions. Things are not stupid, but the value placed on them can be, for one can become imprisoned by his own illusionary objects.

The truly aware entity will bless the gifts given to him, but he will see the illusionary things for what they are, and he will not allow himself to be controlled by them. The true purpose of abundance of non-essential gifts is actually to free you to seek the higher non-physical gifts which await you. With an abundance of things it is easy to be controlled by them when you place too much value upon them. And when too much value is placed upon physical things, you can become blocked in seeking the non-physical things which do have value. True value lies in the essence and not in the illusionary manifestation of forms.

Most of Earth's problems stem from the obsessive value man places on physical things—property, money, cars, houses, gems, and so forth. As I said before, an abundance of these physical things should free the recipient to seek higher non-physical gifts. The purpose of the abundance of physical things is to free you from the struggle for survival and to make your life easier and thus allow you to ascend to the higher gifts of life. The trap emerges when one sees things as the substance of life and when one values things more than anything else. Then your abundance becomes a prison rather than a way of freedom.

Enjoy the things given you and care for the gifts you are blessed with, but don't be controlled by them. If something is lost or stolen or destroyed or broken, don't allow yourself to be devastated. Remember that the value that any physical illusion has is only what you choose to place upon it. Remember also that all gifts bestowed upon you are there to assist you in your progression into awareness.

SUPPORTIVENESS

Being supportive of another's mission does not mean that you must totally or completely align yourself with their particular mission or purpose, for if you do this it could mean having to abandon your own individual mission or purpose. Every entity will fulfill whatever mission they entered the Earth plane to accomplish before they exit. But if one does not stay on his own course, it can take much longer.

Being supportive means attempting to understand what others are led to do and aiding and assisting when you are able and when it does not interfere with your own inner directions. If another is preparing to do something which he feels he must do to fulfill his own purpose, it does not indicate a lack of love or non-support if you do not feel led in the same direction. One is both loving and supportive if he understands that the other is being led and is working to accomplish a certain mission. Align yourself with another if your inner guidance directs you to do so, for there are times when you will share a mission or a purpose with others. But do not align yourself if you feel no inner direction and are doing so for lesser reasons.

Sometimes an entity who is being directed in a particular purpose will think that his mission is of such high worth that he will either expect or demand that others share his zeal and enthusiasm. If others do not, he may feel that he is not loved or that others are not being supportive. Think of the times that you've had what you thought to be a wonderful idea and you wanted others to be as excited as you, but they weren't. The ego says that because your zeal is not shared, you are not supported. This is generally not the case. Oftentimes an entity will find his own zeal dampened when others will not share his zeal, and this is wrong. Do not allow others to throw water on your enthusiasm for something.

True love and supportiveness of others comes when you understand that *each* entity has a unique and individual mission to accomplish and when you allow others, as well as yourself, through your understanding, to accomplish what you and they are directed to do. Never judge or assess what another is attempting to accomplish in his life experience. *All* entities have purpose and worth. Support always their right to be and love always the god within.

HOW TO EXPERIENCE NEUTRALITY

Once one really comprehends the fact that he is the creator, controller, and maintainer of his own vibrational climate, it will make the task of merging into an experience easier. As long as one believes or feels that he is at the whim of the Cosmos, he will be buffeted back and forth from positive to negative by the vibrations of other entities. One will be affected adversely or positively depending on both the strength of his own vibrations and the control he exercises over his vibrational level. In other words, if he has a weak vibrational level, he can be overcome by the vibrational levels of others. Weakness in controlling one's own vibrational level makes one more prone to being affected by the vibrations of others.

Human entities have been conditioned to view experiences as either negative or positive. They have been conditioned to believe that the experiences in life are in themselves negative or positive, rather than our responses to them. So many experiences are entered into with preconceived notions and handed-down data from other entities. Most entities who enter your plane of experience are influenced in their early lives to become predisposed to being either primarily negative or positive personalities. Unfortunately, most seem to lean toward the negative vibrational climates. Seldom, if ever, is a child taught neutrality, which is a perfect balance of vibrations.

In order to enter an experience from a point of neutrality and respond positively, remove from your belief system the idea that an experience is negative or positive in itself. It is neither. It simply is. It becomes whatever you elect it to become by your response to it. If you enter with preconceived notions learned from others, then your response is preset. A preset response waives your right to free will, because it will be based on borrowed, preconditioned data, and is not your own. In other words, you enter the experience with prejudice and a preestablished leaning.

This is not to say that you should not listen to the experiences of others and learn from those experiences which do not directly affect you. But in listening and hearing of the experiences of others, remember that what you are really hearing are the responses to the experiences of others. Do some housecleaning. This means examining your belief system carefully and discarding preconceived notions and passed down data which can inhibit your freedom of response and which, in fact, are in control of your vibrational climate. True freedom is really balance and neutrality, not only in thought but in response.

How do you create a positive response when there is already a negative climate present? If you are bombarded by negative vibrations from another, it is best to stay in the neutral zone. This means that until you are fully developed in this art, you must use your will and power to maintain neutrality. Neutrality is rather like a shield which, if it is impossible to have harmonious vibrations, at least will prevent you from suffering from the disharmony of negative vibrations, or from adding more negative energy to an already negative situation.

As you become more comfortable and competent in controlling the state of neutrality, you actually pave the way to learning to increase your positive vibrations. With a neutral energy you have the option to transform it one way or another—positive or negative. If you master neutrality and can stay in balance, you do not deplete energy, and thus it accumulates and grows. If you master neutrality you can form a positive vibrational response to any experience. You then have the power to create, control, and maintain a positive response and a positive vibrational climate through all of life. When you do this the positive influences overpower the negative, transforming rather than destroying them, thus increasing the positive energy. Once you can do this you will no longer be affected by mass vibrations of negative energy. Then you are really free.

The first step toward being in control and creating positive vibrations is to master neutrality. Positivity is the goal, but neutrality is the way to the goal. Within the state of neutrality you will be balanced and free of stress, able to use inherent wisdom and intuition, and to draw nearer to the essences contained within created life. Your vision will become clearer, your perception more accurate, and your power and potential stronger. A neutral state of mind is an uncluttered mind which allows only relevant data to flow in from the external world. It is an open channel to the Universal Mind. A neutral state of mind is in control of the ego and thus does not judge, but only assesses from a spiritual point the most beneficial way for the human organism to respond and grow and express the God spirit within.

HOW TO LIVE LIFE

Life itself is a vibration which moves like waves upon a great sea. Let me share with you some positive thoughts which will help you to live your life experience more fully and joyfully:

1. *Begin with love.* Love is light and thus cannot enter valleys or be under the darkness of a wave. It shines on peaks and crests. If you feel darkness in your life, analyze your own vibrations of love. You will discover that you entered this state because of some lack of loving in your own being. Do all things with love. Love trusts and believes and has a knowledge of from whence it came. Love restores balance to your life and renews all things.

2. *Try to see things for what they are and render unto them only the importance they deserve.* You can magnify situations and create

thoughts which, when given enough power, can manifest into form and self-created action. Take life as it comes to you without attempting to image the future. Do what you are able with love and trust.

3. *Accept your life experience and know that you are where you must be to learn what you must learn until it is time to move into a new direction.* Let the spirit lead, for the ego may pull you from the path. Even if you leave your path at the ego's urging, be patient, for the spirit will come and guide you back. Do not envy or begrudge another's life or think that their life is better, for they are where they must be for their learning. Be patient with yourself and with others and wait upon the will of your Creator, knowing that He will act always to your benefit and highest good.

4. *Become one with creation and flow in its rhythm.* See no beginnings and no endings, but rather an eternal flow from dimension to dimension toward Oneness and perfection. Lovingly accept the changes as you move through your space-time dimension. Do not allow the changes to become obstacles to your growth, and do not perceive in them the darkness of valleys and undertows. Do not resist, for you will suffer and drown in your own self-created waves. Take your life one moment at a time, shower each moment with vibrations of love, and flow in Cosmic rhythm.

5. *Do not worry or fear.* Follow your inner guidance with regard to experience. Be concerned, if necessary, but not worried. Use caution if inner guidance dictates, but do not fear. Worry and fear create negative illusions and forms.

Remember that you have been given all the equipment necessary to ride the waves and stay upon the peaks. You have intelligence, you have seven levels of consciousness to direct you, you have the direct connection to Universal Mind and thus to Universal Wisdom, you have many entities assisting you, and you have the qualities to call upon to keep you in the light and above the darkness. But it is all for naught unless you surrender to spiritual control so that you will flow and become one with the rhythm of your own life experience and thus one with the rhythm of Creation.

These are affirmations which can assist you on your journey:
1. I will do all things with love.
2. I will see love in all things.
3. I will accept what is and where I am as the garden of my learning and my growth.

4. I will trust in divine will and be patient, knowing that all things will be for my good.
5. I will not worry or fear and will not give negative thoughts power.
6. I will become one with Creation and flow in the rhythm of eternal change, knowing it is for my growth and good.
7. I will see things as they are and will give them no more importance than divine will dictates they should have.
8. I will surrender the negative aspects of my ego and I will let my being be controlled by my spirit.

DEVELOPING INNER STRENGTH

When you feel depressed and boxed in by negativity around you or when you feel discouraged with yourself for sometimes entering into negativity, become quiet and still and strive to connect with Universal Mind.

Try to stay clear of the disagreements of others. They are not your problems unless you choose to take them onto yourself. If others try to push them onto you, resist them. By taking on the problems of others which are not really there for your learning and growth, you also take on any Karma associated with them.

Become more aware of your own special uniqueness, your own feelings, your own thoughts, your own inner awareness, so that the assessments of your being expressed by others do not give rise to defensiveness by your own ego. It doesn't matter what others think you are or believe you to be. In truth, only you and the Source within knows the truth of your own being. The Source alone knows what you are destined to become and unfold into.

Let the world see you as it wishes, and allow others to perceive you as they will based on their own life experiences and visions of the world. Just as you cannot perceive the truth or essence of another, so also is it true that another cannot perceive your essence. Only when you reach the awareness of seeing the God within the All can you ever hope to catch a glimpse of the true essence of anything within your dimension.

You know more about the truth of your own being than anyone else can. Another cannot feel your feelings, think your thoughts, dream your dreams, or feel your pain. And you cannot express adequately enough so that others can perceive *your* truth. This is because you are all changing and unfolding at different rates and in different and unique ways.

Don't be upset when another labels you or assigns certain qualities or false feelings that you may or may not have. Remember that others are seeing you from their own sense of truth and their own individual perception of the world. No one's perception of another can be truly accurate. One's perception of another is generally based on his own individual vision of the world and his own life experiences and belief system.

Be still and know that God is expressing uniquely through your being. Be still and know that you are unfolding according to His plan, as are all others who allow Him to unfold within their beings. Use the power within you to grow and expand and flourish. Be gentle in your assessments of others and seek to see the God within them. Be at peace and know that guidance is ever present and that Universal Love flows constantly in a continual replenishment of your spirit. Be gentle with yourself and seek to know the *I AM* of your own being. Be gentle with yourself and you will cease to be concerned with what the world may think of you. Rise up and walk in trust of the One who created you.

TRUST YOUR OWN PROCESS—LOVING YOURSELF UNCONDITIONALLY

There has been a lot of discussion about that which is termed unconditional love. Many human entities desire to love without placing conditions on that which they have selected to love, but most fall short simply because they try to define what "Unconditional Love" is. The mere attempt to define it places conditions on it and it becomes conditional.

As with all things on Earth, what is or is not "unconditional love" is perceptual and relative to each individual entity. The truth is that unconditional love, in its purest form, cannot be defined because it is the God Essence which is woven throughout the tapestry of Creation. It is That which Is.

However, to bring it to the level of human comprehension, I will attempt to tell you what it is on the Earth plane and what it is not. First of all, it is not a feeling; it is a state of being. Perhaps the key quality within the state of unconditional love is that of total acceptance and complete allowing. In the area of relationships, for example, it is the acceptance of and the allowing of another to be and to express whatever he may be without judgment or criticism. Very few human entities are able to offer this on a continual basis. This type of acceptance and allowing means that one is emotionally nonattached because unconditional love comes forth from the spirit and not the ego. It is not enough to simply allow something to occur or be outwardly accepting of a situation if your thoughts are not aligned to your actions. If you say, "I'll be unconditionally loving and accept this outwardly, but this (situation) really 'bugs the heck' out of me," you are not in a state of unconditional love.

Although most human entities do not attain this state on a conscious level, they need not be dismayed or frustrated or see the attainment of unconditional love as an impossible goal. At your very heart, in your very essence, you are already in that state. At your highest level of beingness, you are already in a state of unconditional love. Each unselfish act or expression of love is a fragment of your highest state of being. What is an unselfish act or expression of love? It is simply expressing the best of yourself at your present level of awareness without expecting or demanding anything in return. Love, however, is like a boomerang which, when sent out, returns again to you. It is the Law of Cause and Effect in action, as well as the Law of Attraction.

You express the very best and highest part of your being when you love your own beingness. Human entities oftentimes have great difficulty in loving themselves, and they are frequently harder on themselves than they are on others, or they believe that loving themselves is somehow wrong. You must remember that you cannot truly offer to another what you cannot or will not offer yourself. If you say to another "I love you," and yet you despise your own beingness, you are not truly loving the other. You are your own first experience—that which projects outward and reflects back inwardly. You are your own mirror.

Human entities would have less difficulty loving themselves and hence, loving others, if they could see themselves as they are instead of through the dim light of their created illusions. You are Creative Expressions, which means that you express the Creator—Love—Light. You are like flowers in the garden called Life, and on this part of your journey are growing in the rich soil of planet Earth. As with the flowers of any beautiful garden, you are all at different stages of development—some still struggling to push through the soil, others just beginning to feel the warmth of the sun, some in tiny bud form, some struggling against weeds and insects, others in full bloom, and still others withering and dying and preparing to move to a higher dimension of Life.

Be gentle with yourselves, for you are in process; you are changing, growing, unfolding, and becoming, in manifested form, that which you already are in essence. If you can come to acknowledge and love the beauty of your own expression, you can express this outwardly to others in your world; if you can learn to be less critical and judgmental of yourself, you will be less critical and judgmental of others. If you can learn to become more accepting and allowing of your own beingness, you will offer this gift to others; and if you can learn to be more forgiving of yourself for your own perceived flaws, you will be able to forgive others for theirs.

You are God Expressing and gods experiencing, and through the experiences you create on Earth, if you choose to allow it, you will unfold into the essential truth of your being—which is unconditional love. As with all guidance, it always begins with you. Connect with the *Truth of You,* and you connect with the truth of All Creation. If you can truly *Love You,* there is nothing you cannot empower with the Love Energy. Human entities have the potential to be their own best friend or their own worst enemy, and what they are to themselves, they project onto their manifested world.

You may ask, "How can I love myself when the outer world keeps telling me that I am no more than a worm in the dust? How can I love myself when the world is the keeper of such a great catalog of sins and flaws that man seems to be heir to? How can I love myself when the world keeps impressing on me that I am imperfect?" A great many entities, most in fact, have been programmed from entrance into form by the judgments and criticisms of others. Collective mind has, indeed, created the catalog of what is right or wrong, good or evil, normal or abnormal. You have been influenced greatly by this, and this is why so many entities feel "bad about themselves" and, projected outwardly, do not feel "good about others." So many walk their journey with their heads down, feeling insignificant, insecure, fearful, lacking confidence or a sense of self-worth, unable to love. Others mask it and project egotism, aggression, dominance, hate. Neither of these types reflect the truth of beingness; they reflect their programming. To overcome programming which does not allow you a vision of who you really are requires a lot of conscious effort to release from it. It requires a willingness to examine those areas which cause you to feel "bad about yourself" and release from them. There are always blocks to growth, barriers to unfoldment, and weeds and insects threatening to strangle and suck the Life from your bloom. To become what you are in essence, you must be free. A human entity is always his own jailor and the keeper of the keys which will unlock his prison door. A lot of human entities keep themselves locked up because of things they've done in the past which they or others considered as wrong. The past is not you—it was part of your unfoldment, lessons created *by you for you* to move you into greater beingness. Do not become stuck in the

69

mire of what you consider to be past mistakes. Look at the past from an observer position, pull from your experiences those lessons which can make you a better you, forgive yourself, if that is necessary for you, unlock your cell door, and move forward toward your own light.

You have so much power and potential which is of little value if it is not used. You are each a significant and a valuable part of the All, and without you, the All would cease to be the All. If I could, I would show you what you, in truth, are. I would show you your essence, your light, your love. But I can only tell you. It is the journey each entity must take, and sometimes it takes lifetimes of lessons to connect with your Absolute Essence. The journey is to become what you already are, to see and acknowledge who you really are, and to project this outward.

Some might say that it is wrong to elevate man so, for fear that he might consider himself to be equal to God. But at the highest level of his beingness, in his essence, he is God, and when he expresses the best part of himself at whatever level of awareness he is on, he is God Expressing in manifested form. There is nothing egotistic about this, for when an entity expresses the best part of whatever he is in a now moment, he is coming from spirit, not ego. This is the goal: to express the best of yourself, always with the knowledge that you are in a beautiful process called Life and that you are changing, growing, unfolding, becoming more, becoming finer, becoming what *you are*. Lighten up on yourselves and enjoy the process. Follow your own inner guidance and your own sense of truth, release from all those gods which no longer serve you well, and, most of all, trust in your own process. This done, you will offer to your outer world all that you have gifted yourself with. You will, with greater frequency, discover that you are in a state of "unconditional love."

TRUE PERSONAL POWER

True personal power is "knowing" who "you" are and acting and living in accordance with that knowledge. One of your wise Earth entities shared, "This above all: to thine own self be true, and it must follow, as the night the day, thou canst not then be false to any man." One's point of power is his awareness of the truth of his beingness. When an entity enters into the knowingness that the truth of his being is that he is God expressing and when he begins to allow that innate and essential God energy to flow through him onto the material plane, he is then connected with his own power. It is important that one realize that "knowingness" is much different than just believing or hoping or affirming that the power is available. It is always there, but one must know it is there in order to

70

use it. True inner knowing with respect to one's personal power is really something which cannot be verbally expressed. Knowing who you are and what you are in truth is awareness of your power. Acting upon your own truth and expressing it is holding your own power.

In your world and in your interactions and relationships with others, an entity may discover that he is being defined by others. At some point or another, you've all been defined by those in your life. How many others have you defined? Human entities define those others in their world according to their individual perceptions which are oftentimes inaccurate, or they try to define others according to what they want to see rather than what is. In other words. they create illusions.

Now if another is defining you in a certain way and you attempt to be that way for some reason—perhaps to gain approval, make someone like you, prevent a relationship from breaking—and this is not the truth of "you," then you are giving your power to another. This is really more common than not, on your plane. Most human entities try to live in accordance with the expectations and demands of others. Most human entities give up their power. This in one reason why so many entities are unhappy and spend their lives in chaos and inner conflict.

At the core of the human entity is the God essence, the point of power. In the heart of each man there is a subtle yearning to know who he is and express that to the manifested world. There is no greater joy than knowing who you are and being that and allowing yourself to become and grow and unfold. Being who you are does not necessarily mean getting to do what your ego wants to do all of the time. Remember that what is called ego is the survival programming for the human vehicle. The results of the force of the ego can be negative or positive, depending on the use or the abuse of it. Unless it is very balanced with spirit, the ego seldom expresses the truth of one's being. So much of what man calls power emerges from the ego base. Power is not control over others, although this appears to be how many entities define it. If an entity is the head of a government or an organization or things of that nature, he has authority. Whatever power he may have in conjunction with that authority is given to him by others.

It is not uncommon for human entities to give up their individual power to others for various reasons. Oftentimes a human entity is not even aware that he has personal power. This is usually due to cultural or societal programming. Examples might be the submissive wife who gives her power away to a dominant husband or the individual entity who gives away his power to please those in his peer group. The base reason why human entities give away their power is rooted in fear. When you give up your power to someone else, you will most likely discover that you are

71

afraid of something in your external world. And fear, of course, is born of ego, not spirit.

There are no real benefits to surrendering your own power to another. When you give up your power to another, you are not expressing in accordance with your own truth. It is rather like a daffodil trying to be a rose. As hard as you try, you will never become what you are not in essence. If your essence is that of a daffodil, you can only pretend to be a rose. You will only try to pretend to be that which you are not if you think others prefer roses or if you fear that springtime's golden flower is a lesser expression than a summer's rose. Whenever you do not express the truth of your being, you are in a type of bondage. How free one really is on your plane is dependent on the degree to which one has surrendered his own personal power to the manifested world. This is something to think about. How much of yourself, your power, have you given over to the manifested world? In the Christian holy writings, it says, "Seek ye first the kingdom of God..." It also says, "The Kingdom of God is within you." In other words, seek your own truth of beingness, the realm of your spirit, your individual Kingdom of God, your place of power within and you will be connected with your power.

Many entities surrender their power to the manifested world simply because they do not know the truth of their beingness and have not taken the time to journey within to discover it. This inner journey in search of self is not always an easy one. As one sifts through layers and layers of programming and self-created illusions, he will discover that he must release from a lot of what he considered to be the truth of himself. He finds that he must surrender the pretenses that he has given in order to please the material world. The realization that he has not been true to himself is not always an easy thing to accept.

However, once you enter that sanctuary of self, your own individual kingdom of God, and see the light of your own truth and essence, you will realize that this is what you really want to express outwardly. It does take courage to express who you really are and to be and act in accordance with your own truth. It does take courage to say: "This is who I am." The most powerful words denoting one's individual power are: I am.

The benefits of taking the inner journey into self are: (1) discovering who and what you really are; (2) releasing from programming which blinds you to your truth; (3) being able to define your own self; and (4) being released from bondage into freedom. Knowing who you are, being that, and expressing that is a freeing experience and a way of reclaiming your own power.

So many human entities struggle and are in great inner conflict. Man yearns to know who he is and to be what he is in essence and in truth. Deep within him he knows that the lack of knowing his own truth of beingness makes him vulnerable to surrendering his power to others. This pulls him into bondage, and creates great conflict in his life.

What is an entity like when he has reclaimed his own individual power, when he has connected with that point of inner power, and has become centered in it? Is it noticeable to others in his world? Yes. The strongest and greatest power in an entity is always very subtle and quiet. It is not overpowering and aggressive to others. You can tell the entity who holds his own power by the way in which he expresses himself outwardly. He walks his path with sureness and with a sense of peace. These are always the qualities of one who knows who he is and who expresses it outwardly. He no longer needs to seek who he is, but rather seeks to unfold into greater "isness." One must always remember that the human entity is continually changing, unfolding, flowing, and becoming, but that essence only expands. The one who is connected to his own power sees it as his own unique gift and is unwilling to give it away, yet is willing to help others to discover their own power. He has no desire to control others with his power; he wishes only to stay centered in the power of his own light. Reclaiming or connecting with one's inner power takes work, perhaps, but it is the path of bringing one to the point of peace with himself and of allowing himself to express the truth of his beingness to the world. If you are true to yourself, really in truth, you will not be false to others, and when you say, "I am," you will be vulnerable to no one.

WORRY

To worry about anything is of little value, dear entity. Have I not told you this so many times before? For to worry serves only to change the energy of that which is in the process of unfolding. If there is positive energy within the unfoldment process, your energy of worry but peppers it with negative energy. And if negative energy is already within the process, you only add more negative salt to the gurgling pot. If you can't, in your truth, affirm and manifest positivity to that which is unfolding, then truly it is best to merely stay clear and quietly allow that which will unfold. Always there are choices for you: you may simply watch the pot simmer or boil, you may start adding more and more seasonings, or you may jump right into the pot.

A good cook, however, follows the recipe. You who are aware know what the recipe is, for you have master chefs to guide you, have you not?

Once you have blended the ingredients and have followed directions, what is there to worry about? Worry comes in when you doubt the recipe and begin changing it. What could have become a feast becomes crumbs for the table of your life. The meal, be it a feast or crumbs, is your own life experience, and you are the preparer. Think on this.

Each moment you prepare a meal for yourself. If you have prepared but crumbs, you hoard them instead of eating them so that by eventide you are weighted down by the burden of the weight of the crumbs. And crumbs, no matter how many there are, never a feast do make. If you have created crumbs in a now moment, consume them and then move to prepare a feast. For even on crumbs one gains from the nourishment of learning.

So many times you have heard, "Do not worry. All will be fine. This, too, shall pass." So many times entities have replied, "What do they know? They are not struggling through this school!" But we know, for we have chosen to be connected to your confusion, your doubt, your suffering, your agony, and all those things which your ego tells you make you human. If we did not choose to be connected, we could not teach you the truth, nor could we assist in lifting the veils which cloud your understanding.

When I say to you "Do not worry," I do not do so merely to pacify you or console you or to offer you some dim glimmer of hope. I do so to offer you a truth—a truth which, if accepted, will serve to strengthen you. Truly, what is there for you to worry about, particularly since it serves no valid purpose in your life? Worry is a child of fear, and fear is a manifestation of your ego's survival programming. One who trusts, who walks in the light of his own God essence, who allows his own process, has nothing to fear and hence nothing to worry about.

When you are thus connected, you become more aware and more attuned to your external world. In this state, who can harm you? You may say, "But there are deceivers and betrayers and those who would seek to do me harm in my world." In the physical realm this may be an illusionary truth because there are so many levels of awareness present. But if you are aware, you will see the deception, the betrayal, and those who might seek to harm you. And if you are a god, you will not judge them but will allow the Law of Cause and Effect within the Cosmos to restore balance. Think about the Master Christ. Did He not know that He would be deceived, betrayed, and harmed? He knew because He was connected, and when one is connected to the All, he enters into a oneness with even those who would seek to harm him. Even with foreknowledge, which always comes with Total Connection, He allowed it all to unfold. He did not seek to prevent it and He did not fear and He did not judge and He did not seek revenge. He simply allowed and loved and forgave. Why? Because in this Complete Connection and Understanding of Universal Laws, He knew that all would be restored to harmony and balance.

To worry about anything creates a resistance to the natural flow of one's life. It's like building a dam on a river to hold back its flow. Build no dams of worry, doubt, or fear. Trust in the river of your life and allow it to flow unhindered. I promise you, it will not fail you.

A NEGATIVE STRUGGLE IS THE SAME AS A POSITIVE CHALLENGE

Since so many entities are perceiving themselves as experiencing inner or outer struggles, let us discuss the nature of struggles from a different perspective. A struggle, like most Earth creations, is based on one's individual perception of a particular experience, and it is relative only to the one who has the experience. What one sees as a particular struggle is simply part of a process to ensure growth and continued unfoldment. In spite of what you may think, the lotus flower experiences struggle with the unfoldment of each new petal, and a tiny shoot struggles to break through the soil to greet the sun.

A struggle is something a human entity will create to challenge a particular level of his being—physical, mental, emotional, or spiritual. You've heard how the butterfly must struggle to break free from the cocoon which imprisons him. Remember, as well, that the butterfly was once a caterpillar who spun his own cocoon. The caterpillar who resists spinning his cocoon will never be a butterfly. The butterfly imprisoned within the cocoon who will not fight to break free from his self-made mold will never experience flight. It is the struggle for freedom that gives strength to the wings which will carry him aloft. You have only to remember the time when, as a child, you found a cocoon and broke it open to find a butterfly inside. If you recall, that butterfly never flew. He died because you removed the struggle necessary to strengthen his wings.

Human entities tend to view a struggle, whatever it happens to be, as a negative experience. Seldom, if ever, will they recognize the growth which is occurring until long past the time of the experience. Then perhaps, after they have passed through the darkness into the light, they may look back into the darkness of their experience and see where growth has taken place.

Back to the butterfly. During the cocoon experience, a part of the time in that limiting darkness is spent in quiet transformation. In that darkness, metamorphosis is occurring; great inner and outer change is taking place. The caterpillar is actually becoming a new creature with new qualities and a new dimension to his being. In that dark prison, the old is being shed away to prepare for the new.

As man spins a cocoon around himself, he creates an experience in which he is challenged at some level of his being. And he struggles against that by which he is challenged. Why? Because on a higher level he knows that the experience will create a transformation in his being—a new dimension to what and who he really is.

So many human entities will try very hard to avoid the spinning of the cocoon. It's as if they would prefer to remain in the caterpillar stage content to nibble leaves for the rest of their days. Now there's nothing wrong with caterpillars, I suppose, for they, too, have their purpose, And I suppose there is some peace and happiness to be found in simply crawling around nibbling leaves. However, there's something inside a caterpillar which drives him to spin a cocoon around himself and enter the darkness and patiently endure the stages of metamorphosis. There is something inside the entrapped butterfly that knows when it's time to struggle free to the light. The caterpillar and the entrapped butterfly do not resist the process. They allow and flow with the process to its completion.

True pain enters the process when one is resistant to the flow of the process, and does not allow the experience. One of your philosophers said that "man is a bridge, not a goal." One meaning for this is that Man is evolving into a higher and higher being. Evolution requires stages of development which involve struggle and the continual breaking free into higher dimensions of beingness.

Struggles would seem less threatening, less painful, and less confusing if you would perceive them as something you have created for your own growth and unfoldment. Struggles would be more understandable if you would see them as a process or part of your own individual evolutionary development.

Have you ever wondered what a caterpillar does inside the darkness of his cocoon? Is he impatient? Does he fear the unknown Does he miss those wonderful days of nibbling leaves? The answer is no. He patiently flows with the process and with a natural trust allows the transformation to occur. He does not bemoan his situation and think, "Oh, why is this happening to me?" He does not fear that he is imprisoned in eternal darkness. He simply allows his unfoldment moment by moment. He may not know why he was led to spin a cocoon or why he entered the darkness or even what is to become of him. But, like all of Nature, with the possible exception of Man, his own God essence trusts in the process and flows with it without demand or expectation.

Sometimes humans spend too much energy in the analysis of why they are experiencing a particular struggle instead of utilizing that energy in breaking free from the cocoon. The result is that they stay in the darkness longer than they need to or they become too tired to break free. I agree that some self-analysis is always beneficial in a growth stage and seems to be necessary for such an intellectual animal as Man. On the other hand, you sometimes overanalyze experiences and your relationship to them. Sometimes greater growth is attained if one says, "This is what is in this now moment. I am what I am in this now moment." Then stay with the experience, flow with it, learn from it, and move away from it.

Man is such a subjective being that he has difficulty in being objective about himself. And so often, particularly in times of struggle, he either wants to remember a better past or envision a better future. When he does this he is not staying with the now experience, and this not only intensifies the struggle, it also prolongs it. There is nothing accidental in the creation of your cocoons. You choose and create them for your own individual growth, and you continue to create them until you are ready to unlock the butterfly within and take flight. How you deal with an experience of struggle and how you meet the challenge is dependent on your attitude, what kind of energy you give it, your perception of struggle, and your willingness to flow with the process of your own life. A negative struggle is exactly the same thing as a positive challenge. It's all based on how you perceive it. Change your perception and you transform the illusion. It's really all up to you. If there's any magic, it is you who are holding the magic wand.

VALLEY EXPERIENCES

At times you have noted that relationships become strained, and you have felt the desire to withdraw and enter a state of isolation. You have felt your integrity being challenged and as if you were being driven to your knees. You have thought, "What is this all about? What have I done to draw this to me? Why do I feel so powerless to transform the situation? Why does it seem so difficult to rise above my own ego and its creation?"

When an entity is experiencing a valley phase in his life, he seeks an external cause at first. It's really only necessary to exert one's energy seeking the cause if there is a recurring pattern of obstacles on your path. Repeated negative situations usually mean that the base cause is within you and will continue to trigger patterned situations to occur in your life experience if not dealt with on an internal level.

There is an acceleration occurring whereby Karmic resolutions can take place. Aware entities are creating situations in order to produce Karmic resolutions more quickly in their lives.

It is helpful to remember that the valley periods in your life experience can provide you with great insights into your own nature if you go through them quietly instead of kicking and screaming. Many entities learn their most valuable lessons in the valley periods, but only if they enter quietly into themselves. Frequently, however, one will follow his ego emotions and become angry and hurt and thus become blind to the lessons. Under this guidance one might attack, defend, lash out at externals, make accusations, challenge others, and make rash and oftentimes unsound decisions. Already in a valley, the entity begins to dig a deeper hole for himself. The only decision which should be made while in a valley period should be the decision to move out of it. Remember the wisdom that "when fishermen can't go to sea, they mend their nets."

In a world of duality there will always be valley periods in your life experience. The length or severity of a valley experience is dependent on how you choose to experience it. Sometimes being driven to the ground or having your integrity challenged are really gifts if they are accepted as lessons, since they can actually move you into a state of inner balance and harmony.

Think, if you will, of the phoenix. It is consumed by fire and disintegrates into ashes. After a time it recreates itself and arises from the ashes as an even more magnificent creature. It should be the same with unfolding human entities. You should be consumed by the fires in your life which insist that you evaluate your inner self and allow that which is no longer right or true for you to die. This done, you are able to rise again, renewed and recreated, a more magnificent bird than before. In the valley periods allow yourself to be quietly consumed by the fire. See the fire as purifying rather than painful. Pain is always self-chosen. Learn from the fire, from the valley. Let those things die which must, so that you may grow. Release from those things which can no longer be your truth.

Do not fear the valley periods, for they will aid in your unfoldment if you will allow it. A valley period is a time to withdraw and enter a state of inner reflection. A warrior is perhaps a greater warrior if he has the wisdom to know when to retreat. And a master is a greater master when he knows it's time to enter the solitude of his being. A valley is a space of stillness and solitude; a place to reflect and get to know yourself, and a place to strengthen, heal, and prepare for your ascent to the next peak of your life.

FACING THE MEDUSA OF THE INNER SELF

It has been stated by one of your wise Earth entities that "A state of consciousness, consistently maintained, will produce a corresponding result." This is true, Beloved Ones, and this is why it is so important for you to step back on occasion and evaluate where you are in consciousness. To do this with honesty and integrity, you must become the observer of you. It's difficult to take the journey into self because the only way one can make this journey is by becoming the unbiased observer. Many refuse to take the journey into the inner self because of fear of what may be lurking in those unknown realms beyond the world of illusion.

Concealed in your self-created darkness are the very things which affect and influence your present consciousness. It is the *unwillingness to look* at your Medusa which allows you to maintain and sustain your present state of consciousness. Your Medusa, children, is a collection of your fears, anger, resentment, hostility, aggression, and a host of other dark angels that you keep alive and empowered within. The outer world is always a reflection of your inner world, and what you allow to live and give power to in your inner realm will be experienced in your outer world. If the dragons of anger and resentment reside in your inner world, this will be the state of your present consciousness, and you will attract these things back to you. If the demon of fear resides within, it is fear that you empower and give birth to, causing you to exist in fear-filled lives.

As the observing self, rather than the vulnerable subjective self, you become the shield capable of seeing the reflection, the illusion, of your own self-created Medusa. As the observer you are able to see that the things that you fear to face are illusions, and yet, as empowered energies, real enough to influence your present consciousness. As the observer you are able to meet those things you fear to face, and thus destroy them.

I have spoken only of those things you perceive as negative, but the same holds true for those things you consider as positive: love, faith, trust, and joy. When these have their home in your inner world, they also influence your present state of consciousness, are maintained by your empowered thoughts, and attract those things back to you in your manifested world.

What you attract back is parallel to what you put forth. It is simply the great Law of Cause and Effect. Know that each entity is responsible for his own life and what he shapes it into. The beauty of Man is that he has the power to change his consciousness and redirect his thinking whenever he chooses to do so. He is always the guard holding the key to the door of his own self created prison. He is free to fly whenever he chooses to *release* and lift himself to the sky. And that, Beloved Ones, is the power inherent in each one of you.

VICTIM OR VICTOR

For the human entity on his Earth journey, many experiences occur which may be perceived as negative, unbearable, or devastating. There are often times when it appears that the universe and Life Itself is against him. The human entity is faced with such things as illness, death of a loved one, broken and severed relationships, financial problems, pain, suffering, fear, rejection, and other such situations which are perceived to be negative life experiences.

Many who are experiencing what they perceive to be negative life situations label themselves as victims in Life. Beloved Ones, as long as you hold a vision of yourself as a victim in Life, you will be that and you cannot move. The more one continues to empower his belief that he is being victimized by Life, the more he will attract experiences which confirm the self image he has of himself. There is great wisdom and truth in the statement, "You are what you think." You are what *you* think, and your thinking leads to believing and empowering those thoughts about yourself. Thus, you create and attract into your lives those conditions which conform to your own self image.

Why do so many human entities choose to play the role of victim in Life? It is because they see the world and those in it as being responsible for their life experiences. They blame the outer world not only for the experience, but for their own reaction to the experience. In perceived negative situations, it is always easier and more comfortable to blame something or someone outside yourself. One who perceives himself as a victim must always be able to justify that role, and the only way to do this is to point his finger away from himself.

Is there any reward for perceiving yourself as a victim in Life? Yes, but it is not really a fulfilling one, and it doesn't bring forth wholeness. Many victim portrayers enjoy the attention and sympathy they receive from their enablers. The ego can achieve limited fulfillment in having others agree with the perceived self image of the victim portrayer. Frequently the victim portrayer will use his victimhood as a way of manipulating or controlling those around him, particularly if they are the ones being blamed for the victim portrayer's negative life experience. One of the patterns of a victim portrayer is the attempt to make those he perceives as the victimizers feel guilty for what they have done *to* him. Sometimes this works, and it becomes another way to manipulate and control others and gives birth to unhealthy relationships.

Victims continue to attract and bring situations and experiences which support that self image. They continue to manifest dis-ease and suffering. Victimhood itself is a disease. Beloved Ones, when you experience times of perceived injustice or unfairness, do not think of yourselves as victims, but only as experiencing a perceived unfair or unjust situation. Do not hold onto the anger associated with the perceived injustice. Remember that you are not the experience, but only the student of the experience. Learn what you need to learn from the experience, release from it, and move forward in Life. It is only when you move out of your choice of victimhood in Life that you are able to enjoy victorious living and accept the heritage which is already yours, royal sons and daughters of Life. How much happier, freer, and healthier you will be when your self image is that of a victor in Life rather than a victim of Life. Remember, children, you are what you think, and Life moves into alignment with your thoughts in order to serve you, so choose to be a victor.

HOW TO HANDLE ANGER

Anything manifested in the outer world must first be experienced in the inner world and what applies to individual mind applies to collective mind as well. Can you truly place your energy into visions of global peace if you are filled with anger and conflict with those who share your smaller world, such as your family, friends, neighbors, co-workers, employees, and employers? Your individual world is but a microcosm of a larger world and a larger world beyond that.

To understand what global peace truly is, you must experience it in your personal world, for how can you seek to achieve on a planetary level something you have no knowledge of? Many of you define peace simply as freedom from any conflict. It could be that, but it could also be defined as being able to resolve conflict when it appears so that it becomes as some say, a win-win situation. Most non-peaceful situations are based in anger, but remember that anger is a child of fear.

There is a lot of anger in your world, to be sure, and it's difficult for the human entity not to be influenced or touched by these vibrations. So let us for a bit discuss the element of anger which you may experience both in your inner and outer worlds. What should you do when you feel angry about something? The first thing you should not do is suppress or deny the feeling. Anger is like a coiled rattlesnake, ready to strike. If you try to pretend that the snake doesn't exist, you will be bitten. You have to face the snake and see it for what it is. To resolve and deal with any emotion, no matter how negative it may appear, you have to face it and allow it to be what it is in that moment. Suppressing anger doesn't make it go away. If you suppress feelings of anger they fester in your inner being, and if not treated, manifest in the outer world in the form of dis-ease. Many illnesses are really due to suppressed and unresolved anger.

Because it is an ego emotion, anger is not an unnatural emotion in your world. When the human entity becomes angry, it produces conflict in the inner beingness. Anger, in and of itself, is neither good nor bad but depends on how the human entity chooses to deal with it and express it. There is a wide range of ways to resolve anger—from blowing up and becoming violent to suppressing it and pretending that anger doesn't exist. Both extremes contain danger. The aware entity will not deny the feeling but will allow it. He will express it as calmly as he can. If you are able to talk about what it is you're angry about, the feeling subsides, and becomes less impactful, and you are able to move toward resolution of the conflict, whatever it is. Expressing the feeling defuses it. You can write about the feeling or verbalize it to a friend who will listen, or simply settle back and think about it. Then you will perceive it differently, and it will lose its impact.

As an aware entity, what do you do when someone is expressing anger toward you? The most difficult thing to do is to maintain control over your own ego. Another's anger threatens the ego, and its natural response is to take up its own sword to do battle. The truth is that you give your own power away when you respond in like manner. The most powerful entity is the one who can remain silent during another's moment of anger. Once the situation has calmed, then you have a chance to respond to the anger.

Any of you who have been the receiver of another's anger knows that real communication is not possible during an angry outburst. The person who is angry doesn't want to talk or listen to what you may have to say. At that moment he feels justified in his anger, and he only wants to express it. If you can remember that verbalized anger is only words coming from one who is momentarily out of control, you will be able to remain silent. If, however, the entity is expressing in such a way that you may be physically harmed, it is wise, of course, to physically remove yourself from the space or take whatever appropriate action is necessary.

82

The only anger you are responsible for is your own. You will learn, as you become more aware of those moments of anger, that you have the choice to control the anger or let it control you. There would be less anger in your world if entities would face their own feelings and express them at the time of the feeling and allow others to do the same. Anger tends to build if it is suppressed so that oftentimes when an entity expresses anger, he is expressing accumulated anger. Since you are only responsible for your own feelings and resulting expressions, it would serve you well if during those times of anger you would attempt to move past the triggering incident and seek to discover the suppressed anger. This is part of doing the inner work and resolving and clearing yourself of deep angers which harm you and prevent you from the wholeness you deserve to experience.

Knowing yourself means looking also at the shadow parts of yourself. It requires no judgment, but simply facing those things that perhaps hurt and keep you imprisoned. Remember, as well, that the deep level hurts and angers lie in the realm of that which you call the past. You are no longer your past, yet so many carry it with them, and it becomes a heavy burden, weighing down the present moments. You are children of *now* and should be free to move like wind. So many are chained to old angers, old hurts. Go within, release from that which does not serve you, resolve those angers which weigh and wear you down and deny you joy. You were meant to have the joy of Life and feel the beauty of Life, but you must be free to claim this, and you cannot do so if you have chained yourself to the rock of old anger. Move forward, children, for Life is too precious to live imprisoned.

BE STILL AND KNOW

There will be times in an entity's life when he feels that he lacks direction. He may feel scattered about making decisions which have the potential to bring forth major change in his life. He may feel he lacks purpose in his life, and may feel frightened by the future, particularly if his attention is being drawn to personal finances, job changes, or relationship changes.

Beloved Ones, there is never a time when direction and guidance is not available to you. There are times, however, when you may not be quiet enough to hear the inner guidance. Sometimes there is too much static coming from your external world for you to be able to hear. "Be still and know that I am God" is the advice I would offer to you in these times of confusion. Consider how powerful the words *"Be still and know"* are. To become still requires your conscious, active will. It means that for a time you must shut yourself off from your outer world of activities. It means that you must clear your mind of your own thoughts and the thoughts of those around you. When you feel a lack of direction, those around you, in their desire to help, want to tell you what they think your direction should be. Abandon even the world and your own programming for a short while, for they produce the "shoulds" and "should nots" in your thinking. Becoming still means shutting down from your outer world for a time and being quiet so that you can hear. It's rather like turning off your radio or television set and becoming aware of only the sound of silence. Focusing on that silence, that calm stillness, you will listen and begin to hear. You will *know*. This is why daily meditation or centering, after periods of high activity, mental and physical, is beneficial. It reconnects you to your own essence and your own inner guidance center. *Be still and know that I Am God*. This is a power-filled directive containing a powerful promise.

Remember also, children, that listening and hearing are not the same. Many listen but do not hear, for hearing is understanding, and it is through understanding that you come to the place of knowingness. You can listen with your ears, but hearing is done with the heart and the mind. It is in the hearing that you will receive your answers and know your direction. Once you have received your guidance, your direction, your inner knowingness, you then have the choice of whether you will follow it or not. As individual entities, you will always be responsible for your choices in Life. If you receive the direction to move or change something in your life and you choose not to do it, that is fine. There are no bad choices, for you will learn from all of your experiences, but there are better choices which may create a greater sense of fulfillment.

Beloved Ones, you were meant to live fully and fearlessly. You were meant to be happy and abundant. You were meant to be unique and express the beauty and gifts of that uniqueness. *"Be still and know that I am God"* is the directive and the promise that will lead you into greater Life—a life *lived* with faith and fearlessness.

FORGIVENESS

Forgiveness is allowing another to become new and free after you have been harmed or damaged in some way; it is a process of healing. Regardless of whether the hurt was the result of maliciousness, ignorance or insensitivity, forgiveness is necessary for healing to occur so that both entities may move forward.

Forgiveness heals both individuals involved. The one who needs to forgive a hurt perhaps benefits the most because the longer one holds a hurt, the more damage it does to your total being and keeps you from enjoying your now moments. Sometimes entities will hold a hurt in order to manipulate the one who hurt them or to attempt to produce guilt in another. This imprisons both parties and prevents growth. Forgiveness should be given whether it is requested or not. When you forgive, you release yourself and the other person to go on.

If human entities loved with unconditional love, and if human egos were not so fragile and sensitive, there would be no such thing as a need for forgiveness. At your present time there is a need for this type of healing since no close relationship can survive without it. If you love, you must be willing to forgive not only others, but yourself as well. When you hurt another you must be willing to not only accept his forgiveness if it is given, but also be willing to forgive yourself. Guilt is every bit as destructive as holding onto a hurt.

As for how often you should be willing to forgive, do so continually if this is what is necessary to keep you free and moving forward. I can think of nothing which would not merit forgiveness. And do not expect to be forgiven if you are unwilling to forgive others. Remember always that forgiveness is a process of healing and of release and that it is vital to the movement and understanding of love on your dimension, because an entity needs a forgiving heart to experience true love.

BEWARE OF ARROGANCE

You've been told many times that you have been created by and from the Creator, God, the Source of All, that your spirits are of God and that this is your true essence, and that your individualized expressions began first with a thought within Universal Mind before you became a manifested form. If you say, "I am God," this is not wrong; if you say, "I have power," this is not wrong; and if you say "I contain divine knowledge and wisdom," this is not wrong. But do not say these things in arrogance, lest your brothers who have not reached this awareness misunderstand.

Remember that a drop of water, though it contains the same elements as the sea, is not the sea. The branch on a great tree, though it contains the same life-giving energy as the tree, is not the tree. A grain of sand upon the shore, though it has all the properties of the sand upon the shore, is not the shore. The flower within the garden is not the garden. The ray of sunlight which touches your head is not the sun.

85

You must realize your fragmentation if you are to understand your unity. You must realize your separateness if you are to understand your completeness. You must realize your disconnection if you are to understand your connection. You must realize that you are a part of God if you are to understand that you are God. When this awareness comes there is no need for words. There will be only a silent knowing, a deep love for All Creation, and a desire to lift all others up. When this awareness comes your power will be of gentleness and quietness and your wisdom and knowledge will be shared with loving sensitivity to those around you. When this awareness comes there will be a quiet humility in your manner.

RELEASE FROM ATTACHMENTS

Be in the world, but not of it. This does not mean that you are to give up all that you have and garb yourself in sackcloth and ashes. It does not mean that you are to become detached and withdrawn from the commitments and responsibilities that you have freely accepted. It does mean releasing yourself from those things which block growth and unfoldment.

Release from attachments means letting go of the illusions that dominate us. It means that you must look at the things you consider important and assess whether these things are blocking your growth. You live in a materialistic culture. There is nothing wrong with this because this is the culture you chose to enter into for your learning. The damage comes when you are so attached to the things of your culture that you would be devastated if these illusions were removed from your life experience. I'm not just referring to material things, but people as well. Some entities are so attached to loved ones that when the loved ones exit they are devastated. The fewer attachments one has, the happier he will be. An attachment is anything physical, mental, or emotional that you hold and feel is necessary to your existence. It is anything which has such importance to you that its loss would devastate you.

First ascertain what your attachments are. It can be a person, a thing, an attitude, a feeling, a habit, and so on. It can be anything which you feel you cannot live without. After you have determined what your particular attachments are, then retrain your thinking.

Everything and everyone in your life experience is temporary on the physical plane. All material blessings are gifts to use on your physical journey. They are as illusionary and temporary as your own physical form, and you will not take them with you when you exit. The people who enter your life experience are there to teach you, to learn from you, and to journey with you for a time. You are all there for growth and unfoldment. And as you cannot, in truth, possess or own a manifested object, you cannot possess another entity.

You are spirit; you are God energy expressing in manifested form. Your only attachment should be to that God energy which expresses through you and all creation. The only importance should be that of allowing that God energy to express through you. Once you realize this beyond your intellectual level, you will release yourself from all attachments which are barriers to your growth and unfoldment. If you align yourself with your own God energy and place your importance and attachment there, then you need not concern yourself with anything else.

When you are in the world but not of it, it means that you will do those things which you agreed to do prior to entering the earth plane, and that you will do them without attaching yourself to those things which create barriers and retard spiritual growth and unfoldment.

DRAGONSLAYER OR ARCHER?

When anger is being directed at you, you may wonder what lesson you are to learn. The primary lesson is how to handle another's anger without being hurt by it. On the human level this is oftentimes difficult because the ego, feeling threatened, will put on its own battle armaments, readying itself, not only to protect and defend, but also to draw some blood of its own. Once this is done, the war of egos has begun.

This need not be so if you will but understand the nature of anger, not only when it is being directed at you, but when it rises up in you as well. Anger, if you will step inside yourself and follow its course, will lead you to a fear of something. What the fear is will vary, but the home base of anger is always a fear. Most entities will not, however, step inside themselves and follow their anger home. It's far easier, the human entity believes, to look outside himself at his external illusion-filled world and issue the arrows of anger outward from himself.

For some reason, the human entity feels that the curse of his anger will be dispelled if another is pierced and wounded and blood is drawn from the chosen victims. Even though the archer of the arrows of anger may think he feels better, the anger will remain inside until he journeys within and deals with it on an inner level. Like a sleeping dragon, it will continue to raise its head until an entity has the courage and the will to become the dragonslayer and not the archer.

When anger is being directed at you, there is a finer and stronger shield available to you than the darkened armor of your own ego. It is the golden shield of your spirit which radiates with understanding, love, and compassion. It is the shield of the sun (Son) which cannot be penetrated. The spirit will not wield a sword, but simply stands firm radiating the power of Love, against which all arrows will melt.

You do not have to be wounded by the anger of another. If you are wounded it is because you have chosen to allow yourself the experience of this pain. The best choice is to step behind the golden radiating shield of your spirit and send forth love, understanding, and compassion. These expressions will be heightened if you can realize that the one who is angry is in great pain somewhere deep within his own being and that anger is but a manifestation of this internal pain. You can feel compassion for one who is suffering, and you can do what you can to ease the suffering, but you need not suffer. You cannot take another's pain unto yourself, and pain can only be released by the one who has it.

When you feel anger rising, do not pretend that the dragon does not exist. Realize its existence and acknowledge it, and then follow it home. You cannot slay the dragon outside your own self because it lies within. If you will use this process, you will discover that there will be fewer and fewer dragons. You will become more neutral, more centered, less attached, less affected, and more capable of generating greater love and wisdom to others. You can walk through your world without hurting others and without being hurt by others. It will be helpful to you if you always keep in mind that the real journey is not an external one; it is an inner one.

THE ART OF NOT FORCING

In the "Book of Runes" there is a statement about practicing the art of not forcing. This is good advice to follow in the area of human relationships. I would add to that statement one about practicing the art of not being forced.

Upon your third dimensional plane of life there are many dominant and domineering entities who will, if given the chance, attempt to force their will upon the wills of others. Some are obvious in their attempts; others are far more subtle.

Most human entities have an ego tendency to desire to have things done their own way. It is human to want things to go the way which is smoothest for you. And it is common to attempt to force your will by using either obvious or subtle methods.

When alone, entities will generally do those things that make them the happiest or the most satisfied. But when relating with others there will always be subtle or obvious expressions of exerting one's will over them.

There will be in human interactions a yielding to or a being yielded to experience.

The art of not forcing refers to human interactions. It will require the use of your own will for a time in order to release yourself from attempting to force your will upon another. You must understand at a deep level that in order to practice this art you must be willing to accept and allow another to freely express. It does not mean that you cannot offer opinions or suggest alternatives. It merely means that you allow the other person to *be*. You do not have to like it, and you are free to move from the situation if you find you totally disagree with what is being generated by another or if you are unable to yield. Sometimes if you force your will upon another you will incur Karma. The prime purpose for human relating is, as you've been told, for learning and teaching, both of which are needed for growth. If you force your will upon another, then it is possible that you will move them away from a much needed lesson. A conscious intent to force your will definitely incurs Karma because this is a manifestation of the ego and has to do with the negative aspects of pride and the ego need to prove superiority over others.

When you practice the art of not forcing, you may express your opinion, and if it is not received by another, you pull into a neutral condition and allow the other to do what he chooses. If you agree with another, you may yield to his opinion, but not to his will. Never yield to the will of another if it goes against your inner guidance. It is possible to allow others to be, without being part of whatever they are generating.

You can express opinions and feelings, you can guide, or you can offer aid and assistance. But, if rejected, do not seek to overtly or aggressively force your will upon another. Allow others to do as they choose, for therein lies their learning. There are many entities whose egos want to command, dominate, be in charge, and who think that no one can do things better than they can. This is one of the reasons your world is in such chaos. Do not allow your own ego to place force upon another. Follow your inner guidance as to what is best for you upon your own path of learning.

If you align your individual will to Universal Will, you will live and work within Universal Flow. Once you learn to accept what is within any given moment without wanting it to be anything other than what it is, you will cease to force your will on anyone, and you will not be under the force of another's will. Then Divine Will is operating in your life, and It is spirit-based and not ego-based. Once this is operating in your life, there will be harmony, peace, flow, equality, and balance.

DECISION-MAKING

When there are decisions to be made, with varying opinions, and your space is filled with discord and disharmony, always do the loving thing. This is true, for when you move from a point of love you will make a decision which is love-based. A love-based decision will always be the appropriate decision for any given life experience.

You may say, "How do I know for sure that what I decide is the loving thing?" All I can say to you is that you will always know. The human entity always is aware of his individual intent and motive and knows when he is moving from a point of love. He also knows when his decisions are ego-based, for he will move from fear, greed, lust for power, lack of trust, selfishness, defensiveness, and so on.

Within groups and human relationships when there is a need for a decision and there is discord present, it is probably best to become quiet and move to your own individual centers and attempt to move jointly from a love base. What happens when individuals or groups make decisions which are ego-based is that they are never certain that the most appropriate decision has been made. Love-based decisions are always appropriate. If all entities in a group or within a human relationship are moving from a point of love in the decision-making process, there may be differing opinions as to which is the best loving way. Just let me tell you that it's less difficult to discern the best and most appropriate loving way than it is to sift through all the ideas coming forth from personal egos.

I would also like to add that if you know a decision being made is ego-based and you are asked to participate, it would be better for you to abstain from participation. Decisions which are ego-based indicate that the decision maker has a less than loving intent and motive, and this puts the Law of Cause and Effect into action. If you know a decision is being made which is not love-based and you agree, you become an accessory and subject to Karmic Law. It is important in the decision-making process to ask yourself where you are with regard to your intent and motive and to assess the feelings and vibrations you are manifesting. Cosmically, if you are unable to do the loving thing, it is best to do nothing. Actions which are void of love are empty actions. Decisions which are not love-based serve no real purpose.

HOW TO SOLVE PROBLEMS

When you have a problem that you can't seem to solve or one in which there seems to be a myriad of solutions and you don't know which way to turn, the best thing to do is to release the problem and allow the Higher

Force to dictate the solution. In this way you can be assured that the most appropriate solution and the most beneficial to your particular growth needs will be manifested. Release, or the freeing of oneself from the action of resistance, brings the individual will and Universal Will into alignment.

On the human level release is sometimes very difficult and the ego or intellect truly wishes to be the discoverer of the solution to a problem. But in the search for a solution or in the analysis of many possible solutions, neither the ego nor the intellect will move from the objective, impersonal state. This is human and natural. Coming from the subjective, personal state, the solution to a problem sometimes creates greater problems. For learning purposes this, of course, is allowed. Many lessons can be learned as one moves through the maze of possible solutions to problems. This is one reason why problems are sometimes called opportunities.

We encourage you to flow, to utilize the process of neutrality, to follow inner guidance or place yourself under spirit control, or to align your mind with Universal Mind. When you are aligned with Universal Mind, you do not have to do anything but allow things to unfold. When you are in alignment you do not have to expend any energy in trying to discern what to do next with respect to a problem you are having. You release from the problem and start using your time and energy more creatively. Alignment opens the door for the most appropriate solution and the one which will provide for the greatest growth. If you remain connected you can rest assured that no matter what the solution proves to be, it is always for your highest good.

If you are truly in alignment, you will be able to completely pull away from the problem and will become the observer to your own life experience. In this position you will be able to see the solution unfolding, petal by petal. You will be able to see new patterns forming and new energies pouring into the potential manifestation of the solution. If one is really aware he will be fascinated by the beauty of the simplicity of this process. In truth, you do not have to find solutions to any of your perceived or self-created problems. All you really have to do is release yourself and allow the solution to unfold before your eyes. This is what you *must* be willing to do. You must also be willing to totally trust in the process.

If you are under alignment and you have allowed a solution to unfold, you most frequently will be surprised by the solution. The solution may be one you never thought of or it may be one which you intellectually or egotistically do not like. But it will always be the one which will promote the greatest growth and will be for your highest good. So if you choose to enter this process, you must continue to trust no matter what the solution proves to be.

NEGATIVE SPACE

You are wondering what you should do when someone close to you is experiencing negative vibrations and seems to be beset by varied problems and mental chaos.

It is easy to get caught up in another's vibrations and just as easy to attempt to take on their problems. It is human to want to solve the problem, lift the vibrations, and release another from mental chaos. Most frequently, however, when you try to do this you lower yourself into the mud puddle, and then there are two struggling to get out. It's far better to have one standing by the mud puddle with an outstretched hand ready to pull the other to shore when he is through fighting with the mud.

What most human entities either do not realize or do not wish to admit is that they control their own vibrational waters. When you are experiencing negative vibrations which are accompanied by various negative manifestations, don't look outside yourself for the cause. Somewhere and in some way you brought this into your present conscious state. If you have the power to usher it in and bring forth its manifestations into your life, you also have the power to move it out of your life. It's not magic. It is will and a willingness to take control of your own individual world.

Likewise, when another is experiencing negative vibrations and manifestations, you also have the power to shield yourself from them. This does not mean that you offer no aid, consolation, or compassion to another who is struggling to find his way. It means simply that you do not share his negative space. These negative spaces which humans create for themselves are learning areas. On some level of consciousness the entity determines that some lesson is needed to be learned and thus creates this space for himself in order to learn it. If you believe that there are no accidents, then the creation of negative space likewise is not accidental. You create the space, stir up the waters, jump in the mud puddle, flounder around until you are ready to be released, and then you get out. But if you don't analyze the entire situation and understand the lesson, you will continue to recreate the same mud puddle.

Being in a mud puddle is pretty lonely, as you well know, and oftentimes an entity will try to bring others into the negative space with him. It is not a sign of love if you opt to share the negative space. It shows greater love if you don't. Remember that you don't have to enter the prison cell to communicate with the prisoner. Remember also that you don't have the key to open the door to his cell; he is always holding the key to his own release.

Remember that an entity's life experience is a solo flight, and even though other birds may choose to fly beside him, and he may choose to fly with others, and even though wingtips may touch, for each bird it is still a solo flight. You cannot ride upon another's back, and you cannot share your wings. And if one becomes caught in a thicket or lost in the fog, you cannot share that space. You can only wait, with patience, love, and understanding, until the bird is free or moves from the fog and is ready to soar toward Home once again.

BEAUTY IS WAITING TO BE DISCOVERED

Is the rose beautiful of itself or is the beauty of the rose, or anything else for that matter, merely perceptual on the part of a human entity? Each aspect of Creation is the Creator expressing. Thus, the essence always contains beauty, for beauty is one of the children of Love, and the Creator is Love Expressing. One of the benefits of living in a world of duality, a world of opposites is that you can be aware of beauty. You are aware of beauty because you can also be aware of what you perceive to be non-beautiful. I prefer not to use your term ugly, just as I prefer to use non-love rather than hate.

"You bring beauty to the rose" and "Beauty is in the eye of the beholder" are true statements for your particular level of awareness. How much beauty you are able to perceive is dependent on your individual level of awareness. If you can perceive the external beauty of any creation, you add power to the essential inner beauty of it. In this way you, in your awareness of beauty, do bring beauty to the rose. Being aware enough to perceive the outer beauty of something brings you closer to connecting with the essential beauty of it. If this connection is ever totally completed, you become one with that aspect of creation. Love and its children, truth and beauty, are the connectors to Essence—the link between your outer and inner worlds of awareness. The more beauty you are aware of in your external world, the more connected you are to the Essence of Creation.

If you journey through your life experience and perceive little or no beauty within it, it is apparent that you are far from connecting with the Essence. It would also be wise to analyze and evaluate how you are vibrating. If you cannot see beauty, you are vibrating negatively and are not growing in your understanding and expressing of Love, which is critical for your unfoldment into Oneness.

The more aware you become and the more you can understand your connection to the Whole of Creation, the greater your capacity to perceive beauty will become. The goal is to be able to see beauty in all aspects of Creation. The one who seeks to perceive beauty in All is well on his way to achieving unconditional love.

To perceive beauty you must travel beyond the external forms. So many human entities will not do this. Oftentimes in your world of duality, an aspect of Creation may appear in your perception as grotesque and distorted to the physical eye. It is easy to turn from it and perceive it as non-beautiful. If you will but open your inner eye and journey beyond the external form without fear, you will experience its beauty. But you must want to do this, and you must be at a level of awareness where you *know* that all external form is illusionary. Go beyond the levels of form, with love, seek the essence, and you will always find the beauty waiting to be discovered and perceived.

BECOMING ONE WITH THE DANCE

In thoughts about the Baryshnikov concert, you said that it seemed as if the dance and the dancer became united—became one. This is the secret of success in anything you choose to do. Many are concerned with executing certain movements at certain times, but the dancer and the dance are not united. The result may be a flawless performance, but the ones who excel and enjoy it are the ones who become one with the dance itself.

In writing, in painting, or in any act of creating, one will excel if he unites with what he is doing. In the process of creating, the Creator became united with not only the process of creating, but also with that which He created. No matter what you ever undertake to do, no matter how mundane it may seem, you enter the process of creating. If you can consider this when you are going to do something, you will not only enjoy it more; you will experience results greater than you would have imagined.

The reason that you oftentimes find life to be mundane and boring is because you allow yourself to separate from what you are doing. The actor and the action are not connected; the artist and his painting are not united; the writer and his writing are not one; the dancer and the dance are separated. When you choose to separate from what you are doing, you become robotic. You may expend energy, but not all of your energy. You may achieve seemingly positive results, but you will not receive full joy. Separation denies you this.

Think of the times you have put your whole self into a project and become one with it. Didn't you experience great joy? Then consider the times you entered into doing something, but mentally separated from it. Did you experience joy? This is one of the secrets of living life to its fullest: becoming united in the process called life, to become one with its energy.

Humans tend to separate themselves from things, situations, and people they don't like. Remember that *nothing comes to you that is not meant for you.* If you enter into those things you don't like with a new approach and new energy, you may discover that you have been denying yourself great joy and learning. Even if you should discover after leaving an experience that you still have the same dislike, you have learned, and the new knowledge, in itself, will give you joy. Become one with the dance of life in the process of dancing. When you release all of your energy into the process of life, you are best expressing the Creator who expresses through the entity called *you.*

ANY ILLUSION CAN BE ADDICTIVE

The basic reason for any addiction is the fact that the human entity simply does not either realize or recognize who he really is: God expressing in form. When one is truly aware of this in his deeper levels of being, he will neither be addicted to nor obsessed by anything in his external world. When this awareness of one's true beingness is realized and accepted, one is released from all his prisons, and he is, in truth, non-attached to all his created illusions.

Human entities become unsure, uncertain and insecure about who they are. This confusion creates greater inner unhappiness. They then find themselves seeking something that will make them feel better or produce happiness, a magic balm to soothe the inner pain and confusion. They seek it in the external world, and soon have created an addiction. All addictions are caused by internal wounding and self-created suffering, because you do not know who you are.

Heaven is within; Paradise has not left you—you left Paradise. The only way to re-enter Paradise is to return back through the gates of your own being and stand face to face with your own God essence that so long ago you wandered away from and thus became lost in your world of illusions. It's an inner journey into self and sometimes an arduous one because the beautiful voices of the Sirens of your illusions keep singing to you to come back to your outer world. These are but false voices promising you peace and fulfillment.

To be free, it is vital to become non-attached to all your illusions. Look carefully at your material world of form. What is really yours? What do you really possess? What can you take with you when you journey beyond the veil of your present realm of life? The answer is *nothing*. You leave it *all* behind you, for you will have no need of any of it. You will not take your physical baggage with you, but many will carry their attachments to that baggage beyond the veil of illusion. Sooner or later, in terms of time, one will have to release from the thing itself (whatever that happens to be) or from his attachment to the thing.

When human entities use the term addiction, they are usually referring to some of the things which are known to be harmful to the physical vehicle, such as drugs or alcohol. However, it goes far beyond this, for one can be addicted to or obsessed by any illusion in his world. Because of not knowing who you truly are, because you will not see your own God essence, you create a void. To fill that emptiness you fill it with other gods, other idols, because you so want to feel whole and complete. You bow down before drugs, alcohol, money, sexual pleasures, other human entities, and anything else within the world of illusions. You try to create permanent happiness from vaporous air. So it is with *all* illusions. You live in an ever changing and temporary world, and to cling to any illusion will only deepen the void that you try so desperately to fill.

You cannot fill that which is already full. In truth, there is no void in your being. That is also one of your illusions. You create the illusionary void because you will not acknowledge your own God essence. You must want to be free and you must be willing to acknowledge who you really are: *God expressing as you.* When you understand this you also understand that there is no void, that there is only your perfect God essence. There is no space that needs to be filled with the opiates of the material world. Knowing this, all that flows from the world of form, all the beauty, love, and pleasure, are blessings to you. They become tools to expand your growth and unfoldment rather than prisons. It is the Father's good pleasure to give you the kingdom and all that lies therein. But an entity must know where the kingdom is before he is able to accept its gifts. Seek first the kingdom of God and all else will be given you.

BECOME A DIVER

I am sometimes amazed at the way your culture and other advanced cultures still assess or judge one another on external appearances. Sometimes human entities become so caught up in the external appearances of both themselves and others that they become completely blinded to the internal appearances. The idea that the exterior presentation is always parallel to the interior is completely amiss.

Learn to move inward beyond the illusionary exterior to the interior. Do this not only with yourself, but with others as well. You can tell very little about another by the choice of costume or mask he wears for a particular role he is portraying in a life experience. In certain cultures life is akin to attending a huge masquerade ball. You don't really know who anyone is until the masks are removed, and you don't and won't learn their identities until you are willing to go beyond the veil of illusionary reality and reach out and touch the essence of another.

You can break through this tough shell of external illusionary reality. First of all, consciously acknowledge that nothing is ever as it appears on the surface. When you look at the ocean you might think that all that you see is its surface. But what about the depths that cannot be seen? How do you know more about the ocean than its visible surface? Become a diver and enter its depths. Then you know more of the ocean. The deeper you are willing to go beneath the surface, the closer you come to essence, for there is a point in descending into the depths where essence is ultimately touched. Once touched, there is transcension. Transcension occurs when essence is touched because all essence is the same. It is the Spirit of the Creator, the Lifeforce of Creation. It is the Creator and Creation becoming One.

To become a diver, trust completely and have great courage. You must trust that there is nothing to fear as you dive deeper toward your own essence or the essence of another. If you fear increased awareness or are passing through murky depths filled with self-created illusionary phantoms, first dispel your own darkness and ignorance. This is where courage comes in. If you have the courage to enter your own darkness and challenge your own phantoms, you will see a light awaiting you. This is your essence, the place of your true reality. If you have the courage to enter your own darkness, you will not lack courage to enter the dark spaces of others.

True spiritual connections in relationships lie beneath. Only by going beyond the surface will you discover the love, the beauty, the truth, the reality of another. And though you might have to journey with another into the depths of his pain, confusion, fear, non-love, and all the other phantoms he has created, it is worth the journey. This is the process of the true human and spiritual connections within human relationships.

DISSATISFACTION IN LIFE

You have been feeling dissatisfied lately. Remember that what is being perceived within your external world has its base within your own being. You are dissatisfied with certain inner realities, and these are being projected outward to your external realities.

You are aware of being out of alignment and unable to reach your own center. In your external life you are doing a lot of things with internal resistance and without true willingness or love, creating resentment, frustration, and even guilt. This is why it is advised that you act with love or refrain from the action. Cosmically, the only duty you have is to allow the Creator to express through you, and the only obligation you have is to strive to perfect the expression of the God Self. Any other duties, responsibilities, and obligations you have are self-chosen. In truth, you owe no one, you are obliged to no one, and you are responsible to no one.

If, in your external world, you have assumed responsibilities, duties, and obligations but are not performing them with a loving heart, then it's time to examine them and yourself. First comes the awareness of dissatisfaction with certain elements within your internal and external worlds. The human approach is generally to analyze the external manifestations and seek to distinguish them. The spiritual approach is to then move inward from the external manifestations and seek to know what your spirit is trying to tell you.

When dissatisfaction reaches the conscious level of awareness, the spirit is attempting to trigger the entity into creating an inner change which will assist him in fulfilling the individual mission with greater effectiveness. Change and transformation must occur within. The inner world must be changed for dissatisfaction to be alleviated. And as you know, when the inner world is changed, the external world also changes.

To change the outer reality you must begin by changing your inner world. You may wonder why life doesn't seem smooth sometimes. It's because you get too caught up in your externals and expend all your energy outward, saving nothing for your inner world. You concern yourself with people and finances and cars and so many things in your outer world. So often you don't move outward into these areas from a place of trust. You do not always trust that everything is working for your growth and good in all areas of your life. You do not always see your world as a place of learning and teaching.

If you understand at the gut level that the inner journey is the important one and that you are the creator of your world and the author of your script, you will not place undue importance on the outer. You will do those things which you need to do to live in your world, but you will do them with inner wisdom. Nothing is without purpose; in all external situations you are there to learn or to teach or both. In your connections with other people, you are there to learn or to teach or both. Don't allow your frustrations, irritations, and fears to block the process. Be serious about your inner growth and learning, but don't take your outer world so seriously that you become blind to your true journey. Work from a center of peace and love and trust in your Creator, and bring these into your outer world.

SCALING THE WALL

Human entities, within their life experiences, appear to enjoy creating negative space filled with fear, frustration, irritation, confusion, resentment, and anger. They create these spaces primarily because they have been programmed by other human entities to do so. It is not a part of Cosmic programming.

There has been much emphasis in recent years on reprogramming yourself, of retraining your thought patterns, of making a conscious effort to see the world in a new light. Entities striving to lift the consciousness of the world must learn to lift their own consciousness first. In truth, mass consciousness will not be lifted; it will be pulled up by a few who are willing to pull themselves up first. It will take a few to scale the wall first so that they can pull the others up. The seekers are the ones who must scale the wall. You have the knowledge of what you need to do; now it must be applied.

When you enter a negative space you should really analyze why you are there. Why did you create it? What purpose is it serving? How is it manifesting before you? With acceptance, which is really non-resistance, you can analyze and evaluate why you have allowed yourself to be in a certain space and why you created it. Acceptance does not mean that you must sit and do nothing. Acceptance does not mean that you cannot employ the powers of affirmation. What is affirmation? It is simply the consciously willed procedure of reprogramming yourself and your thoughts. And it works. It is more than hoping, dreaming, or wishing, and it is not magic. It is a technique which, when used, will change your perception. When your perception shifts, so also does your world and its manifestations.

You see, much of your perception is based on your prior programming which is based on the life experience of yourself and others who have been and are now your teachers. If this programming is not filling your journey with joy and abundance and fulfillment, then I should think you would be eager to change your own programming. It takes work and time to affirm the things you want for your life, and it is hard to break habits and patterns, but it can be done. When scaling the wall you might fall to the ground a few times before your fingertips reach the ledge and you are able to pull yourself up and stand upon it. Many entities make the attempt, and when they fall back upon the ground, they sit there and do not try again. Or they may try a few times and give up.

Blaming the external illusions for perceived lack and limitation is the primary mindset within your world, and this is the continued programming of the young. Those who are initiators of the New Age awareness must begin changing their own programming so that it can be taught to the young. It is critical that you learn it yourselves, if you are ever going to teach it.

Along with positive affirmations, work on seeing with clearer vision. You came across a saying which is so true of your world about two men looking out through the same bars and how one saw only mud, while the other saw stars. Granted, you can learn from the mud, but it can be far more pleasant to learn from the stars. It's so much nicer to look up rather than down. It's important to begin to see and perceive anew as it relates to the kind of journey you experience and what kinds of manifestations you create. You have the knowledge on how to change and how to shift and how to reprogram your thought processes and patterns. Have the wisdom and incentive to apply it.

HURT FEELINGS

When you experience hurt it is better to express those feelings immediately rather than to hold onto them because unexpressed hurt will become anger. Anger, when allowed to build and grow within, is more damaging physically, mentally, and emotionally than any hurtful experience could ever be. Anger can trigger irrational actions which can lead to disastrous effects. Anger can manifest physical maladies if allowed to fester. Most anger begins as an unexpressed hurt.

When you experience a feeling of hurt, you must remember that you are allowing yourself this feeling. Nothing within your external world can hurt you that you do not either allow or choose. You can also allow yourself to express the hurt, because in the expression comes the release. Releasing it through expression will prevent anger from settling in and holding you in bondage.

Most human entities will experience what they perceive to be hurt until they realize that nothing in the external world can hurt them and that hurt feelings are created by one's individual ego. Hurt usually comes as the result of a lack of understanding in our communication with others, whereby the ego misinterprets or misperceives or misreads intent. The ego is both very strong and very fragile. More hurtful feelings seem to come to those entities who take the external world and themselves too seriously, to those who do not love themselves enough, and to those who have many expectations of others.

Now, I realize that there are entities who attempt, through word and action, to produce hurt in others. This is only your concern if you are the one attempting to hurt another. An unloving, knowing intent to hurt another places you under Karmic balancing. All suffering which you knowingly or unknowingly create will be balanced because of the Law of Cause and Effect, but those conscious, intentional actions designed to create suffering are more severely dealt with.

If you say something to another with no intent to hurt, and yet another is hurt because he misinterpreted your words, there will be an effect, but there will be no incurring of Karma. Intent is the key factor within Karmic balancing. If you are of such a nature that you will not allow hurt to occur even when another's intent is to hurt you, that person will still incur Karma even though no hurt was created.

It is not really necessary for you to suffer from hurt feelings if you learn to understand that no one and nothing external to yourself is the cause of them. They are triggered by the sensitivity and fragility of your own ego, and your choice to allow yourself the experience of hurt. Learning to communicate and express your thoughts more accurately to others will also create a condition of greater understanding so that fewer misperceptions occur. Learning to be more accepting and understanding of the diverse unfolding personalities and natures of others as you travel your own path will make you a happier and healthier being. Walk softly with understanding.

THE GIFT OF LIFE

There are times within the Life experience when human entities are separated from others through death, divorce, broken engagements or friendships, and so forth. Closures of relationships can be extremely painful because of the seeming loss which is experienced. Some entities become so very devastated that they become physically ill and are never

101

able to move forward again. There are many accounts of a husband or a wife making a transition, only to be followed by their spouse shortly thereafter. There are accounts of entities committing suicide after a divorce or a broken engagement. There are accounts of entities grieving so after the transition of a loved one that they become reclusive, fearful, and unable to find joy in life.

These are sad accounts and although I do not lack sympathy or compassion, they are entities who became so attached and dependent on another that they could not continue without the other. They are entities who never grew to the awareness that although one will journey with many others in a lifetime, he still walks alone. They are entities who did not understand that with each closure there awaited a new opening if they had been willing to move through the doors of new experience. They are entities who focus all their attention and love on another so that when the relationship is over, they feel that life is over. Christ said, "Where your treasure is, there will be your heart also." This can apply to relationships as well as to your material possessions. To give up the beautiful gift of life because of another person is just as much idolatry as any other manifested idol one may have. There are times when one may die or give up his life for his friend, or his brother, but for and because of are two different things.

All human entities will experience closures of relationships within their lives, for this is part of the Earth walk and part of your learning. Closures, although they are an ending, are also a beginning, a start of something new. A closure can be a strengthening experience if one allows it. You are on a wonderful journey, and you need never fear that you are unprepared or lack direction. Trust your own guidance; know who is at the helm, be willing to risk, and be adventurous enough to pass through the doors which open for you. Be willing to love, be willing to be who you are, and be willing to become. On this wondrous sea of Life many ships will pass in the night of the soul's journey, yet others will draw alongside you and you will sail in a parallel direction.

This does not mean that you will not feel sadness during your closures or that you may not mourn the passing of a loved one. You are human entities and you have the capacity to feel and to be touched deeply by your life experiences. But when you reach a certain level of awareness you will mourn, and your mourning shall transform itself into the joy of knowing that your loved one has moved to a higher and finer dimension of Life. You will feel sadness when you must release from another, but that sadness will transform itself into the joy of knowing that you each have grown and have the potential to unfold into finer beings. Your pain will yield to healing if you are but open to moving from your own darkness to the brilliance of a new dawn.

Never fear being alone or soaring into the open skies of your own beingness, for that is where the Source of your self is; that is the core of your own unique essence. Life is meant to be lived—it is a gift. You are a gift. You are life giving unto Life. Throughout the closures in your life, continue to cherish the gift of your own life. Remember, as well, that closures (and openings) are but illusions and lessons on your life walk. You are all interconnected and woven together into the tapestry called Life. It is only a dream on your physical plane that the threads appear to be broken. What has been woven together in Life is of strong fiber, God fiber, and cannot be broken or severed in the Truth of Life.

LIVE FEARLESSLY AND YOU WILL LIVE FULLY

In your world there exists an immense collective fear base. This collective fear not only influences the individual entity, but the individual is, in part, responsible for its existence because collective consciousness is the accumulation of the thoughts and energies of individuals.

Your culture is extremely stress filled. If it were not, you would not spend so much collective and individual energy and time attempting to discern ways to reduce or alleviate negative stress. Negative stress results from worry, and worry is but an extension of fear. One who does not fear does not worry. Worry, rising up from your fear, is active in your manifested world. It depletes your energy, and it robs you of your time. It can affect your health on all levels—physical, emotional, and mental. It imprisons you and oftentimes paralyzes you from living life.

So why, Beloved Ones, does fear exist if it is so destructive? Does fear have any positive reason for being? Fear is born out of the ego whose primary function is to protect and maintain the physical vehicle in the manifested world. When the ego's protective programming perceives a threat (real or unreal), it produces the emotion of fear so that the entity will respond to protect or defend the vehicle. The human entity has within him basic survival programming in order to respond to situations which physically endanger him. This programming was necessary for the survival of the species on your planet. It is not this kind of situational fear that causes the problem on your planet.

The kind of fear that causes the greatest amount of stress and worry is that which you create by your own thinking. Most of the things that you fear in your lives are the result of a lack of faith and trust and a lack of knowledge about who you really are in truth. Think about those things you worry about. You worry about not having enough money, about being rejected or not loved, about what's going to happen in the future, about illness and death, and about the lives of others. You spend a lot of time in the world of what if this or that happens. You worry about old age, not being a success, living in poverty, and not being able to leave your children anything. You worry about being killed in an airline crash or an earthquake, getting an incurable disease, the IRS, your car breaking down, paying your bills, and on and on and on.

Let's look at this a bit, children. You're powerful energy beings—individual expressions of God—experiencing Life in a manifested world of which you are the co-creators by your own thinking. In spite of what you may have been told, you are not worms in the dust. You were not created to be paralyzed, fear-filled beings. You are powerful beings, but this can only be manifested when you trust in the Universe and in the God you express. You live in a world of consciousness, Beloved Ones, and you are spirits journeying through a world of forms. If you could understand at your deepest level that the world of form is transitory and illusionary and that spirit is the reality, your perceptions would change. When perceptions change, your world changes.

Is it possible for you to live in a world where there is no fear? At this time in the process of your world's evolution, probably not. But it is possible for you to experience a life filled with faith while journeying. One of your wise Earth entities, Mark Twain, said: "Courage is resistance to fear, mastery of fear—not absence of fear." Mastery, however, does not mean pretending a fearful thought does not exist. Mastery of a fear means to acknowledge its existence, to bring it into the light of your own awareness, to examine it as a scientist might under a microscope without an emotional attachment. Write down the fearful thoughts which come to you and look at what you have written carefully. Sometimes it's hard to discern its origin because some lie in childhood or even in the far reaches of prior lives. Most of your day-to-day fear thoughts and worries can be mastered by looking at them carefully and asking yourself: "Is this something I really need to be afraid of? Is it threatening my life really? Is it something which my fear or worry can change, or will my fear or worry only add power to the situation? What, in my perception, is the worst thing that can happen to me in this particular situation?" If one really looks at his life, he will see that the majority of things he projects to happen, don't.

It takes great courage to walk the human walk, Beloved Ones, and courage is not the opposite of fear; it is the mastery of it. When a fear-filled thought comes to you, attempt to move from the emotion of it and into a higher place where you are able to view it from a higher perspective. When you are but the observer of your fear, you examine it rather than empower it. Living fearlessly in a world that is filled with fear vibrations requires attention and work. As time passes you will begin to know the difference between the fear which insists on action for your physical well being and the fear that is unreal until you give it life through your empowerment. You will learn how to dismiss fearful thoughts and replace them with positive thoughts.

You were meant to live empowered lives. One who lives in fear does not live fully and denies his own joy. You were meant to awaken each day exclaiming: "What gifts does this day hold for me? What shall I give to this day?" All you have is *Now*. Yesterday is done and tomorrow is but a dream. Empower your *Now* with love and trust and fill your consciousness with faith, because what you do *Now* will impact all the *Now* moments you will experience. It's time *Now* to become the master over what and how you think and what thoughts you will empower. Live fearlessly and you will live fully!

THERE IS NO FUTURE

Most human entities do not value their present moments to the degree that they should. *Now*, in truth, is your golden moment, because it is the one moment on your plane of experience that you are guaranteed. Past moments are gone, fluttering like ashes in the winds of your life, unchangeable. They become stored away in the vaults of your subconscious to await your beckoning, and they come to you in the form of remembrances or lessons learned. Future moments are yet to be determined and not yet guaranteed and if they do arrive, they become your *Now*.

Many attempt to live in the future, and this can be the cause of great stress and disappointment. So often you attempt to live your life in that which is not guaranteed, and in so doing you rob yourself of your present. How many times do you say, "Someday I'm going to. One day I will. I'll do it tomorrow, or next week, or next year?" How many times do you plan your life around an event which may never occur, such as winning the lottery or a sweepstakes?

The human entity must have dreams and visions, because this is part of his creative nature. It is what keeps him stretching and growing into greater beingness. To grow he must empower his visions in order to bring them to manifestation. Empowering a thought or vision, however, is not the same as trying to live in a time which has not yet come. Empowering requires your connection to your *Now*, because empowering insists that you use the energy of your present consciousness. A seed does not dream of becoming a flower; it uses the energy within its present state to become that flower.

What comes to you, children, is always based on the state of your present consciousness, and it is through this that you empower and bring forth what is contained in your *Now* moment. You draw to you what you are in present consciousness. This is why it is so important for you to examine your present consciousness and determine how you really feel about the various elements of your life. Ask yourself:

How do I feel about the people who share my life?

How do I feel about money and prosperity?

How do I feel about myself on all levels?

How accepting of Life am I?

What are my fears?

What is it that I truly want?

Do I live my life hoping or *knowing*?

Do I know who I am, in truth? Do I trust that?

Do I understand that my outer world is but a reflection of my inner world?

Do I understand my own power and how to use it for the highest good, or do I give my power away?

Am I imprisoned by my past?

Do I perceive myself as a victim in and of Life?

The answers to these questions will tell you a lot about where you are in present consciousness, which is the instrument through which you empower and ultimately manifest. The key to that which is called the future is in how you think *Now*.

Now is your power moment. It is the moment you can waste in either the past or in that time not yet come. *Now* is the only moment you can use to energize and empower that which you desire to manifest. Remember always:

Now is your moment of power.

Now is your gift.

Now is when you can love and forgive and give.

Now is when you can change your reality.

Now is when you can empower your thoughts and visions.

Now is when you can choose happiness.

Now is when you can create.

Now is when you are most alive.

Let the wind catch the sails of today so that you may fully enjoy this day's delights and insights. Be the seed which energizes in the process of beingness, in the journey, not the destination. Do not use your energy in dreaming of what you will become, but rather remain connected to what you are within the process of becoming.

YOU ARE STUDENTS AND TEACHERS

If human entities would open themselves up to Universal Mind, Earth teaching and learning would be simplified greatly. All knowledge is within each of you. Earth teaching is intended strictly to trigger this knowledge into manifestation on the physical plane. We teach by channeling through your brain computer, but you must teach using those faculties which you have on a human level. You must teach verbally, you must teach by example, and you must learn through experience on a physical dimension.

Human knowledge is passed from generation to generation through the process of sharing in some form, through writings, creations, words, and so forth. New knowledge is always channeled to one or more human entities so that it can be passed in the traditional Earth ways. Higher learning must always come from Universal Mind, from higher dimensions. Any new idea must first be channeled to a human entity before it becomes manifest on your dimension.

The more open and aware you are of higher dimensions, the more likely it is that you will be one of the selected entities to bring new knowledge to your own dimension. You learn best when your mind is uncluttered and open, and you learn best when you are under spirit control and not ego control, for the ego is more inclined to accept traditional Earth knowledge and is inclined to be more subjective than objective. It is also inclined sometimes to be very gullible and will take the easy route over the more difficult route.

From our point of view you will learn the greatest lessons for your progression through meditation; through being quiet, being open, and allowing yourself to be connected to Universal Mind and thus to Universal Knowledge. A lot of knowledge that you have on Earth is inconsequential to your growth but necessary to your physical survival. This is why we are always encouraging sensory awareness. We want you to go beyond your physical senses, but the physical senses are the starting point to take you beyond the mere physical aspects of your senses to the higher aspects of them.

We are trying to guide you to the point of seeing the essence or truth of every illusion. Your planet has had many wonderful entities who have shared their truth and knowledge in the form of writing, art, music, and so forth, and this is why we have guided you into so many varied areas to expand your knowledge. By expanding your knowledge it is hoped that you will be able to transform it into wisdom and to make knowledge and wisdom a way of life and not a mere thing of the brain.

Learning is very important because this is a way of growing and progressing. It is part of the Full Circle journey. It is necessary to learn in each expression you have chosen to enter. All entities learn. Truly aware entities seek to learn, strive to learn, open many doors and follow many paths. They maintain an openness of mind. Knowledge is a cup that can never be filled. You will never, on your plane, learn it all. This is the excitement of life: the continuance of learning. It is what keeps you young and alive and a participant on the journey. Once you have learned something, it is up to you to share it. For sharing is teaching and teaching is sharing. You are both learners and teachers. You are never one or the other; you are both.

BEYOND PHYSICAL PERCEPTIONS

You are primarily spirit or mind or consciousness or energy. What you are has little to do with your physical shell. Even your physical shell is not what it seems. You look at your world and you see only solid objects. But everything which you see as solid is alive and moving at incredible speeds. If everything you perceive as real and solid were to become unbonded as atoms and their components flew apart, you would see nothing. This is why it is called illusion. It is all dynamic energy, it is all the Source. Everything in all dimensions is cosmic energy which is dynamic and flowing and eternal.

I am amused by your definitions of inanimate and animate objects. There is nothing inanimate or solid in all creation. There is nothing which is not cosmic energy. There is nothing which is dead. There is nothing which is passive. Everything moves and vibrates in all spheres of life. To be a part of all this action is truly exciting, don't you think?

The spirit-controlled entity has this awareness of living in a dynamic, flowing, and changing universe, and he moves and flows with it. He sees beyond his physical limitations and finds joy in the vibrations of life. When the ego controls he cannot sense beyond the physical limitations of his five senses, and thus he sees barriers and mistaken reality and death. He cannot flow and really experience the existing dynamic energy.

There is a beautiful interplay between the different aspects of creation if you will but begin perceiving yourselves differently and start becoming aware of your part in the Cosmos. A dream is similar to physical life. When you are dreaming, you see people and things and you experience. When the dream ends, all disappear and you may or may not recall the dream. If physical life became unbonded you would see nothing, but the memory would remain.

Basically what I'm trying to say to you is that you are spirit, you are dynamic energy, you are part of the Universal Mind, and your path and your journey is spiritual. Do not let your physical senses deceive you or limit you. You are something beyond your physical perceptions, and nothing is really as it seems. Expand your consciousness, transcend your ego, and experience the dynamic energy of life and the creative interplay of all that is. Let your spirit lead. Become one with your spirit who is traveling in your dimension through your physical manifestation. Do not hinder your spirit's movement. Do not fragment yourself from spirit for its journey is yours.

GIVING AND RECEIVING

You've been told that if you cannot give with love, it is best to withhold, for the gift without the giver is bare. For your own personal growth and to keep the Law of Karma from affecting you, it is best to refrain from giving unless you can do so out of love. Sometimes it's appropriate to refrain from giving, because there are times when the greatest gift can be to force another to do something without your support. This can encourage greater growth, self-reliance and God-reliance. Connect up with the Universal Mind and determine whether the gift you're giving will help or hinder the growth of another entity.

In order for entities to grow, it is important that there be a balance between giving and receiving. There will be times when you will be required to give more than receive. Likewise, if there is balance, there will be times when you will receive more. On Christmas all give and all receive, and this is essentially balance. But on one's birthday all give and one receives. This is not balance, but eventually all are placed in the position of receiver, and thus there is balance.

From a cosmic point of view, all will ultimately be balanced. Those who have been primarily giving out of love will receive more than they have ever given. And for those who have primarily taken for their own benefits, much will be taken from them. This is the Law of Balance which is no more than a part of the Law of Cause and Effect.

This does not mean that you should never request anything of another. But you must request out of love and not simply out of a sense of trying to make your life easier at another's expense. When you receive something given in love, you should accept the gift in love and be willing to give out of love. It does not mean that you owe the specific giver something. It means that when someone requests something of you, you must be willing to respond out of love.

You owe no one and no one owes you. But in the area of giving and receiving, you owe life. You take from Life and you must give to Life. Some feel that when someone does them a favor or gives them a gift that they are obligated to return the favor or a gift to the particular giver. This is not true. If the gift or favor was given in love and if you have received in love, then you pay tribute to this love by passing the love on. All gifts should be given in love or not be given at all.

WHO IS YOUR TEACHER?

Who is your Master? Who is your teacher? Who is your guru? Is it a spouse or a friend? Is it the book you are reading or the television program you watched? Is it a Beethoven symphony or the song of a bird? Is it the Bible or the Koran? It is all of these and more. Your master, your teacher, your guru is Life and all that it contains. You are all masters, teachers, and gurus, for you are Life. At times you feel you are doing neither, but the process of learning and teaching goes on whether you are consciously aware or not. You are learning at either a supraconscious or a subconscious level. On the supraconscious level you have the ability to teach the supraconscious of others. The subconscious level is basically a storehouse, although it acts as teacher during hypnosis and dreams.

At the conscious level of teaching and learning, you teach best when you share yourself in openness and love and give the wisdom and experience of your own being, and when you exemplify whatever truth is yours. Never fear to share the crystal of a new facet reflecting a new light. Those who are your students change and transform and thus will accept change and transformation in you.

You can learn from others best when you are quiet and listen to their truth with love and do not judge their truth. Let them share the wisdom and experience of their being and know that the crystal of their mind may turn and show a new facet reflecting new light. Accept change and transformation in those who are your teachers as you accept it in yourself.

Be gentle as teachers and eager as students. Gentleness and eagerness are two beautiful qualities in the exchange of wisdom and knowledge.

Without eagerness, the teacher cannot teach. Without gentleness, the student will not learn. Since you are both, be both gentle and eager.

TO WORRY IS TO BE SELFISH

Worry is a waste of time and energy. You all know this. Seldom does worry accomplish anything but the giving of power to negative thoughts.

There is great selfishness in worrying because of the negative thought energy which is produced. Through worry, particularly if it is about another entity, your negative energy could manifest into a situation which might not have occurred had you not added negative energy. If something happens which you deem to be unpleasant and you have not created negative energy prior to its manifestation, then it was part of the flow. It was meant to happen as part of a lesson. But worry is based on selfishness and ignorance, and you have reached the point in awareness where you are no longer ignorant of the powers contained in thought.

Just as negative thought energy has the potential to manifest and change a situation, so also does positive thought energy. Positive thought energy has as its base love and unselfishness. It is of God. And because it comes from love, it is good. So when a situation appears which your ego tells you to worry about, dismiss it and begin creating positive thought energy. This is the most helpful and loving thing you can do both for yourself and others. It is a love born of trust and faith. It shows a loving concern and not a selfish worry. Use one of the most trusting statements you have: "Not my will, but thy will...."

NEUTRALITY AND PROGRESS

Never confuse neutrality with apathy for, indeed, there is a great difference between the two. Apathy denotes an attitude of non-caring, whereas neutrality provides time to assess all the data prior to one's response. Neutrality in one sense simply means entering a life experience with a free and open mind and provides the opportunity to respond in a fresh and unique manner.

Neutrality is a way to move into a life experience and view the data with clear and uncluttered vision. Your reaction to the experience after assessing the contained data will most probably be either negative or positive, and will seldom be neutral. Basically you begin as the outside observer of the experience from the point of neutrality, and you become the subject of the experience when you choose your reaction or response based on the assessed data. If you have entered from a point of neutrality, you are seeing the fresh and unique aspects of the experience, and your chances of responding positively are increased as opposed to patterned responses which have been based on your reactions to similar experiences in the past.

Everything which occurs to you in your present life experience is different not only from past experience but also from the experiences of others. Similarity may be present, but not exactness. So when one says to you, "Oh, the same thing happened to me," this is inaccurate. Something similar may have happened but not the exact same thing. Also when you have the feeling of experiencing something before, yet on your conscious level you know you haven't, it is simply that you have either experienced a similar situation in another expression or that one of your aspects has experienced or is experiencing it, and somehow your conscious mind has filtered the data from another level of consciousness.

Awareness is truly the key to seeing the unique differences between similar experiences, and awareness is brought about by your own position of neutrality. Your response will determine whether similar experiences will need to be repeated. Neutrality truly provides the means for faster progress in the learning of lessons in your present expression.

TRUST YOUR OWN PERCEPTION

Do now allow yourself to be confused by basing your assessments on the assessments of others. Trust your own inner guidance. One entity may present an entirely different picture of another than that which you have. Do not allow this to influence or color your own picture.

Just as you relate to the various entities within your life experience with individuality and uniqueness, so do others. If someone tells you that a certain entity is selfish and unloving and yet that entity has never been anything but giving and loving to you, then trust what has been rendered to you. All entities come to one another from different levels of awareness, and all perceptions of a singular entity are based on an individual's awareness level and his own level of truth.

You will never be able to see the totality of another entity while in a three-dimensional world. A human entity is multi-faceted, and you will only experience single facets of the human crystal. So the facet which is shown to you may be different from the one shown to another.

If you turn one of your lighted facets to another, you raise them up, for they will seek to reflect that light. On the other hand, if you show forth a muddied facet, this too may be reflected back to you. Sometimes entities who say negative things about another are only verbalizing a reflection of their own nature.

Don't be confused. If your perception of another entity is positive, hold that vision. To you this is a true perception. It does not matter how another may perceive him. Only your own perception is of value to you.

You can cause the lighted facets of others to turn toward your own light facets, or you can cause their dark facets to appear. Seldom will a muddied facet turn toward a lighted one. You will bring into your life that which issues forth from you.

If another's perception of an entity is also perceived by you sometime during your life experience, do not say, "Oh, I was wrong. I thought he was giving and loving, and he turned out to be selfish and unloving." There is no wrong or right except as you perceive it. Because the human entity is multi-faceted he can be, at differing times, selfish and unloving and giving and loving. He did not turn out to be anything, for he is not yet completed, anymore than you are. He is growing, expressing, and becoming.

Be open to a human crystal's rotation and know that you will perceive both muddy facets and clearly lit ones, and that neither represents the totality of the whole crystal. Seek always the light of the crystal's core, the true essence, and make no firm judgments about the facets which appear to you, for they are but illusion. The power and the reality lie within the core. Concentrate on expressing your own lighted facets outward to your world, and know that one day all crystals will be surrounded by Light flowing outward from their own crystalline cores. One day there will be no reflected light—only Light from the All, the Light of the Cosmic Core.

ALL HUMAN ENTITIES ARE GIFTED

Each human entity is blessed with numerous talents and gifts completely individual and unique. Since the Source expresses through the individual aspects of Creation, the gifts and talents are likewise expressions of the Source. Some of the gifts and talents of an individual expression are recognized and used by the individual expression. Other talents and gifts may lie dormant within the individual expression until the entity grows to that awareness and is able to recognize them. Sometimes the awareness of unused talents and gifts is never recognized because the individual expression does not seek to become aware of them. The potential of one human expression is beyond your comprehension. Most human entities do not realize their potential because they have a belief that they are limited, and it's this belief in limitations which prevents them from realizing their true potential.

Human entities sometimes block their potential by taking their realized gifts and talents for granted. They think that because they have a particular gift or talent it can never be taken from them. But if a gift or a talent is not used or expressed, it loses its power and is sometimes totally removed from the individual expression. Unique gifts and talents are given to individual expressions for the sole purpose of being used. If an individual expression will not allow the Source to express a certain gift or talent through him, the Source will find another instrument to express through.

A gift or a talent that one has been blessed with or gifted with should always be used to express the Creator in the highest way possible. This should be the basic motivation behind the expression of any gift or talent that one may have, whether it is in the arts or music or cooking or gardening or healing. Anything that you do can be a gift and can be developed to its highest potential. If you use a gift or talent strictly to make money or to become famous, then it's possible that your gift or talent will never reach the potential that it could have if your motivation had been simply to express the Gift of the Source. Money, fame, prestige, and so on are added blessings to one's physical life, which come if the motivation to express the gift has been a high one. The Creator is aware of your physical requirements to live in the world in which you reside, and if you trust and continue to express your gifts and talents out of love for the Creator, an abundance of blessings will be given unto you.

So many gifted human entities do not realize this, and they strive for fame and fortune and prostitute themselves for temporary illusions. And, yes, some of them achieve those temporary things they seek, but they never realize the highest potential of the gifts or talents which have been given to them.

Go within and assess what gifts and talents have been given to you, and determine whether you are using them to express the Creator. When you express them, what is the basic motivation behind your expression? Are you expressing your gift or talent out of love for the Creator or simply to attain some temporary illusionary goal? It doesn't matter what it is, for all that you express can be a gift if it is expressed out of love for the Giver of the Gift.

Now I suppose you are thinking that everything you do should be spiritual. What is spirituality but the expression of love to the Creator? It is not just speaking divine phrases or acting religious or anything that you might consider to be spiritual. It is the act of placing Love into everything you do. It doesn't matter if you are a Michaelangelo painting the ceiling of the Sistine Chapel or scrubbing floors or collecting garbage. You are correct in your thinking when you say that nothing in itself is spiritual. It is man who puts the element of spirituality into the aspects of life. And spirituality emerges when love for the Creator enters whatever a human entity happens to be doing. Whatever you do out of love for the Creator is a gift or a talent and carries with it, by its very nature, the element of spirituality. It is acting within this Love for the Creator which gives all your gifts and talents the potential of being expressed more fully and completely.

Perform all actions thinking of yourself as an expression of the Source. Think of all acts of your life as gifts and talents given to you by the Creator. If you will do this in truth and sincerity, you will see your gifts and talents rising, you will realize more of your potential, and you will see the added blessings within your physical life.

HOW TO HANDLE DISILLUSIONMENT

Disillusionment is not a negative experience if you perceive correctly. In fact, with correct perception it is a positive experience. What does disillusion mean but a freeing from an illusion? You live in an illusionary world created by your own mind and the minds of others; more accurately, in a world created by your thoughts and the thoughts of others.

When you experience a disillusionment you are freed from an illusion you had or a thought which you created, and you will do one of two things. You will be bathed in the light of a new truth or revelation, or you will seek desperately to create another illusion. When you experience disillusionment the veil is lifted, the blinders come off, and you are brought into the light of a new truth, a greater sense of awareness. It does not matter whether you like the new vision of truth or not. "The truth will set you free." For one who perceives the experience correctly, disillusionment gives birth to enlightenment.

If you feel sad and depressed during a disillusionary experience, it is because your own ego wanted things to be different than they were or you wanted things to be the way you had created them with your own thoughts. When your own illusions are unveiled and you have a vision of a truth totally alien to your own preconceived truths, then you will feel sad and depressed.

Perceive disillusionment and disappointment as positive experiences and not negative ones. Feel blessed when the veils of illusions are lifted to provide you with the light of a new truth, no matter whether the ego part of you likes the new vision of truth or not. All relative truths are fragments of Absolute Truth, moving toward oneness with the Absolute on your journey to enlightenment.

RISK SEIZING OPPORTUNITIES

Once upon a time there was a princess who lived in a beautiful white castle which sat high on a hill overlooking a large lake surrounded by many trees with large and long branches. Winter had come and the lake had begun to freeze. The trees had lost their leaves, and the bare branches extended over the lake like long, spidery fingers.

One day the princess was standing near the lake's edge, looking across the frozen waters. In the distance she could see another castle sitting upon another hill. On the opposite shore she could see a young man staring back at her. "Come across!" he shouted. The princess carefully stepped out onto the ice. Upon hearing a creaking sound beneath her tiny feet, she quickly grabbed a nearby branch and pulled herself back to safety. "Perhaps tomorrow," she called back to the young man.

The next day she tried again to move out onto the ice, but quickly retreated to the shore's safety when she again heard the creaking beneath her feet. The young man across the lake shouted, "Don't be afraid! The lake is frozen solid!" But the princess simply would not go beyond the branches which represented her safety. Each day she would go to the lake and do the same thing. How she wanted to meet the young man in the distance.

This scene continued all winter long: the princess stepping onto the ice; pulling back and grasping the branches at the first creaking sound; and the young man in the distance calling to her and telling her not to be afraid.

One day in early spring she went to the lakeshore and looked longingly across to the opposite side, hoping to see the young man. The castle on the hill was gone and there was no one on the distant shore. The princess went down to the shore for the rest of her life, but she never saw the castle nor the young man again. A part of her always wondered what would have happened if she had not been afraid to walk across the lake. And another part of her was always a little sad.

This is a tale of letting go of security, of taking risks, of trusting. Many times within an entity's life there will appear in the distance great opportunities which will beckon and call to you.

Sometimes in order to seize these opportunities, it is necessary to move beyond the edge of what you consider security. It may require

116

walking alone out onto the ice of a new frontier beyond the branches of safety. It will always require trust in the voice of opportunity and becoming deaf to the creaking sounds of your own inner fears.

As happened with the princess, if you do not move outward to seize an opportunity which has been presented to you, it will disappear and may never reappear again. This, of course, does not mean that if you do not grasp one opportunity that there will be no others. There will always be opportunities, which are actually gifts of the Creator, presenting themselves to you. But if you do not accept these gifts, they will disappear from your view.

Do not become habitually fearful of seizing the opportunities presented to you. Although you may miss some opportunities, risk seizing opportunities more often than missing them. Go beyond the edge of your security and fears and move out upon the waters of life. Never be afraid of losing what you have already gained, for you can never lose what is truly yours. Remember that there is always more to gain than to lose if you are aware of the abundance of opportunities available to you. Move toward them with courage and with trust.

When you see the castles of opportunity shining and hear the voice calling and asking you to trust, move out and leave the branches of safety and security behind. When you do you will discover that you are on solid footing and that you will not fall or sink or fail. The key is always trust, for when there is trust there is also courage.

DO NOT PLAY GAMES WITH LIFE

Sometimes the hardest thing human entities have to face is a deep sense of loneliness which can even occur when there are lots of people surrounding them. Even when one is surrounded by others, there can be a time when there is no real connection with them. It is this lack of connection which causes the feeling of loneliness. And this feeling can be deepened if the entity also feels disconnected from higher realms. Loneliness can lead to a sense of frustration, despair, and desperation which can lead to violence against oneself or others. Suicide is the result of a lack of connectedness.

This loneliness, this lack of connection, has as its base cause the games human entities play with one another. Think about your world and the games that are played. Can you look beyond the flesh and blood of each human being and sense the spirit of God within? When your ego allows you to be hurt by the words and actions of others, can you forgive as God eternally forgives you? Or do you withhold your forgiveness as a method of punishment? Do you keep the Karmic Wheel constantly turning? Do you seek to raise others up with your love, or do you see only the flaws and center on them to keep others down? Do you have prejudices? Do you make demands on others because you feel they are somehow less than you? Do you expect to receive without having to give? Are you envious of the gifts and talents of others, or do you want the best for them? Are you supportive of others? Do you listen to others, or do you shut them off if your ego does not wish to hear? Do you see yourself as both teacher and student? Do you use love as a weapon and not as a key?

These are just a few of the mind games humans play with one another. Because of the games the human condition continues to be chaotic, and many live in a constant state of confusion and disconnectedness, both with others and with the Source.

It is preferable that one gets his own house in order and does not worry about the houses of others. Encourage and support others, but do not think that you can clean their temples. Each entity is responsible for clearing away his own cobwebs and clutter. And this is as it should be, for each entity has been the creator of his own cobwebs and clutter. If you want to see bright light, clean house and don't play games. If you want the world to change, start changing yourself and stop expecting others to change first. If you want to be gods, then act like gods. If you want the world to cease to be filled with loneliness, start filling it with love. It begins with *you*.

I AM WHAT I AM

The reason so many will not reveal their true name, *I Am What I Am*, is because they fear rejection. Or they feel they will hurt or disappoint a loved one. Or they doubt their own sense of God-direction. It's hard to be what you are because of the risk you must sometimes take. When you dare to be yourself—when you dare to be free—you are willing to risk. In taking the risk, people will misunderstand you, you may lose what you consider love, you may be rejected, and you may be labeled by your society as strange, selfish, or unloving.

All entities at some point in their physical life experience desire to fully express the God within, but it's hard to know the God within one's own unique expression because so many have narrowly limited their definition of God. They say God is love, God is forgiveness, God is merciful and just, and so on. He is all of these things, but He is much, much more. Then sometimes a human entity is admonished to strive to be like God within a limiting human definition. If you strive to grow within societal limitations, you restrict the unique and natural flow of your own God expression.

To be able to *say "I Am What I Am"* takes courage, but it requires even greater courage to *be* what you are. It is not society who should determine what you should be. It is you and the God expression of you who should determine not only what you should be, but what you should *become.* An entity will never be happy or healthy or free until he can say *"I Am What I Am."* He must also trust when he says *"I will be what God directs me to be."* If he is unable to do either, he is restricting his own God.

There will be no real growth unless an entity can take the risk and say *"I Am What I Am."* This acceptance says *"I Am What I Am"* in my present moment which is all that you of space-time dimensions are assured of. This acceptance acknowledges your trust in the God of your own being. It allows God to direct you and flow through you, expressing Himself without limits. It also ensures growth and enables the God qualities to manifest from within naturally rather than exerting energy to will them into your consciousness.

To you who would live free and express your own God essence, be what you are, accept what you are, trust in the direction of the Source, and know that you will become One. Take the risk of being free, remembering always that He made no other gods for you to serve. He said *"I Am What I Am,"* and you are His children who bear His name. You can say with joy, *"I Am What I Am!"* Say also, *"I will become what my Lord God directs me to become, and He directs me to become One!"* Though waves may lash and leap, and the perils may be many, with the Master at the wheel, you will soon be Home.

YOU ARE RESPONSIBLE
FOR YOUR OWN HAPPINESS

When you experience unhappiness and discord, it's time to look within and discover what is causing these feelings. It's easy to look outside of yourself and blame externals, but externals are not the cause of inner unhappiness. They are only illusionary creations you have manifested into your life experience. You create your outer realities based on your inner realities. What you bring into your outer reality or what you manifest is parallel to what you extend from your inner being. You are the creator and controller of your individual outer world.

Many unhappy entities blame people and situations because they have within their belief systems the idea that the outer world is supposed to bring them happiness. These people expect others to create happiness for them. You already know that having expectations brings disappointments. The world owes you nothing. And you are not responsible for creating happiness for others. You are responsible only for creating your own happiness. When you create happiness for yourself from within, it extends outward from you, thus manifesting a happy outer world of reality for yourself and others.

The bases of unhappiness are often rooted in fear and its children—resentment, anger, jealousy, prejudice, guilt, self-pity, and so forth. One who deals with these emotions and feelings will be released from them. But if you pretend that you have none of these and still wish to blame your externals, you have chosen your unhappiness.

If you are unhappy and make no effort to seek the truth of your own inner being, you will continue to manifest unhappiness into your outer world. It takes great courage to face your own inner reality—that world which is filled with both light and shadow areas. It takes great courage to be truly honest with yourself. It takes great courage to face your fear, your guilt, your resentment, your prejudice, your jealousy, and your anger. In facing these ego creations, you will also find your beauty, your goodness, your love, and your own God essence.

The Creator did not create His Creations to be unhappy. If unhappiness is part of your life experience, you have created it from your own inner world. Find the light of your inner being. With inner happiness, you bring outer happiness to you. With inner love, you bring outer love to you.

DOING NOTHING IS SOMETIMES PREFERABLE

If you cannot help someone, make certain that you do not knowingly hurt them.

If you cannot lift another up, make certain that you do not knock him down.

If you cannot offer your hand in peace, make certain that you do not raise your sword instead.

If you cannot love another, make certain that you do not hate.

If you cannot fill another's hunger or quench his thirst, make certain that you do not take what little bread or water he has left from him.

If you cannot help another carry his burden, make certain you do not add more weight to his present load.

If you cannot give to another, make certain that you do not rob him of what he has.

If you cannot respect another, make certain you do not take his dignity from him.

If you cannot add joy and happiness to another's life, make certain that you do not knowingly create sorrow and unhappiness for him.

If you cannot set another free, make certain you do not imprison him.

If you cannot help another in his understanding, make certain that you do not add confusion.

If you cannot bring light to another, make certain you do not create darkness.

These statements simply mean that if one is unable at a present awareness level to offer anything to another, it is preferable to do nothing rather than to do the reverse or to attempt to offer something which is not coming from the heart center.

Continue to evaluate your awareness level within all your relationships and life situations. Examine what you believe, think, or feel in any situation and with respect to any human relationship. If you cannot, in the truth of your own being, offer your hand in friendship and in peace to another, peace is better served in your doing nothing at all until you reach the point in your awareness where you can make a sincere offering. Feigned offerings are empty gifts and serve no one, least of all the one doing the offering.

There are situations within life where you might wish to help another, but you do not have the resources, the knowledge, or the abilities. In this case, doing nothing would be preferable.

In closer and more intimate relationships, human entities will offer out of a sense of obligation. They oftentimes offer because they feel they have to. On the external level, obligatory offerings appear to be beneficial, but on a higher level they are but half full and are not complete. You must always remember that giving and receiving are really the same thing. When you offer, you will receive back—so it is very important that you are aware of not only what you are offering, but also how you are offering.

Attunement to your own inner guidance will always create the knowledge of what you should do in any given situation and within the framework of any human relationship. Guidance, of course, will never urge you to do the reverse, such as offer hate when you are unable to love. But it will, if you will listen, oftentimes instruct you to do nothing if it is not coming from the heart center or if your offering would create greater problems.

Remember, as well, that what you offer may not be returned to you in like manner, but how you offer has a great effect on your individual growth and unfoldment. Offerings from the heart center unify giving and receiving and make them one.

Whenever you offer any part of yourself, it is a commitment to the now moment. For your own growth, be very clear about what you commit to and about your inner intent and true attitude. If there is any lack of clarity, then it is preferable to wait for higher guidance. When you offer yourself in the truth, sincerity, and love of your heart center, you receive these back into yourself. A wise master gave his young student two prettily wrapped boxes each tied with golden ribbons. The student eagerly opened the first and found a shimmering pearl inside—a beautiful treasure. With the same eagerness, he opened the second box and found nothing.

The wise master asked his student, "Which gift do you like the best?"

The student replied: "Why, of course, the one containing the treasure. The other one was empty; there was nothing inside."

And so, dear ones, when you offer yourselves, think of yourselves as prettily wrapped gifts, for whenever and whatever you offer, you are really offering *you*. You are the gift! And only you are aware of the contents or lack of them.

THE PURPOSE OF MIRROR VISION

Mirror vision is alluded to primarily in the negative sense that those things which you dislike in another can likewise be found within your own self. This is true. To discover this you must be willing to explore the deeper levels of your being. On the other side of the coin, those things which you admire in another are likewise to be found within your own being. You limit your concept of mirror vision through your limited vision and limited understanding.

Don't you see by now that everything that "is" can be found in your own being? Everything that you are able to conceive or perceive is a part of you. If it were not, you would not recognize it; you would not know it. Oftentimes you look at one of your brothers and you say, "I dislike his negativity or his dishonesty or his lack of punctuality." Your ego then proceeds, after your judgments, to tell you that you are free of these perceived flaws within another's humanness. This makes you feel very good, does it not? The ego is forever trying to convince you of your perfection in your movement upon the Earth plane. The more convinced you become of your Earth perfection, the more judgmental and critical you are apt to become.

In spirit, in essence, you are perfection. There is, in truth, only Oneness, and in this Oneness with All Creation you hold within your being the potential to manifest every created illusion that you have awareness of. Whatever you can see is within your own being. This is why so much emphasis has been placed on the advice of not judging and of allowing. If you are connected in Oneness, then when you do judge or condemn another, you are judging and condemning yourself as well.

All that you see within your third dimensional world, all that you perceive and charge with negative or positive thought energy, is illusionary. Only you are real. When you look into a mirror, you reflect back into yourself the image that you project out from yourself.

To work with the concept of mirror vision so that it can benefit you, you must reach the awareness that you are in Oneness with those qualities you both like and dislike. You cannot perceive that which you have no knowledge of. For example, you cannot dislike negativity unless there is, somewhere in your being, the element of negativity. It's not necessary to try to discover where it, or whatever you dislike, is lurking in yourself. It is there. That is all you need to know. You see, if there were no consciousness of negativity within you, you would not be able to see it in others.

I would ask the seeming impossible of you: that of allowing your brothers to be without your judgement of them. Do not, in arrogance, think that you are beyond anything which you perceive in your world. You are not, in spite of what your ego may tell you. In your perceptions of your brothers remember that you are disabled with limited vision and can view but a few facets of their totality. When looking into a mirror you can see but one reflection. Even when you are surrounded by mirrors, you are unable to see all the reflections at once. No matter how hard you try you will never see the totality of any entity, not even yourself.

What is the purpose of mirror vision? To teach you and to help you to grow. The primary lesson contained in the concept of mirror vision is to move you to release yourself from the habit of judging. Once you can perceive without judgment or allow without criticism, you become free. In the allowing of your brothers to be, you allow yourself to be. Once judgment has left the space of your being, you will see and perceive anew, and you will see beyond the surface and into the core of your brother where, in Oneness, you will feel the connection of the God centers. The true purpose for mirror vision is not to make you aware of your negative flaws so that you may overcome them. Flaws are just manifestations of your ego and are not real, and the purpose of mirror vision is merely to teach you to release from your judgments.

THE POWER OF WORDS

Frequently human entities enter learning phases in which suffering of some type is manifested—physical, mental, or emotional. All that suffering means on a higher level is "undergoing." Thus, one's entire life is a process of undergoing—be it joy, sadness, or whatever emotion one chooses to experience. Your word suffering in its Earth meaning generally means something which is negative. When you think of suffering, you think of something which is negative or painful or uncomfortable.

If you could raise your awareness to the place where you could redefine it and call it undergoing, you would probably not become so caught up in the experience in which you think you are suffering. The word undergoing is in itself neutral, just as suffering really is. Collective mind, however, has charged the word suffering with negative energy. It always refers to the experience of pain and discomfort.

What I'm trying to make you understand is that oftentimes the mere exchanging of one word for another to denote the same experience or process can change your perception of an experience, and a change in perception can change the experience. Suppose you have a dis-ease which when in manifested form causes you to experience pain. The pain will lessen if you perceive yourself as undergoing a process rather than if you perceive yourself as suffering. Why? Because you have been programmed to perceive suffering as negative. Most entities relate to the word undergoing with more neutrality.

In the vocabularies you use in communication, you never really examine the words that you utilize. If you would really begin analyzing the words you use, you would come to realize that many of them have already been positively or negatively charged by the collective mind. Many have been collectively defined and charged with certain energies. An individual entity is then programmed with not only the word itself and its accepted definition, but also with the collective energy assigned to it. Then if the entity accepts what the collective mind has determined, he adds his own energy to the word, either negative or positive. Much of what you think is your individual perception based on experience is really programming by the collective mind.

Most entities do not realize how much power words have in their lives. You already know that words produce certain effects when used in communication with others. But what you oftentimes do not understand is that the words you use in communication with yourself in your thoughts energize and connect to your perception of your external and internal worlds. For example, I much prefer to use the word non-love rather than hate because the word hate is of a high negative charge within the collective mind. Non-love is not so highly charged.

Begin thinking about the words you use. Which are neutral? Which are negatively or positively charged by the collective mind? What should you do after you've made the determination? The only ones you need to concern yourself with are words of negative power. If there is a word which causes you to perceive negatively, exchange it for one which is either positive or neutral. Rather than saying "I'm suffering," say instead "I'm undergoing." It doesn't mean that you will not experience what you have chosen to experience, but it means that you will alter your perception, which can lessen the perceived negative aspects of the experience. Rather than saying "I feel terrible," say instead "I feel out of balance." One phrase is charged with negative energy; the other is neutral.

Most people take words for granted; they use them loosely without thought or consideration of their effect on either themselves or others. Words, in themselves, have no power. But when they are defined and used, they have incredible power. These energized symbols have the power to heal or destroy. And that's what words are—energized symbols used for communication. And anything with energy contains power and should be used with care and wisdom. Think carefully of the words you use with yourself or others. Release from some which have no benefit to you or others. Exchange negative words for neutral or positive ones. This requires a lot of discipline and probably a lot of reprogramming, but you will discover that as time passes you will learn to control the words you use within communication, you will begin to perceive differently, and you will feel better emotionally, physically, and mentally.

THE HOLY GRAIL OF YOU

From the time he first began to question Man has asked, "Why am I here?" and "What is my purpose in Life?" So many human entities spend their life journeys seeking the Holy Grail of themselves and only find it when they reach the awareness that they are God expressing uniquely and perfectly as themselves. Until that awareness is reached, many human entities wander, oftentimes aimlessly, searching for a reason for being.

Beloved Ones, so much of your earthly journey is spent in trying to validate your existence. It is no wonder that there is so much stress and confusion present in your lives. The fact that you are is validation enough for your expressing on planet Earth. Your primary purpose for being in form is to teach and learn and to express the godness of you. Remember that your Earth walk is but one leg of the Cosmic journey, one second in time and space. Beyond that there are myriad dimensions and planes of Life to experience. Life is ongoing, eternal. There is no death, Beloved Ones, in spite of what your illusions may tell you. There is only a release from form as you pass through the doorway to a higher dimension and frequency of Life. If you only knew what you are a part of and connected to, you would not fear so, and you would not run hither and thither like mice in a maze.

Prior to your entrance to the Earth plane of Life, you knew what your individual and collective missions would be, and you knew what lessons you needed to both learn and teach. On the present conscious level it is not necessary that you know what your missions are. On the spiritual level you know, and you will not exit until your mission is completed. Therefore, Beloved Ones, no one exits before his time.

Yet you are formed beings, energy beings, beings with consciousness, beings with dreams and visions, beings with needs and wants and desires, and you think and act and do. You need to be active and contribute to the betterment and advancement of your individual and collective life, so you need to be doing something with your life in manifested form. You already have purpose simply because you are expressing, so what you seek is knowing what you are supposed to be doing on the mundane level of manifested life. How do you determine what you are supposed to do and where you fit in?

One way is to evaluate your individual gifts and talents. Each individual entity contains within himself gifts and talents unique to himself which, if developed, will sustain his life and supply his needs. Many human entities do not take the time to discover their gifts and talents, or if they do, they do not take the time to develop them. Many lack patience to develop them, or lack trust in their gift and enter jobs they hate. They live lives in quiet desperation feeling unfulfilled and without real purpose. Not all entities will be artists, musicians, or writers or those roles you assign as gifted. A gift is anything that you love to do and are willing to take the time developing. It can be anything from scrubbing a floor to composing a symphony. It is whatever creates a feeling of satisfaction within you. When you love what you are doing, work becomes a joy and adds to the advancement of not only your own life, but to the lives around you and to the culture you have chosen to express yourself through.

To determine your true purpose on the mundane level really means knowing yourself and honoring and being true to that self. Success or the lack of it is based on how you feel about you, not on how the outer world evaluates you. Success in Life is felt when you are doing what you love to do, and this is when you express yourself best and to the fullest. This is when you give your best to the world: when you're giving your best to you.

Beloved Ones, do not fret so over the purpose of your lives. The purpose of a seed is to produce the fruit and the flower. Do you think the seed frets over its purpose? No. It merely allows Life's energies to touch it and activate it. It simply is and unfolds into new beingness. And this is what you should do, for are you not seeds of greater beingness? Allow Life's energies and your own inner guidance to direct your feet upon your Earth walk. Remember, children, that the importance lies not in where you walk, but rather in how you walk. Begin living your lives in the fullness of who you are in truth. That which you seek—the Holy Grail of you—is already in your hands. Look within and *See!*

THE TRUE GIFT

This is the time when many celebrate the birth of Jesus the Christ, the expression of God who made the greatest impact upon your planet in your culture. Christmas is characterized by greater love and caring, the offering of gifts, goodwill to men, joy to the world, and peace on Earth— positive vibrations.

Yet at this time many experience their deepest depression and greatest sense of loneliness. For many the Christmas season becomes a time of great pain and intense disillusionment. Why, Beloved Ones, does this happen to so many entities at a time which appears to be so positive?

One reason has to do with the illusions which are created. Your stores and shops are all decorated in glitter and tinsel and colored lights offering the illusion of elegance. Your television advertising creates pictures of well fed families laughing around perfectly decorated Christmas trees under which perfectly wrapped gifts are arranged in perfect order. Or perhaps you see a horse drawn sleigh merrily trotting through powdery snow heading toward the warm, welcome lights of a beautiful home. Or you see the exchange of gifts—furs, diamonds, material finery. The mental pictures that are recorded insist that Christmas means perfect families, beautifully decorated homes, elegant gifts. On another level these pictures exhibit family, home, togetherness, sharing, giving, joy, relaxation, love. A collective image is being created of what Christmas should be if it is to be right.

For so many entities the depression, loneliness, and pain settle in when they realize that their lives are not like those images and that their Christmas is not going to be like it should be. These televised dreams also cause memories of happier times to surface—Christmases experienced as children or with your own children or with a mate who has left your life. A present Christmas always invokes memories of past ones and oftentimes creates a deep longing for another time, and the knowing that you cannot return produces loneliness and depression.

Let this time which acknowledges the entrance of your greatest Master upon your planet be a time when you enter the manger of your own self to witness the birth of the newness of you. Leave the outer world of illusions and enter into the Presence of the true Light.

The true significance of this event and what the Gift really is was not the birth of a baby that was so magnificent; it was the entrance of the Christ Consciousness upon your planet. Jesus didn't change the world; the Consciousness He expressed through His manifested form did. The expression of this Consciousness on His earthly walk was an example, not an exception. This Master expressing the Christ Consciousness exemplified a powerful and power-filled way to live. This was the Gift offered to mankind, to each individual willing to accept it. Jesus the Christ showed through His earthly walk how He exemplified true love, true forgiveness, true giving, true compassion, true connection, and oneness. He experienced life on the outer level, but He lived it on the inner level. The Christian world calls Him its Savior, but the Consciousness which He expressed has no religious or philosophical boundaries. The Gift is for All.

During this season in your Earth year, do not allow yourselves to be prisoners of memories of happier times or become victims of expectations of dreamlike should be's. Take the journey to the manger of your inner self where the Christ Consciousness within you lies waiting to be realized. Go within and accept the true Gift and then move outside yourself and share it with a hurting world. This, Beloved Ones, is what the season should be about. Dream illusions are magical in their appeal to your senses, but the real magic comes from your loving and light being expressed by the Christ Consciousness in you. Allow this to be born in this joyous time!

HAPPINESS IS FOUND IN THE INNER WORLD

Happiness is based on one's individual perception, and that which is termed as happiness varies from individual to individual. Happiness to one may not be happiness to another. Strange as it may seem, there are individuals who are happiest when their lives are filled with drama and trauma. Essentially happiness is a feeling of peace, contentment and fulfillment in one's life. It is a positive emotion. On a higher level happiness is more than an emotion; it is a state of mind, an expression of consciousness. From the higher perspective then, it is possible to experience happiness no matter what may be occurring in one's outer world.

True happiness must come forth from the inner world of being, from one's god self. If you seek happiness in the outer world only, you will discover that it is transitory. The entity who believes he will be happy if he has more money, for example, will soon discover that his happiness is but temporary. The entity who seeks his happiness in the form of another entity will find his happiness to be short lived. Whenever you look to the outer world as your source of happiness, you will ultimately be disappointed. Happiness, Beloved Ones, moves from your inner being to the outer world of manifestation and not the other way around.

One of the primary reasons that so much unhappiness exists in your world is simply because many entities do not understand that each individual is responsible for his or her happiness or lack of it. So many entities believe that their primary role in life is to make others happy. You never make another happy unless that other chooses to be happy. Seeing your individual mission in life as that of making others happy can oftentimes become an imprisoning experience because frequently the entity trying to make others happy denies his own self. One's responsibility is to create happiness for himself on the inner level. When this is accomplished, the happiness moves outward touching other lives. At the other end of the spectrum, there are those entities who expect others to create happiness for them. Each is responsible for creating his own level of happiness and no human entity is responsible for making others happy.

How many times have you heard someone say, "You have made me so happy!" because of something you've said or done? It's a wonderful experience to bring joy to another, but it's not a responsibility. Adding joy to someone's life and enriching another is a gift. Creating happiness for yourself or others is always a gift—never a responsibility or one's mission in Life.

The lines of a current Earth song say, "Don't worry, be happy!" and this is good advice. Worry will always deny you joy in Life. When you are worrying, you are not trusting, and when you are not trusting, you are out of alignment with the true source of your life. Worry is a negative emotion based in fear and, as an empowered energy, becomes a magnet for more negative situations. When you worry you set yourself up to

129

attract exactly the things you really don't want in your life. Happiness is a state of mind born of your inner god essence. Seek happiness in your inner world, for then it can be manifested in your outer world of form. Do not take your life and yourself so seriously. Those situations which you allow to cause you unhappiness today will be but memories tomorrow unless you choose to hold onto your pain and continue to build upon it.

Within your life journeys there will always appear valleys and peaks and plateaus, for Life is movement and the primary purpose for living is to learn and to teach and to unfold into greater beingness. Sometimes you will perceive struggle and challenge, but these need not be negative, and they need not create pain and unhappiness. It is only your own perception that makes mountains out of molehills and causes you to see boulders instead of pebbles on your path.

So, Beloved Ones, when you are feeling unhappy, examine the cause of your unhappiness and determine how important and serious the situation really is in the totality of your life, remembering always that no situation is forever. See your life situations as simply opportunities for greater growth. The tiny plant must struggle to break the hard shell of the seed and must push through the soil in order to stretch to the sun and unfold its petals. The plant within the seed has an inner knowing that the struggle is for its highest growth and good. You can feel joy during your struggles if you know that you are growing and unfolding through experience.

There will be times when you might question, "Why should I be happy?" You should be happy because you have been given the gift of Life. You should be happy because each of you is expressing God uniquely and beautifully. You should be happy because you are Life Itself expressing as you. Go within and know who you really are, and with this knowing you cannot be anything other than happy.

OPENMINDEDNESS: A KEY TO GROWTH

It is important, Beloved Ones, to explore all the knowledge which your world has to offer and to allow your minds to be open for the purpose of increasing your conscious awareness. There is so much knowledge available and so much to be open to that you may sometimes wonder if *everything* can possibly be true. The answer is yes. To some entitiy on some level of awareness there exists truth.

Truth is not absolute in the physical dimension. Like the entity seeking truth, truth itself is in a process of Becoming. Truth is flowing to Absoluteness just as you are flowing to Perfect Oneness.

But what happens to an identity who reaches a point in the truth-seeking process where he believes he has discovered all the answers? What happens when an entity decides that he can no longer accept certain ideas and concepts? What happens when an entity begins to tell others that what they might believe is wrong? What happens is that the entity begins to start closing in on himself. An open mind is a light which not only emits light, but receives light as well. The entity who begins closing his mind receives no light, and as this entity begins closing in on himself he becomes like a collapsing star and ultimately a "black hole" where light is not even emitted; a self-contained entity incapable of being fed or of feeding others.

This situation may be more prevalent on your planet than you realize. The ego has created the closure of many minds through its manifestations of fear, guilt, prejudice, hate, and even ignorance. It can immmobilize the entity and prevent new experiences and new learning. It can numb the mind so that new awareness is impossible. It can imprison the consciousness in a thick, protective shell. It can retard growth and ultimately stop it altogether.

It is important to keep your minds open to all that is, even if your Earth logic is mistrusting. If a pathway is not right for you, you will be led from it. Being led away from a particular path does not mean that it is a wrong or untrue path. It means only that it is not correct for you. It is best not to judge rightness or wrongness or truth or non-truth on any basis except in relation to oneself.

Truth is like a lotus flower, or any other flower for that matter. The total or absolute truth or essence cannot be discovered in a single petal, but must be seen in the whole, complete flower which is a combination of petals. And who among you has the wisdom and knowledge to know when the last petal of the lotus has unfolded and on what dimension it will unfold?

Your minds are like lotus blossoms, and with each new truth a new petal forms, and sometimes an old petal which is no longer your truth will fall away. The process of your Becomingness will ultimately reach the state of Beingness when the entire flower will be present. You cannot hope to achieve this state if you close what petals you presently have and refuse the Light. All of you have the choice to be either collapsing stars or unfolding lotus blossoms.

SPEAK FROM A POINT OF DIGNITY

How you speak to another is a way of expressing love and caring. Think of how you speak to others. Does your speech reflect dignity or arrogance? Words spoken with gentleness reflect your dignity and are filled with power. Words spoken with arrogance can be abusive and commanding, have little power, and are met by resistance, defensiveness, and ill feelings. One loses his power when he speaks from arrogance.

Oftentimes one may feel that in order to make a point or create an impact he must yell. Again the speaker loses his power. The power is lost because the one hearing the words becomes more focused on the loudness and the tone rather than on what is being said. When the hearer focuses on the tone of voice and the loudness, it produces fear, anger or a feeling of being intimidated. The ego sees itself as the protector of the human vehicle. When threatened, it prepares to both defend itself and wage war against what it perceives to be an aggressor. So, whatever the speaker was originally trying to convey is lost. His words and his message have lost power.

Within the framework of communication one must also consider the intent behind the words. When you speak, what is the purpose or intent of your words? Are you trying to create fear? Are you trying to hurt or slay another with your words? Are you trying to make another feel stupid or inadequate? Or are you trying to share your wisdom, knowledge, insights, thoughts, feelings, dreams, awareness, love, and self? Are you trying to uplift another with your words or bring him down?

How you speak to others is quite often a reflection of how you perceive yourself. For example, if you try to create fear in others through your speech, it means that somewhere deep within you are very frightened. If you try to make another feel inadequate, it means that you have an inner sense of your own inadequacy. If you try to bring another down, it is only an attempt to elevate yourself in your own perception. But if you speak with gentleness and dignity to others, it reflects a respect for your own being, a gentleness toward yourself, and an awareness of your own inner power.

If you wish to communicate your words which are but expressions of your thoughts with power, do so with gentleness and dignity. If you wish to have your words heard, empower them with love. Because there is an innate goodness or Godness within human entities, they will respond to gentleness. The seeking entity striving for greater awareness should become more attuned to how he verbally communicates. Know what words you wish to convey and consider your intent. If you discover that your intent is not to uplift or assist in another's growth and unfoldment, go within and seek to discover how you feel about yourself. Determine, when you speak, whether you are reflecting inner dignity or inner arrogance.

All the great masters and avatars have spoken and acted with quiet, gentle dignity, and they have respected the dignity contained within the God selves of others. To become a master one must become a humble seeker and become a speaker with gentle dignity.

BE PATIENT

I have been giving you the thought: "You must be patient, entity." Why do I offer this thought to you over and over again? Because part of being a warrior requires patience. Patience requires the entity to maintain an inner stillness and a calm knowing that the Universe truly is for his highest good. Human entities have a very difficult time developing and maintaining a patient state of mind. Most want everything *Now*. Developing patience and having the discipline to maintain it is truly an art.

There are many advantages to being patient. Patience allows the emotions to settle so that when action is required, the entity will act and move from a point of clarity and spiritual direction. When this occurs nothing is ill-timed or hasty, and there is no loss of inner power or energy. You see, you can't find a solution if you are not clear as to the nature of the problem, and you can't find the answer unless you know what the question is.

Patience requires stillness, a stilling of the emotions, a quieting down within. "Be still and know that I Am God." What does this mean to you? What should it mean to you? It means quietly going into the aloneness of your own being and connecting with your own God essence, for therein lie all your answers and all your joy and all your peace. You will not find your truth anywhere else. When the advice is given to release all the burdens you have chosen to carry, you must not release to anything external to yourself. This is why release, surrender, giving it to God or to the Master sometimes appears not to work very well. When you try to release it external to yourself, you are separating from the All. You are expecting someone or something beyond yourself to somehow transform your life and give you the answers to your questions. You are then like a child asking a physical parent to fix your broken bike or to repair your broken doll. When you truly know that the Christ Spirit and the God essence is part of you and, indeed, is you, you will stop going outside of yourself. You will then know that you must quietly enter the temple of your own being, for this is where the power is, and this is where your truth is. It's nowhere else.

Many do not have this awareness at the heart level or what you term the gut level. Many are just too impatient or too afraid to journey into the inner temple of their being. It's much easier and quicker, they feel, to seek the answers from their external world. It's not that you should never seek guidance from other beings. The wisdom of another, however, will never be as accurate as your own inner guidance and wisdom.

Why don't human entities want to journey to their own inner temples? Some do not accept anything but a God external to themselves. This is their truth, and they live their lives in separation, either praising or blaming an external God for whatever happens in their life experiences. Others actually fear going into the inner temple of their being because the first thing you must face is your own reflection. You have to stand naked before yourself, stripped of your ego garb. You have to be willing to look at yourself honestly in this inner world. As you move through the dark places and the shadows of yourself, you will come to your light, the place of your treasure, and in the mirror you will see the face of God. It takes patience, courage, and a willingness to accept responsibility for your own life. Sometimes it's difficult to shed the ego garb and see yourself as you project outward. The ego garb can be as thin as a soft veil or as hard as a coat of armor. Remember that what you project outward is only a small portion of your total beingness; it is a few facets, some shining, and some dark. But your inner core is the God essence, the Christ Spirit, the Heaven of your being.

When I say to you, "You must be patient, entity" I am trying to direct you into a state of mind which will move you to enter the sanctuary of your own inner temple for a time. Then you will know the problem and the solution, the question and the answer. In your own stillness and in the silence of your own heart you will understand your own truth and your own wisdom. There will be no desired outcomes, no preconceived ideas. You will simply be in the place of your truth, and in patience you will wait for guidance.

PART IV

I WANT TO FEEL GOOD

The ancient Greeks spoke of a sound mind in a sound body, and this means a proper balance between mind and form. The spirit/mind needs the physical form on this Journey, so it is important to value our forms and care for them. We suffer from imbalance when we focus so much on our form that the spirit/mind is neglected. Likewise, our physical form suffers when we allow our consciousness/mind to become stressed and negative. To feel good and live our lives fully, we must learn to balance these two aspects of our person.

YOUR VEHICLE IS NOT YOU

The primary purpose of the physical vehicle is to enable the spirit to express in a world of manifested forms. Manifested form is the illusion; spirit is the reality. As Mind created or brought forth the organic brain computer to serve as a transmitter to and receiver from Universal Mind, so also did Mind create the physical vehicle in order to express through it. Therefore, the vehicle is of importance in the manifested world because it is that which carries you through your world to your destination, thus allowing you to fulfill your individual mission, whatever that may happen to be.

In your world there oftentimes appears to be an imbalance with respect to where a human entity's primary focus should be: on the body or on the spirit. The vehicle is amassed with sensory receivers and transmitters which are controlled, as you know, by the organic brain computer with its intricate programming. You are sensing, feeling entities; you see, you touch, you smell, you taste, you hear, and you then interpret the incoming data from your outer world. You also receive data from your vehicle itself. You know when you're thirsty, hungry, tired, ill, or hurting. When you really think of the vehicle itself, it is a marvelously constructed form. When it is in balance with spirit, there is little that surpasses your form in the manifested world.

There is no reason why you should not love your form—the vehicle which transports you. But in loving it it is important to remember that the vehicle is not you. To express that which is you in the manifested world through your physical vehicle, learn to become attuned to what it needs in order to operate properly: things such as water and sustenance, rest, the need for exercise, and so forth. Each form also has individualized requirements, which is why attunement to your own unique form is vital.

All forms require sustenance, but not all can ingest the same kinds of food. One entity may be able to ingest chocolate, for example, with no adverse reactions. Another entity may ingest it and become ill. Your individual form will tell you what works well within your individual system and what does not work well. But you have to listen and be aware of what it is telling you. Many human entities ingest food items and pay no attention to the body's reaction to those items. They wonder why they don't feel just right or why they may lack energy. Your body also communicates when it needs fuel, or food intake. It indicates this with sensations of hunger. Many human entities eat primarily out of habit patterns rather than hunger, and frequently eat more than their form requires. Ideally, the best time to ingest food is when you are hungry and to take in food only to the point of satisfaction. To gorge or overfeed the form is stressful to the digestive system. And, as you know, too much food for your individual structure creates added weight which adds stress to all the other systems in the form.

Perhaps the key to loving or enjoying the vehicle that you have chosen to express through is your awareness of its primary purpose. Your vehicle is your automobile on your road of Life. You choose your vehicle and you maintain it. It doesn't matter whether you choose a Volkswagon or a Cadillac. It doesn't matter what the exterior appearance is; what matters is how well it runs. Many human entities, however, are unhappy because they compare their vehicles with others and are never satisfied with what they have chosen. Does it really matter if you are tall or short, black or white, beautiful or non-beautiful by the standards of your world? No. The form is not you.

Once you truly understand this at your deeper levels of awareness, as well as the primary purpose of the human vehicle, you may change your thinking and your attitudes regarding your form. You may one day look into your mirror and exclaim, "Wow! Look at me! There's no other form exactly like mine. I am a totally unique expression traveling in a vehicle totally my own!" And you might say, "I'm going to study this form of mine and find out what it takes for it to operate at peak performance. In your study you might release from addictions such as drugs, alcohol, smoking, or from foods which distress your systems. You might release from weight which burdens your structure; you might begin exercising, and you might begin meditating or centering to create greater balance in the form. Whatever you do, you will do it to better express the truth and beauty of the essential you.

When you feel physically good, you not only have increased energy, but you also have more positive thoughts. You begin to reflect outwardly what you are in mind. Your body and your mind work very closely together. One of your wise Earth entities said, "A sound mind in a sound body." There is great truth in this. To have a sound body does not mean that you have to become a body builder or a health nut or run five miles a day or take a mass of vitamins. If you are aware of what your own body tells you and are attuned to your own unique requirements, you will have a sound body.

A sound mind has to do with how and what you think: your consciousness, your perception of your world and of your self. So, which comes first, a sound mind or a sound body? The thought or the manifestation of the thought? The answer is the thought. What you are in form began first as a thought. Much of what you think has to do with your programming and what you feel about yourself. If you received a lot of negative input about how you looked or if you were compared with other forms, you may have negative thoughts about yourself which you express outwardly as unsureness, a lack of self-esteem, or insecurity. You may then try to cover this up with masks, such as undereating, overeating, addictions of various kinds, excesses and stresses which abuse the form. This is a circular effect: negative thought leads to negative manifestation which leads to more negative thought and so on.

Is it necessary to change your form in order to feel good about it? No. Change your thoughts about your form and it will reflect your thoughts. Accept who you are and love what you are in your present moment. Attune to your own vehicle's individual needs and requirements and it will transform itself. Focus more on your God essence, your inner beauty, and this is what will be expressed in your outer world. True, essential beauty has nothing to do with the exterior shell. You are spiritual beings traveling in a physical vehicle. Don't compare yourself with others, for when you do this you will always perceive lack. When you begin perceiving lack, you become blind to your own gifts.

Health is no more than wholeness, and this is achieved when your levels (emotional, physical, mental and spiritual) of beingness are in balance. Soundness of mind is no more than a positive awareness of and attunement to these levels and an ability to energize these levels with

Love. You are what you are; you become what you think and choose to be. But always you are unique and beautiful God expressions traveling in wondrous vehicles from one plane of experience to another. Work to bring your levels of beingness into balance and harmony so that you can, with greater ease, enjoy your Life journeys and fulfill your missions.

INFLUENCE OF NEGATIVE THOUGHT
ON HEALTH AND HEALING

Most physical problems start in the mind and then manifest as illness, discomfort, and dis-ease. Actually the mind, which is non-physical, is never unhealthy. It is neutral with respect to health.

Except for preestablished Karmic purposes, most physical problems are the results of improper thinking. One's health oftentimes greatly parallels one's thoughts. If there is an overabundance of negativity, physical manifestations can occur in the form of ill health. The shell was designed in such a way that it must release energy, both positive and negative. If the body is holding too much negative energy, it must release it. Sometimes its release comes in the form of illness and disease. Illness is your release into wellness if you understand its basic cause. Strength and health return upon the release of the negative energy contained within the shell.

When you are dealing with a physical manifestation of ill health, it is advisable to examine your own thinking. As your body goes through the process of illness and discomfort in form, it is releasing the negative energy which has been built up. So illness and disease are forms of release. If you feel negative about the release, you continue to add negative energy to the form which must continue to release. Thus, some illnesses linger on and on, oftentimes affecting the entire form.

Sometimes the physical manifestation caused by the release of negativity becomes so uncomfortable that you must seek external assistance. The external assistance can be termed either a catalyst or a catalytic converter. All healers have procedures designed to convert the negative energy into positive energy, which is what is called healing. The healer attempts, through his own positive energy input, to convert the negative energy into positive energy, thus restoring health and balance to the form.

If the one who is ill continues to create negative energy by his thoughts, healing either takes longer or is not affected at all, unless the healer's positive energy is more powerful than the negative energy being produced by the patient. Healing has a greater chance of coming into being whenever you begin adding positive thought energy to your life. The most positive thought energy you can have is love. If your being is filled with love, this is what the form will release to the external world. If you are filled with love energy, nothing will invade the form.

Healing occurs when you choose to release the negative thought energy you are holding. Understanding the process, its purpose and your part in the process can help you to control the state of your own health. Thoughts can create ill health, and thoughts can bring you back to wellness. You have far more control over how you physically feel than you realize. How you think is one of the primary factors in one's state of health and well-being.

PHYSICIAN, HEAL THYSELF

Complete healing can occur, and there is no disease which is considered by us as being incurable. Within the mass consciousness of Earth, some illnesses have been designated as being incurable, but this is only your relative truth based on your lack of spiritual awareness. As you ascend into understanding and grow in awareness, you will realize that All is Perfection.

When the great Master Jesus performed what you consider to be His miraculous acts of healing, He was seeing perfection of form, not disease-ridden bodies or crippled and deformed limbs. When he told a man to take up his bed and walk, He saw a perfect form, not a crippled one. He commanded with authority. He did not beg, pamper, or plead, and He did not take the suffering onto Himself. He worked with the spiritual, mental, and emotional levels of the patient, and when these were touched, the physical responded. The great element in the healing work of the Christ was that of complete and total love. No one can heal or be an instrument of complete healing unless two things are present: (1) seeing the one to be healed as perfect; and (2) loving that person totally and completely.

Since most disease or illness with the exception of pre-established Karmic choices begins first in the mental and emotional areas of an entity before manifesting in the physical form, healing of the physical form is only temporary if the other levels remain untouched. Many Western healers work primarily with the physical form. While this is necessary, it oftentimes does not result in complete healing. When there is physical damage, it is good that there are those trained to physically repair physical damage. We are impressed with the advent of holistic medicine within your Western culture. Holistic healers are learning to treat not only the physical damage, but the whole entity as well.

If you are the one in need of healing, there are some things you can do to assist in your own healing. Physicians, holistic doctors, psychic healers, and so forth are but instruments to help you trigger your own healing energies into action. The Christ could trigger the healing energies in others by the touch of His hand or a word, but always He saw perfection of form, and He was a channel of total Love. You can assist in your own healing by seeing yourself as perfect and by loving yourself totally and completely. Examine your own emotional and mental levels. To be healed and to remain healed, one must make changes in his life experience. One cannot remain healed if he continues to hold negative thoughts and attitudes. If the emotional and mental levels are not dealt with, the healing is not complete. When the spiritual, mental, and emotional levels are brought into calmness, balance, and joy, the physical will respond. *You are perfect spirit, not imperfect form.* It is only your ego which keeps trying to convince you how imperfect and fragile you and others are. It keeps you centered on the imperfection of yourself and others, and in doing so, keeps you imprisoned by the illusions of sickness, despair, death, and chaos.

All entities can be channels for healing, but they must first raise their levels of awareness to see perfection in All, and they must Love. Start first with yourself. As the Master Christ said, "Physician, heal thyself!" so also do I say this to you. See the perfection of your own creation and love your own creation. Remember that you have been created by and out of the Lord Most High, and if you do not love yourself, you are denying love to your Creator. Once you love yourself and see your own perfection, you can no longer see others as imperfect, and you will love all men and all creation. You are then completely healed and can become a true channel of healing for others.

WHY STRIVE FOR BETTER HEALTH?

You have an allotted time in which to work in your dimension, and you have a choice as to whether you wish to do it in a healthy shell or an unhealthy one. One's individual mission is smoother if one keeps his physical vehicle in good operating condition. Some entities appear to have no choice, but in those cases it is for their learning or another's learning and was something chosen prior to entering physical form.

If you reach the awareness that something is truly harmful to the health of your shell and you still continue the abuse, you have made a choice. If poor health does descend upon your form, you will still have to remain until you have finished your work. The primary reason for striving to maintain good health has to do with the functioning of the brain computer. Generally, if the body or shell is properly cared for, the brain computer will operate properly. This is important because it is the connector between mind and physical form and physical form and Universal Mind.

Individual mind and spiritual energy exist without form. They are not contained within the brain computer. The brain computer is the transmitter of information from the mind to the conscious level of the human form. It is always to your advantage when the brain computer is working properly because you are then receiving correct information from your mind. If the brain computer is not operating properly due to improper nutrition, alcohol, drugs, or certain foods that your body has indicated it does not positively respond to, then the information from the mind will not flow correctly within the brain.

Always strive for better health. Better health is not encouraged to increase your life span, but rather to make your life within your life span happier and more fulfilling and to make your work easier. When you are advised of ways to improve your shell or when your body tells you something, it is to your advantage to heed the advice. Your Greeks said: "A sound mind in a sound body." The truth is that the mind is always sound, so it would better be stated to read: "A sound brain in a sound body." Sound mind flows through a sound brain contained within a sound body.

FOUR ELEMENTS

Each individual entity is influenced to a degree and on certain levels of his being by the four elements: Earth, Air, Fire, and Water. The degree to which one is influenced by any single element is dependent on his particular astrological sun sign as well as by the number of planetary influences exerting pressure from one of the four elemental triads. I will give you an example: If your sun sign is Aries which is of the Fire Triad and yet most of the other influences upon you came from the Earth Triad, you would experience greater Earth manifestations physically during your life experience than you would of Fire. An entity will experience all four elements to greater or lesser degrees depending on his astrological composition.

Problems occurring within Fire and Air elements tend to manifest physically in brain and mind malfunctions, such as fevers, depression, confusion, headaches, visual disturbances, lung problems, heart problems, and psychotic and neurotic imbalances. Negativity in Water

141

and Earth elements manifests in skin and sensory disturbances, cellular changes, bone and joint problems, digestive and urinary problems, muscular pains, blood disturbances, and imbalances within the immune system.

As I said, each element exerts an influence on each entity, but generally the influences are not balanced. You must also remember that the four elements are symbols of energy. All are born of the One Energy which is represented by Ether. The four elements stream forth from the Ether and connect with creation in differing ways. I agree with the writer who said that Fire is the force of Spirit, Air the force of Mind, Earth the force of Form, and Water the force of Emotion. By force, I refer to energy. These energies divide from the One Energy (the Ether), move out, and give life to manifested Creation.

The elements also have a direct connection to the chakra centers. Fire and Air are connected to the upper four chakra centers, and Water and Earth are connected to the lower three.

When realignment is necessary or growth is required within form, the spirit of the creation may determine that a particular element or energy would be better able to restore balance into that creation. Your Higher Self, God Essence, or Spirit will always know what the best energy is to promote growth and realignment within you.

NUTRITION AND STRESS

There are foods which are both beneficial and non-beneficial to the functioning of the human vehicle. An individual needs to become attuned to his own vehicle's responses to ingested items because each individual responds uniquely to what is taken into the vehicle. This is why some have allergic reactions to certain food items, while others do not. If you are attuned to your individual requirements, your body will always make you aware of what is beneficial and what is detrimental to its unique functioning. Remember that your form is constantly changing and must continually adapt to the environment in which it has been placed. Thus, you may discover a particular food item to be detrimental when once it was not.

Become aware of your individual stress level. Emotional stress, particularly if it is severe, causes the form to release certain chemicals which will react with any ingested food items and produce toxins. This will then create severe physical manifestations within the form. If severe emotional stress is present, it is better to refrain from ingesting anything with the exception of water until the stress is eliminated. If the stressful period is a long-term situation, it is preferable to ingest mild, bland food.

Some entities suffering a severe emotional crisis overeat as a way of compensating for their unhappiness. Doing this not only produces too much weight but also causes the form to become overloaded with toxic chemicals which manifest in a myriad of physical disorders. An attuned entity will deal with stressful situations as soon as they arise within his own life experience without turning to food. Sometimes the prime importance lies not in what you are eating, but rather the conditions under which you are eating. If stress is present, you can sit down to the most well balanced meal and those same beneficial nutrients can become poisons in your system.

I also advise eating in moderation. Many entities, particularly in the more abundant cultures on your planet, ingest far more food than the form actually needs. Those cells and organs designed to break down the food items in the digestive process must work harder if the entity has consumed more food than the form actually requires to function well. Your body gives you signals as to when it needs more food. These signals are termed hunger, and indicate when you truly should eat. Many human entities, again in the more abundant cultures, ingest food when they are not really hungry. This is because of certain societal programming within a particular culture.

Attune to your body's requirements and learn to understand its signals. Being mentally connected to your own form and its special requirements creates a smooth and properly functioning vehicle for you to experience your life expression.

IS SELF-HEALING POSSIBLE?

Is it possible to heal yourself? The answer is yes. But you cannot do it by yourself. You must align yourself with your spirit which is your own God essence.

If you have manifested illness or disease in your life experience, you must try to assess why you have brought illness or disease into manifestation. With the exception of prior Karmic choices and decisions before entering the physical Earth plane, all illness and disease begins first as a thought. In fact, all manifestations and materializations of everything within your world began first with a thought, so why should the manifestations of illness and disease be any different? If a thought, energized and given power, can be brought into the manifested form of illness or disease, then another thought, energized and given power, can manifest into a healing.

The spirit which resides within and without the human entity is always working to release healing energies. It is always working to attempt to bring about awareness to the entity as to why the form is diseased or ill, and to break through to an entity's higher consciousness. Your belief system is critically important in the bringing on of the manifestations of both illness and healing. If you have an illness and you do not believe in healing, self-healing is impossible.

All healing is self-healing whether you ingest medications, undergo surgery, spend time with physicians, or offer yourself to any of the treatments within your current medical technology. To be healed you must believe in healing, you must trust that you can be healed, and you must have faith in whatever method you have selected to trigger your own healing energies into action.

Self-healing begins first through your belief in healing. Healing is a manifested thought which erases another manifested thought of illness and disease. It involves reprogramming. Always when one desires to change how he thinks about something, there must be both the will and the willingness to do so. Healing has to begin in your own consciousness. Since most illness can be traced back to such negative ego vibrations and thoughts as fear, anger, hate, resentment, guilt, and so on, these must be dealt with. It is here that the real healing occurs. An entity might have a properly functioning form which is seemingly disease-free and yet still be diseased if he harbors negative ego thoughts and vibrations. Another entity, on the other hand, may have what appears to be a diseased form and yet may not harbor negative ego vibrations and thoughts. Where it really counts, he is the one who is healed and healthy.

The spirit of an individual entity is always trying to create healing and health; it is always trying to redirect negative ego vibrations and thoughts and transform them into positive ego vibrations and thoughts whose energy is Love. Love is the only energy which can create complete healing, and is the energizer needed to bring health into all areas in need of healing.

Upon your planet most entities are in need of self-healing, so be gentle with yourself and others. Do not feel that you are alone in the process of self-healing, for there are many human and spiritual entities willing to help you in your process toward wholeness. Be willing to help others in their paths toward wholeness. As individuals are healed, so also is the planet healed. Begin first with your own being, for as a healed or a whole person, you are then enabled to help others in their own healing processes.

144

ONLY PHYSICAL FORMS NEED SLEEP

First of all, I shall tell you something which I imagine that by now you are fully aware of: the condition you call sleep exists only in some physical dimensions. Sleep is necessary for the maintenance of cellular forms and for the proper functioning of the brain which is not the same as mind. Mind is composed of various levels of consciousness and exists beyond the brain. The brain is a receiver for the input of mind. It analyzes, interprets, processes, and stores data coming from the external mind. What requires rest or sleep is the physical form. How much rest or sleep an individual entity requires depends on many things such as diet, the condition of mental and physical health, the amount of stress present, prior programming from childhood, cultural programming, and how an individual entity thinks.

In terms of diet, there are many substances which human entities ingest which are somewhat toxic and cause the physical form to require more rest. Examples could be alcohol or sugar. So far as mental or physical health is concerned, many of your physical dis-eases debilitate the cellular structure of the form and create the need for more sleep or rest. Likewise, mental unrest, such as depression or boredom, also induces the need for the form to sleep more. In regard to stress, if there is too much external or internal stress present, either physically or mentally, and if the entity has not learned to control his reaction to stress, the form will require more sleep. Programming from childhood and cultural programming primarily have to do with how one's belief system was programmed. And, if as a child, you were told that the human entity needs eight hours of sleep each night to function properly, this is probably what you will require until you change the programming. Some cultures have established programming for their inhabitants, such as a certain time for a "siesta" or nap. So far as how an individual entity thinks is concerned, we have observed that the more negatively oriented a human entity is, the more sleep he will require to function on his physical journey. A positively oriented entity will generally have more energy and will require less rest and sleep. Positive and negative orientation has to do with how one thinks and perceives his external and internal worlds of reality. If one's orientation is more positive, he will not only have more energy; he will also most likely be healthier and less affected by stress. I would also like to add that as an individual becomes more consciously aware of his own unique physical and mental functionings, he will learn which ingested substances create the need for more sleep and rest. He will also become aware of how his childhood and cultural programming influence his requirements for rest and sleep.

A certain amount of sleep or rest is necessary for the form to exist and function properly on the physical plane, but it's possible that you do not need as much as you think. When you attune yourself to your own individual form, you will know exactly what you require.

In those planes you term spiritual realms, entities or spirits have no need of sleep or rest. We continue to perform whatever missions have been assigned to us by the Source. But even you, when your form is at rest, continue to work with us at the other levels of your consciousness, even though you may have no conscious awareness of the unfoldment and learning going on in the higher levels of your individual mind.

What you present to your external physical world is but one facet of your total reality. There are many other facets of you living and working and unfolding on other dimensions and planes of life. Your true essence is spirit, not physical form, and that spirit is not confined by space and time. Therefore, your true essence does not sleep any more than we do.

Entities who make their transitions at death are said to sleep for awhile. This sleep we refer to is not sleep as you know it and experience it. More accurately it would be a period of quiet release. Oftentimes a human entity will exit quickly as in an automobile accident, or he will have experienced great physical pain prior to exiting the physical plane. In some circumstances he was not adequately prepared for the exit. In these cases, a certain amount of clearing and releasing is necessary as the spirit, with the ego-personality aspects of the human entity, passes through the astral belt of Earth. When an entity has died and you are told that he is still sleeping, it means that the spirit is on the astral plane releasing such things as confusion and pain before moving into the Fourth Dimension.

There are many to assist in this quiet release. The spirit will always release the baggage it may carry from the physical journey; if it did not, the spirit would have to remain on the astral plane. Until the spirit releases its baggage, which may contain confusion and pain, among many things, it may not even realize that the form it inhabited has died. In the cases of entities who did not grow in awareness while on the Earth plane, their ego-personality aspects will remain strong in energy on the astral plane for a long time. Even though the spiritual clearing has occurred, these ego-personality aspects will continue to think they are still in form and will communicate with living Earth entities in various ways. Unless an Earth entity is aware of this condition, it can sometimes create confusion. The Earth entity is not, however, in communication with the spirit of an entity

146

who has crossed over, but rather is being communicated with by the ego-personality aspects of a past human entity. Those forces which you term poltergeists are energies of ego-personality aspects, not spirits. A spirit, in terms of human time, moves quickly through the astral belt of Earth, releasing its baggage, and moves into the Fourth Dimension.

PART V

AFTER LIFE, WHAT THEN?

The process of death, the exiting of the spirit from this plane of life, is perhaps the greatest and most feared of Man's illusions. Many entities have been programmed to think that death is the end, and if they do believe in a beyond and hereafter, they still have great apprehension as to what that beyond and hereafter may mean. Those who fear death are unable to live fully because that culmination, or so they think, always looms on the horizon. Kyros helps us to understand that there is more to us than what we see and that we are part of a Larger Life. He tells us that there is no such thing as death, except in our perception, and that our true selves continue on.

THE FULL CIRCLE JOURNEY

Originally there was only the First Cause or the Primal Intelligence which you have come to term as God, the Creator, or the Source. All manifested and unmanifested Creation began first with a Thought. Creation was born from the only thing there was and is: the Creator. The Creator chose to express through the individual aspects of creation, so you, as an individual aspect of creation, are part of the Creator. You, as an individual spirit with an individual consciousness, are part of the Universal Spirit and Consciousness of the Creator.

You moved out as an individualized expression of the Creator on a journey which will ultimately return you to Oneness. This movement is called the Full Circle Journey.

On this journey your individual and unique spirit, consciousness, and energy will experience all that it is possible to experience, and you will move through a myriad of dimensions, planes, and levels of life. Sometimes you will experience in manifested physical forms as you are doing now, and sometimes you will experience as conscious energy in dimensions void of time, space, and form.

In the physical dimension that you now experience, so many entities see the so-called death of form as finality. But in truth, you are not form. You are energy and consciousness and spirit, and these are eternal. Even the physical form does not die; it merely becomes something else.

Many on the Earth plane would have less fear if they could see their form for what it is: a vehicle which makes it possible for them to experience life on planet Earth; a vehicle through which they can express their individual spirit, consciousness, and energy.

In spite of what you may think, no spirit exits the physical dimension until it has fulfilled what it came to accomplish. Before entering the physical plane you knew what your basic mission was to be, and you knew what lessons were necessary for you to learn.

When you do exit your third dimension, your individual consciousness, spirit, and energy reenter the fourth dimension after a brief journey through the astral plane of Earth. Within the spiritual fourth dimension you have access to knowledge of all the life experiences you have ever had since your emergence from Universal Spirit. You will also have the wisdom and knowledge to know what other lessons you need to learn and what life experiences you need in order to progress on the Full Circle Journey. You may choose to remain and experience in the fourth dimension, or you may choose to re-enter another physical vehicle on Earth or other third dimensional planes in other galaxies in other universes.

It is important to know that even though you experience as a unique, individualized expression of the Creator, you are still connected to the Source of All Life. This is because you are a creation both of God and out of God. I know it's difficult to think of yourself as whole and connected and yet separate and distinct at the same time. Traveling the Full Circle Journey is a journey of unfoldment as you move through the multitude of lives and experiences back into Oneness. Always it is a progressive journey of your own Becomingness whose ultimate destination is Oneness with the Father.

I say to you in this, your present life experience: Bless each experience which you have, and bless each lesson which is given to you. Each precious now moment of your life moves you closer to Oneness.

WHAT IS THE ASTRAL PLANE AND ITS PURPOSE?

Each physical aspect of Creation has a sheath of energy surrounding its form. There are, as you remember, other bands of energy, both within the form and surrounding it. The astral body separates the dense physical form from the higher energy levels. The entire Earth is surrounded by what you call the astral plane, or what we prefer to term the astral belt. This astral belt is a sheath of vibrational energy which vibrates higher than physical form but lower than the mental, etheric, and spiritual planes. The astral plane, though not physical as you perceive it, is part of the third dimension.

Contained within the astral belt is all thought which has been generated from planet Earth. All thought energy borne out of the minds of men from the beginning of Earth's physical creation is held within this non-physical holding area. A human entity, throughout a single life expression, may send forth into the astral belt millions upon millions of thoughts, some positive, and some negative. Although higher vibrational planes and dimensions can sometimes sense Earth's negative vibrations, these vibrations are not contained within dimensions higher than third.

When a human entity makes the transition from his dense physical form, his spirit, which contains all the elements that made his expression unique and individualized, passes through this astral belt in the ascension to the fourth dimension. Within the astral belt the spirit releases the ego and the vibrations connected with it. Individualized aspects of personality are released as well. In a sense this is a cleansing area. The spirit then enters the fourth dimension with individual mind which, as you know, contains all the levels of consciousness. The spirit is free of the ego and the personality aspects of the physical vehicle he left behind.

Usually the journey through the astral belt is rapid in terms of human time. Sometimes, however, if the ego/personality aspects have been very strong during the Earth expression, it will take the spirit longer to be cleansed or freed. The astral belt is the area where any ideas one had on Earth regarding life after death will be manifested. For example, if one believes he will experience pearly gates and so forth, the ego/personality will experience this. If the belief is in a destiny of fire and brimstone, this experience will be allowed. The spirit will work to release itself from the ego/personality and once released will ascend, leaving the illusionary ego/personality to remain with the illusion it has chosen. The astral plane is a kind of clearinghouse. It is a place of release whereby the spirit, which is composed of mind, consciousness, energy, and essence, moves on without the unique ego/personality of a particular Earth expression.

Because the astral plane or belt contains all the thought energy of Earth since physical manifestation, and because of the myriad of illusions present, some beginning channels receive information from this plane. Until the channel is guided to communicate above this level, he will oftentimes think he is in contact with a spiritual energy when, in fact, he is in contact with the vibrations of the ego/personality and past thoughts of an Earth expression. This is also why there are so many myths in your present time warp regarding what you like to term the hereafter.

Now with respect to astral travel, I will try to explain briefly what occurs. When you astral travel a portion of the astral energy which composes your astral sheath is released for the journey, although it is always connected to your physical form. During astral travel in the conscious or alpha state you will experience only physical dimensions, be they on Earth or elsewhere within the Cosmos. In sleep you do not really astral travel all of the time. Part of your unconscious journeying includes ethereal travel, which means that this portion of your journey is spent in non-physical dimensions.

In summary:

1. Spirit leaves Earth at the death of form.
2. Spirit travels though the Astral Belt.
3. Spirit releases from the Ego/Personality aspects and all illusions.
4. Spirit enters the Fourth Dimension with total consciousness and awareness of all expressions since beginning his individual Full Circle Journey.
5. Spirit has recall of all past expressions but is free from all individualized Ego/Personality aspects of those expressions.
6. Spirit expresses more of the Cosmic Essence.

PERSONALITY

Just as there are levels of consciousness, so also are there levels of personality. Think of the word personal. Break it apart to be Person-All. Person-All refers to your total beingness as well as your becomingness or that which you are unfolding toward.

Personality on your physical level generally refers to the individualized expressions you employ to relate to your external world. And your personality is quite frequently assessed by those you contact: "He has a great personality! She has a bad personality! His personality is charismatic!" The personality includes all those qualities which have to do with how you individually express or relate to your world.

Personality is very limiting on your dimension and in your human definition. You not only have a physical personality, you also have an emotional personality, a mental/intellectual personality, a spiritual personality, and a Cosmic personality, to name but a few. Just as you have a Higher Self and a Lower Self, so also do you have a Higher Personality and a lower one.

Personality refers to how you express individually and uniquely within all aspects of your being and on all your levels of consciousness. What you express on your physical dimension is but a fragment of your total individualized expression.

When the spirit leaves the third dimension at the point you call death, it travels through the astral belt and releases itself from the ego and certain personality aspects. The ego creates personality characteristics which it deems necessary for survival on planet Earth in order to protect the vehicle on this part of the journey. The ego program, as you know, is a very powerful influence on how you express and relate to your physical external world.

When the spirit passes through the astral belt, it releases the survival programming or ego which it no longer needs. It also releases personality aspects which were expressed by the entity during that specific Earth incarnation. When you enter the fourth dimension you will no longer express any of the physical personality characteristics that you express now in your present life incarnation. You will retain your consciousness, but it will be united with the knowledge gained from all of your expressions.

So, personality really means all that you are, your complete individualized expression of God, and not just those fragments you show to the world, most of which are based on ego and survival programming. Personality refers to the All of your Person. When you assess another's personality, remember that you are glimpsing but a fragment and that you are assessing from your own human perception, which is frequently inaccurate.

MURDER AND KILLING

Some of your entities believe that since it is impossible to die, it is impossible to kill. Thus, as one of your Earth writers determined, "Thou shalt not kill" is a promise and not a commandment. I would like to go into this a bit further.

On one level there is great truth in that perception. Energy cannot be destroyed, but only changed into a different energy. Birth and death are merely points within the passage of a physical creation's journey. If there is no such thing as death, then you cannot kill because you do not have the power to destroy energy or essence. You have the power to change one form of energy into another form, and you have the power to move an entity from one dimension to another. "Thou shalt not kill" is more than a promise; it is a statement about your power. You cannot annihilate or destroy energy, essence, consciousness, or spirit. You cannot destroy that which you did not create. God is the Creator of a Lifeforce of All Creation and only He has the power to destroy that which He created. But God would not destroy that which He created because He created and creates out of Himself. To destroy any part of that which He created would be destroying a part of Himself. Destruction of any part would remove the Whole and the All. Creation is an eternal process, an unfoldment of the lifeforce of which there is no end.

Now you are wondering, if you cannot in truth kill because there is no such thing as death, why are there so many laws and punishments relating to killing? Why, if there is no such thing as death, do we tell you that it is against Universal Law to kill?

To kill or to murder oftentimes involves an intent to destroy the lifeforce. Cosmically, the wrong is more in the intent than in the action itself. Within the holy writings the law "Thou shalt not kill" is sometimes stated, "Thou shalt do no murder." These two versions are different. Murder bears malefic intent: the ego desire to destroy the lifeforce of another. Killing does not always contain the ego desire to destroy the lifeforce of another. Killing occurs because of Karmic reasons or ignorance or the survival programming of the entity.

You most probably will kill if your form is being threatened because the brain computer has been programmed to assist in the survival of the form until the mission is completed. You may even kill out of fear which is but ignorance of what is and what is not truly a threat to you. All acts of killing bring you under Karmic Law and will be balanced in some way.

The acts of murder where there is a conscious, willful desire to destroy the lifeforce of another form are dealt with very severely. Those who kill and find joy and pleasure in killing are dealt with more severely. One who kills with malefic intent may escape the physical punishments you have established, but no one ever escapes the Law of Balancing. Only through the Law of Balancing can the ignorant be brought into enlightenment and can man's created evil be brought into the knowledge of the goodness of God.

THE GRIEF PROCESS

The most prominent cause of grief that is experienced by human entities occurs when a loved one makes his transition, and is created by a lack of understanding of death. It is not the spirit which does the grieving, but rather the ego. Ego mourns the perceived loss of another ego and knows, at some level, that at the point of transition it loses both its power and its purpose. Spirit, on the other hand, knows that there is no death and that it will continue.

Many human entities do not understand at the conscious level that the spirit-containing mind, which holds data from all dimensional experiences and incarnations, moves quickly into the fourth dimension after leaving the physical vehicle. The individualized ego and personality which were contained within a particular incarnation are left behind in the astral belt of third dimensional Earth. Each time a spirit chooses to reincarnate on planet Earth, a new ego and a new personality are taken on. Many human entities still do not understand that what they truly are is spirit, mind, and energy, and not form. Physical form is merely a vehicle of expression for your plane of experience.

If human entities had a complete understanding of the transition process and if they had trust in what they perceive to be the unknown, it is unlikely that they would ever grieve the passing of another into the next dimension. However, because so many do not have this understanding and trust, they will, of course, choose to experience grief when a loved one moves from one dimension to another during the exiting process called death. Even with comprehension, your ego self may still grieve the loss of another's form. This is alright as long as the grieving does not extend for long periods of Earth time. In fact, on one level grieving can restore balance to the physical form and can be seen as a release and a cleansing process. All too often entities will hold onto the emotions of anger or guilt, which may or may not be a part of one's individual grieving process. If these ego emotions are held too long, they will most probably begin damaging the form of the one who is grieving. To feel guilty over things you may have done or omitted doing while the entity who made the transition was working on the Earth plane is a waste of time and energy. In each now moment you simply are what you are without judgment of any kind. You express what you are at whatever level of awareness you are on. If you place judgments upon yourself, you will always be weighted down with guilt, which is both a nonproductive and a heavy burden for one to carry. If in the linear flow of your now moments you deem something to be in need of resolution, forgiveness, or reconciliation, then do what needs to be done and release it from yourself. In this way, you will not be troubled by guilt at the dimensional passing of another. So many, at the dimensional movement of another, will bind themselves up with guilt. This is totally destructive and purposeless. You cannot change any of your past moments, so it is best to let them go and move on. Everything you do during your transitory journey on Earth is for learning and teaching. The Master said, "Judge not..." and He was referring not just to your judgments of others, but your judgments of yourself as well. If you have acted from a place of non-love toward an entity who has made his transition from the Earth plane, don't you think that, on the higher levels, reconciliation and forgiveness have already been sealed? They have. So if you, in your grieving, are suffering guilt, forgive yourself and move on.

Anger sometimes enters into the grief process if those remaining on the Earth plane feel that the one who has left it has gone before his time, as in the case of young entities or those who exit under tragic circumstances. There are no accidents and there is no such thing as an untimely death. No one ever leaves the Earth plane until his particular mission is completed. When entities understand this, they will cease to feel anger in these areas. There are times when entities left behind on the Earth plane will experience anger if they feel that the one who has exited did so at an inopportune time, as in the case of the breadwinner of a family. The death was inconvenient, so to speak, and does create many problems for those who remain. Again, there are no accidents, no untimely deaths. So, if this type of anger occurs, it emerges from the ego base and manifests as selfishness and fear. If one is able to move from this type of anger, he will discover a great lesson and the gift of a new opportunity. Quite often, the one who is left behind on the Earth plane will feel as if he is the victim. There simply are no victims on the Earth plane. You create your individual worlds of reality, and if you see yourself as a victim, then it is due to your limited human perceptions and judgments.

Oftentimes grief is simply a cathartic and a cleansing process and can be a wonderful way to restore balance to one's form and emotional state. You miss the warmth of another's form. You miss the conversations, perhaps; you will miss the individualized personality. You may weep as you sweep through your memories remembering the physical closeness. This is wonderful, for it clears you and releases you from both pain and stress. And it is healthful and short-lived if it is not bound up with anger and/or guilt.

Sometimes people grieve simply because the transitional movement of another forces them to face their own mortality, and this creates an intense fear. Many people fear death primarily because they don't understand it or else they associate it with pain, disease, and lengthy suffering. Frequently they will grieve not so much for the passing of another, but more for their own journey yet to come. This grief is based, in part, in paralyzing fear.

I would have you see the transition experience for what it is: your spirit leaving physical form and moving into a higher, more beauteous plane of Life. In truth, it is something to celebrate. Yet I can understand why there is so much fear present upon your plane of experience. It is because of the illusions you have created around the transitional experience (pain, disease, suffering) and because of the myths surrounding that which you call the unknown (Hell, limbo, Satan, and so on). Death is only a movement of energy, a movement of spirit into something grander. It's very simple, very beautiful, and nothing to fear. It is really a journey of the spirit, and not of the form which is but an illusionary vehicle.

If you cannot yet see this movement as one to celebrate, and if you must grieve, then do so in order to heal yourself and restore balance so that you can continue on your journey. Do not carry guilt or anger with you. Trust that there is no death and that life is eternal. When you are cleansed, then release your grief and move on with full and complete knowingness that he that you mourned continues on in the Full Circle Journey. Remember, as well, that All Creation is connected into Oneness and that even though forms separate, the Oneness is eternal. One is never separated through death except in your own inaccurate perceptions. If there is such a thing as death, it occurs in life when you are not fully expressing your own being and are not allowing yourself to unfold in your now moments. This is death—death in life.

RELEASE FROM THE FEAR OF DEATH

Many people on your planet fear the exiting process which you term death. In fact, many humans, once they become aware that this process exists, begin to fear. Usually this begins in childhood when a pet or relative dies. Adults try to comfort the child by saying, "Tabby or Fido went to heaven" or "Grandma Pearl went to live with God." But because adults oftentimes mourn so and beat themselves up with guilt by saying such things as, "Oh, I wish I had been kinder to Grandma Pearl," or "I wish I had never kicked Fido or left Tabby out in the rain," children sometimes receive this as a statement of finality or that maybe heaven or going to live with God is not really such a positive thing.

When someone dies and adults weep and mourn and suffer, a child doesn't understand that the sadness is really over the loss of form. An adult might truly believe that Grandma Pearl in her essence and spirit lives on, but will mourn because her form can no longer be with him. A child will perceive this sadness as something negative, and death will take on a new meaning for him. If going to live with God is positive, yet everyone around the child is sad, then the child begins to doubt what the adults have said. Once the doubt enters, fear begins.

Very small children, because they have recently entered from another dimension and still have some dim recollection of it, have less trouble with the process of death. As a child becomes more programmed by the outer adult world, this recollection becomes locked within his subconscious mind, and he begins to perceive as the adults in his world do.

The best way to deal with children in this area is to be, as you would say, up front with them. "Grandma Pearl went to live with God because she had finished her work here. She couldn't take her body with her because her body was designed only for life on this planet. I'm sad because I will miss her form." Children are far more intelligent, sensitive, and understanding than adults give them credit for sometimes.

The problem of fear exists because, as children, most adults were programmed by other adults. They see death as inevitable, mysterious, unknown, filled with pain, and oftentimes as final. Many go through their lives with this hidden fear. As I've said before, you cannot fully live and experience your physical journey if you fear death.

Many people who fear death do so because they do not understand at a deep level that they are spirit, and not form. Your form or body is only a vehicle to carry you through your third dimensional journey. It's like a spacesuit or a life support system for physical life. If you went to the moon, you'd have to wear a protective suit in order to do your work there. When you returned to Earth or entered a simulated Earth atmosphere, you'd take it off because you'd no longer have need of it. So it is with birth and death: you put on a form when you enter at birth and remove it when you leave at death. It's very important to learn that your vehicle is not you. You are energy which cannot die or be destroyed, but only transformed into a different kind of energy. You are spirit, and spirit contains individual mind with all its levels of consciousness, and this is eternal. You were created out of the God essence, and God does not die.

Birth and death in the physical realm are basically the same process. At birth you enter from a higher dimension, and at death you enter into a higher dimension. You think of death as an exiting, but the only exiting which occurs is when the spirit exits the physical vehicle. Both birth and death are processes of entering.

Many do not fear the actual process of death as much as they fear how they will die or when they will die or the physical pain which sometimes occurs prior to the transcension experience into the fourth dimension. Oftentimes, how you will die has been determined by your spirit prior to entering for your own learning or to teach others or for some Karmic balancing. There are no accidents, in spite of what you may think. At higher levels everything has a purpose and a reason and is designed for growth and unfoldment. When an entity dies has to do with his mission. No one, again in spite of what you may think or perceive, ever leaves his vehicle until his individual mission is completed. Except in your perception and limited awareness, there are no accidents or untimely deaths.

I do not wish to sound insensitive about the fears human entities have concerning the process of death. I do understand your confusions and concerns. On the higher dimensions we do not use the term death. We see what you term as death as merely a transition; a movement of spirit and energy from one dimension to another, and from one level of awareness to another. You chose to enter your dimension to learn and to teach so that you might grow and unfold. When this is completed you move on. I wish I could calm your uncertainties, but until man can understand that death is like an effortless passing through a doorway from one room to another, he will be uncertain. Your great teacher, the Christ, told you about many mansions, and he showed you that death is an illusion through His resurrection. If only you would believe.

As for the pain and suffering which sometimes precede the moment of transcension, well, these are the illusions your mass consciousness have created. You have created pain and disease and brought them into manifestation, and they have become part of the mass belief system which continues with each generation. You chose to create a world of duality for your growth and unfoldment. All these negative illusions which you perceive are based in fear. The Master Christ was always saying "Fear not!" Why? Because He knew fear would bind you and imprison you and prevent you from experiencing a full and an abundant life. He also knew that fear of anything is ego-based, and the ego's main function, as you know, is to maintain and protect the physical vehicle. The ego knows that once the spirit is released from the vehicle, it no longer has either purpose or power.

If I were able I would convince you that there is nothing to fear in the process of transcension. You will be released from fear when you come to the true awareness that the real you is energy and spirit and not form. You will be released from fear when you reach the awareness that there is no such thing as death in terms of finality. Even form does not die but merely transforms itself into something new. Ashes and dust return to the Earth Mother and give birth to new life. Nothing dies. All is but transformed. You will be released from fear when you acknowledge who you really are: a spirit of God, His Own Essence. The physical walk is but a short journey in terms of time, and there is so much beauty ahead. Fear is released when you align yourself with your Creator and your spirit and trust that all is for your own highest good and growth. Fear is released when you replace it with Love, which is the healing and transforming energy of the Cosmos. This is your whole purpose on the Full Circle Journey: to love; to learn it, to teach it, and to be it.

In closing, I would also like to add that sometimes humans fear death because of their attachments to the physical. It is human not to want to leave those people and things which you love and have found joy and pleasure in. Fear will leave if you will remember that those people you've loved and journeyed with are also spiritual beings traveling in physical vehicles, and that when you move to another dimension, your spirits are even more connected and attuned to one another. You don't really leave them. As for attachments to physical things, well, they will no longer have meaning in a higher dimension. Physical illusions belong to the physical plane, and one's intent should be to move toward release from attachments to illusions to the alignment to spirit reality. Once you have made this transition, there should be no fear. Joy does not cease at the point of transcension but increases beyond human comprehension.

So, if you fear death, I would say to begin working on release from fear. Think of yourself as a caterpillar in a cocoon preparing to take flight as a beautiful butterfly into a world of sunshine or as a rosebud preparing to open into bloom. Though you may not, because of your current belief systems, think of it as such, it is a beautiful and joyful experience and not one to fear. I would also say that after you have released yourself from fear, begin to live and experience each now moment in your time dimension to its fullest. Life goes on eternally.

PART VI

I WANT TO KNOW

In this section, the messages are informational and cover a multitude of subjects concerning issues in today's world, such as money, drugs, abortion, terrorism, and poverty. In these messages, Kyros takes us to another level of perception and helps us to reach the awareness of knowing how we are all connected and how we are part of what is occurring on the collective level.

EARTH CHANGES:
"CAN WE RETURN TO EDEN?"

With respect to Earth changes, perhaps the first thing to focus on is fear. The Earth is changing, shifting, evolving, and transforming. Your entire sun system is participating in what is called a Universal Transcension in this New Age. This requires the raising of vibrations, not only within your physical vehicles, but in the planetary body as well. Earth, like the beings upon her, has been evolving since her manifestation into form. There have been earthquakes, floods, volcanic action, shifts of the axis, and cataclysmic events since her origin. Some, though not all of what occurs in your physical world is related to the mass consciousness and to the vibrations (negative or positive) with which the collective mind is charged. The highly aware Earth entity is able to see that what occurs in his outer world of experience is also occurring in his inner world of beingness.

Many live in fear of natural disasters. To fear is to be unable to fully live and experience your Earth walk. Some were predicting major earthquakes along the western coastline of your own country. These channels offered specific dates and indicated that these earthquakes would result in the total destruction of the great coastal landmass. Be discerning when you hear such messages and remember that the future is not pre-set. A myriad of futures await, and the present is selected primarily by the collective mind. This is why there has been so much emphasis placed on the shifting and transforming of individual and collective consciousness. Be wary of doom and gloom predictions for your planet and of those who would tell you that the control of natural disasters is in the hands of a spiritual hierarchy or extraterrestrial beings.

If you are filled with fear every time a new prediction of devastation is made or every time a comet passes, you will not fully live. There are things in your outer world over which you have no control. You do have control over what is in your inner world. The Earth, like you, contains a spiritual energy embodied in a vehicle, and as you experience changes within yourself, so also does your planet. Many things which may appear as cataclysmic to your physical eyes and perception are but the Earth herself working to restore planetary balance. As you are learning to respect, love, and better care for your own forms, you should also begin to love, respect, and better care for that greater form called planet Earth. As residents of Earth, you are also called to be guardians and caretakers, and are responsible for her maintenance. It's rather like owning a house. You have the choice of letting that house become dirty and rundown or of having enough pride in it to keep it clean and bright and maintain it in such a way that it becomes even more beautiful because of your care and effort. Essentially, you chose to leave Eden, and you can choose to return to Eden. The decision is completely up to you who are called Earthlings, the residents of planet Earth.

ABUNDANCE INVOLVES CONSCIOUSNESS

Simply put, abundance is that which abounds in an entity's life, and what abounds has its origin in one's consciousness. What and how one thinks determines what an entity has an abundance of, and can be either negative or positive. Overall, abundance tends to be thought of as something good, and means having more of something than you perhaps need.

Frequently entities think of abundance in terms of material wealth, and they limit their thinking to that. They look on the entity who has money and call him abundant and prosperous. This is not what abundance or prosperity is all about; abundance or the lack of it has to do with consciousness as well as with perception.

A great portion of your world's entities live in a state of poverty consciousness and continually empower that which is termed limitation and lack. The more anything is empowered, individually or collectively, through thought or consciousness, the more it continues to manifest itself on the physical, external level of Life. Just because there is the illusion of poverty in your world does not mean that there is not enough substance available to provide abundance for all entities who live and express on your planet. There is an unlimited source and substance available, but in so many cases it is blocked from flowing in by man's own consciousness. Man himself builds a dam to hold back the flow and only allows a little to trickle over the dam he has built.

So why does he build the dam in the first place? Why does he want to hold back the flow of the waters of abundance in his life? One of the reasons is ignorance, and by ignorance I simply mean a lack of enlightenment. He doesn't know what he is damming up or holding back, and he fears the unknown. A second reason is fear that if he doesn't build a dam, the waters of abundance will flow away to such an extent that there will be none left. So he lets a little trickle over the dam and saves the rest, for a rainy day perhaps? He doesn't believe in the constant and eternal supply; he doesn't trust the Source of All Life. Many are the entities who spend their lives saving and conserving, sacrificing and denying themselves joy in life in order to experience some degree of comfort in that which is termed old age. How many entities do you know who have spent their lives working and worrying about the future, only to reach the later years too sickly and tired to enjoy them?

What you attract or do not attract into your life is parallel to how you think, the state of your own consciousness, and what you empower. If you always feel you do not have enough, it will never be enough.

A great many human entities are in a state of poverty consciousness. They look out on their lives and see only limitation and lack. And, of course, this is what is manifested to them, and the more it is manifested, the more they believe in it and empower it. It becomes a circular effect. They fear and exist in joyless living and suffering. This really need not be, for Life was meant to be lived in joyful abundance!

Examine some of the reasons why the illusions of lack are so prevalent in your world. Much of poverty consciousness lies in an individual's attitudes and feelings about his own worth or worthiness. Some entities simply feel that they are not worthy of the riches and abundance of life. Oftentimes entities will experience lack and limitation in their lives because of programming. Many are taught and come to believe that doing without—poverty, and sackcloth and ashes—is a more holy and spiritual way in which to live. But many who live in a state of poverty also live in a state of resentment, want, and anger, and even though they have been programmed to believe that poverty is more spiritual, they do not believe it at their heart level. They try to convince themselves and others that poverty is a more spiritual path as a way of rationalizing and justifying their feeling of deprivation. It becomes an attempt to ennoble, in some way, the external content of their lives.

A third reason for the illusion of lack is the fact that many entities do not trust in the Source of All Life as the Universal Provider and Sustainer of All Creation. When an entity fails to trust, he enters into the stress-filled states of worry and fear, and this is the negativity with which he charges his external world. Worry and fear are the bars to his self-created prison of limitation. Very little of the abundance can flow when an entity's consciousness is centered in worry and fear.

Be willing to move from a belief in lack to a belief in abundance. Begin to look around and perceive anew by focusing on what is in your life rather than what is not, blessing with love and a grateful heart those gifts which you have attracted to you. Release thoughts of lack and limitation and bless that which you perceive as good. In your prayers and affirmations, be clear on what is or is not abundance and prosperity to you. It is difficult to manifest into form if you do not clearly know what you wish to manifest, for what is abundance to one may not be so to another. Remember to seek the riches of the kingdom within first. What is outside in one's external realm of form is usually a reflection of one's inner world. And finally, reach the place of trust: trust in the Source of All Life and in Infinite Substance and Supply, trust in your own worth and worthiness as God expressing uniquely as you, and trust in your unique position in the All of Life. Prosperity and abundance come to those who work with, trust in, and allow the creative flow of Life.

THE TRANSFORMATIONAL PROCESS

A friend said to you that there are no answers to anything that you question, but only alternatives and options. Yet you've been told that all of your answers lie within you if you are willing to seek them. That which your friend spoke was true, for when you choose your option, you have selected the answer. There is never a question of a wrong or right choice, only the choice itself, which is the selection of one option over another.

It's never a question of better. Whatever choice one ever makes is fine, for all choices will always give birth to growth. Life is not a question of winning or losing; it is a question of unfolding and becoming, and this you will always do no matter what you choose upon the plane of experience.

Yet if you stay connected to your own God center and if you listen to your own inner guidance, you will flow with life with relative ease. This doesn't mean that you will never meet with perceived obstacles. You will, because you will create them for your own learning. In connection with your own center you will move over them, around them, under them, and through them, gleaning all the wisdom from them which they contain. If you continue to set up the same obstacles for yourself, it simply means that you haven't chosen to take all the wisdom from an obstacle experience that you want or need for your growth. In an obstacle experience, I would advise meeting it head-on, sapping it dry, and reducing it to dust. Then you are finished with it and will no longer have the need to create that particular experience.

What seems to be perceived as obstacles by many of you is the acceleration of and shifting of individual awareness levels. Throughout your life journeys growth and unfoldment have generally occurred gradually so that changes appeared subtle. With the New Age those elements which produce growth and unfoldment are being accelerated, and the shifts which manifest on the physical-mental plane are intensified. Because they are occurring rapidly, you who are experiencing inner transformation oftentimes feel confused, and those of you who are witnessing changes in others may have difficulty in coping with or understanding the process. This frequently causes feelings of insecurity and a lack of stability in relationships. These feelings emerge from your ego base and oftentimes manifest in relational conflict.

For those who are experiencing these deep, transformational forces, I would advise you to relax and allow the process to unfold unhindered. It is a necessary shift for the work you must do. Many of you have in the past few years felt a sense of urgency which manifested in feelings of unrest, restlessness, and a desire to be free to fly in the wind. This was the inner calling and the advance notice of the beginning of an intense transformational process. For many it was the kiss to awaken the sleeping master within them, for you've been told that many masters have entered human form for the purpose of bringing in the New Age and for the lifting of collective consciousness. The result of the transformation experience is advanced awareness and higher wisdom, and for the masters it means the offering of the gift of enlightenment to others and the flowering of a new age.

For those in the experience of the transformational process and for those awakening masters, know that we are here to help you. Know, as well, that many human entities are more than they appear in illusionary form and will be coming into your life to walk with you and work with you, so do not be resistant to new energies coming into your life experience. It is truly a wondrous journey for those of you who have chosen or been

165

chosen to experience it. Enjoy it, for the day is coming when you will feel completion on the plane of conscious experience.

CONCEPT AND EXPERIENCE

Cosmically speaking, everything begins first with a concept before it is ever manifested into formed experience. This is because Thought always precedes form. All thoughts, concepts, ideas, and so forth originate first in Universal Mind in pure and perfected creative energy. This Thought moves from Universal Mind through the levels of consciousness within individual mind. As it does so it most often loses its purity and perfection as it becomes comprehensible to the individual creation. Individual thought of the creation is the Universal Thought of the Creator made comprehensible and understandable to the level of awareness of the creation. You may think sometimes that experience precedes concept, but this is not the case, no matter what the externals may seem to indicate. Because all creation is connected to the Creator, all concepts, ideas, and thoughts, known and unknown to the conscious mind, are contained within all Creation. As the Creator originates new concepts, ideas, and thoughts, they immediately become part of creation. Somewhere within your individual mind the concept exists, and you may or may not choose to bring it into formed conscious experience. It is possible to experience without having a conscious awareness of the concept, but still the concept is present in your individual mind.

THE POWER OF BELIEF
ON HISTORICAL EVENTS

If the power of belief is strong enough, could it erase a historical event out of existence? Let us use the example of World War II.

The answer to this question is yes, but it would require a change in mass belief. One person could not do it. What you call historical events are illusionary time warps created by the power of mass thought. If mass consciousness continues to believe in these illusionary time warps, they are kept in continued existence by the power of mass belief. The continued empowering of illusionary time warps is history.

Much of the New Age philosophy centers on the power of thought. You've heard the statement, "As a man thinketh, so is he." This is true. But it is also true of mass consciousness which is collective thought power. Most of the entities on planet Earth haven't reached the awareness to understand that there is great power in thought, and most never realize that what they perceive as reality was created by mass thought of which they were a part.

The truth contained within the so-called New Age philosophy is, in terms of time, still in its infancy. Those who know the power contained in thought are very small in number compared with those who do not have this awareness yet. But the numbers are increasing and the day will come when they are great enough to shift the mass consciousness. It must be this way to bring the New Age to the peak of enlightenment. The present New Age initiates must be prepared to battle against many obstacles contained within the present mass consciousness. The New Age initiate, aside from being a lightbearer, must also be a warrior and understand the power of his sword and the protection of his shield if he is to survive the created illusions of his world.

As I stated, your timing for entrance to the Earth plane was critical for the mission you chose prior to entering. The time you chose to enter determined the nature of and the approach you take to your pre-selected mission during your particular life expression. The spaces and situations you choose determine your lessons, and sometimes you enter spaces and situations which are unnecessary for you. The Creator, however, has arranged one's life experience in such a way that all spaces and all situations become either a learning or a teaching experience for each entity. All of one's life experience becomes purposeful and are not without value and meaning. Nothing in your life experience is accidental, for either your spirit chooses for you or your ego chooses its path. Either way, you choose.

The only things which are predestined are your timing for entrance into form and the fulfillment of your individual mission. Once completed, the spirit exits form and moves on to other work.

THE FALL OF MAN

The Fall of Man has many different meanings and is dependent on one's current level of awareness and on the programming within his belief system. Many consider the Fall to have occurred when man became male and female, and thus they think of the Fall in terms of sexuality. But man's division into male and female really had to do with duality, not sexuality.

In the Creation story in your Bible, it speaks of the Creator dividing heaven from earth, light from darkness, water from land, and so on. In the process of Creation it appears that there is a lot of division and separation going on. From your physical perspective, it might appear that duality is being created. Yet in the seeming divisions and separation, there was Oneness; there was not really duality. Heaven and earth were in a state of Oneness, light and darkness were in a state of Oneness, and water and land were in a state of Oneness. They were merely the Creator expressing that Oneness differently. It's difficult for me to make you understand that light and darkness are expressions of the same thing. Your own mind perceives them as opposites. This is why we say you have created duality.

If there was a Fall, and I personally do not like the term, it occurred when Man lost his awareness of Oneness and began seeing Life with divided sight. Paradise or Eden was the state where Man, even when expressing the Oneness as male and female, was aware of the Oneness. If there was a Fall or a descent, it was when Man, in his mind and in his perception, began to create the illusions of division and separation out of Oneness. For when he began perceiving opposites, he also began assigning qualities to his perceived opposites. When he began assigning qualities, he began judging these qualities, so that the quality of light was more preferred than that of darkness, and the male was superior to the female. From his judgments, more and more divisions occurred and more and more creations of illusions of duality were born.

This, then, would be my interpretation of the Fall of Man: it is that point in his evolution when he lost his awareness of Oneness and began to perceive division and opposites. Although you learn from your world of divided sight, you will still struggle to return to your awareness of Oneness. Your journey is back to Eden and back to paradise. You are on your way if you can see night and day as the same, expressing uniquely; you are on your way if you see male and female as one, expressing uniquely; you are on your way when you stop judging the differences. Your great writer, Gibran, said of joy and sorrow, two seeming opposites, "Your joy is your sorrow unmasked." He was discussing Oneness expressing uniquely.

Oneness will always be expressed uniquely in a myriad of ways. It doesn't cease to be Oneness just because you choose to center on the uniqueness of its expressions, rather than on its Oneness. All is One, no matter how much you focus on separation and division. If you wish to remain in a fallen state of awareness, you are free to do so. However, remember that the gates of Eden are always open to those who wish to enter.

STARSEED INITIATES OF THE NEW AGE

In the Earth's time period of the late 1930's and 1940's, a massive number of starseed initiates began to enter Earth's realm. Their collective purpose was to initiate major shifts in consciousness which were designed to usher in the great Aquarian Age. Now just because this time period brought forth a major exodus of starseed does not mean that there were no starseed present upon the Earth before them. There have been starseed upon the planet since the original manifestation of mankind. Massive numbers of starseed have always been present during those periods of increased enlightenment upon your planet. Often the term Dark Force is used, usually to describe what man perceives as evil. The only Dark Force present upon your planet has been and is ignorance. It is only ignorance or the lack of enlightenment which gives birth to all those things man terms as evil.

Always when there is a massive influx of starseed entering the Earth realm to raise the consciousness of the planet, they will be challenged by the Dark Forces of ignorance. If the lightbearers are able to shift the consciousness to a higher state, then Earth herself enters a golden age of enlightenment. Those so called bleak periods in human history where new thought has been stifled have occurred because (1) there were few starseed present upon the Earth plane at the time, or (2) the Dark Forces of ignorance won over the forces of enlightenment.

All present New Age thinkers and initiates are starseed or they wouldn't be involved. Many starseed have not yet awakened, and some will choose to remain within the sleeping state, because at the present time it is the most secure, safe and comfortable position on your planet since it is reflective of the majority views of mass consciousness.

For those who are the New Age initiates and who are the torchbearers of enlightenment, you must realize that the battle with the Dark Forces will rage for awhile. Some of you must be willing to carry a torch of light in one hand and a sword to clear away from the dark and tangled vines of old thought with the other. That is why this phase is also called the Age of the Warriors. It is the Warriors who must clear away the dark undergrowth to prepare a path for the priests and kings.

Many starseed of the great exodus have had to experience many things and have had to remove many blocks in order to reach the path of the collective starseed mission, and many are still undergoing the process of clearing away their individual obstacles. For example, within the culture in which you live there is an increasingly high divorce rate. Not only is there a necessity to resolve karmic situations with certain entities quickly, but there is also a need to release from entities who elect to remain in a safe, sleeping state. You will note that many New Age initiates have, at some time during their life experience, released from entities who chose to remain in the safe state. Rarely, if ever, will a starseed who has awakened return to the sleeping state. You were told a long time ago that once you had reached a critical point on this journey, there was no turning back. The New Age initiates are like specialized brain cells preparing to pour out the new instructions to the cells of humanity. They are like a nucleus preparing to spread outward to all which surrounds it, or a hub around which the spokes revolve. Without the hub, the wheel would never turn.

But you who have at some time in your past released from entities who elected not to go on this journey must never pride yourself into thinking that you are better than they. You must always remember that everyone is a critical and vital part of the All. Bless the lessons which you learn, for they are part of your growth and unfoldment. It's just that when you reached the fork in the road, you each chose a different path. Do not judge another's path, for ultimately all paths merge together into the One Path. Bless those who are still asleep, for it is their sleeping which gives purpose to your mission since you have chosen to walk and work in a world of duality.

As an awakened starseed walks on in his journey, he will begin to feel a strange sense of urgency as his individual mission, which is integral to the collective mission, becomes clearer. New insights and heightened awarenesses begin to fill his conscious mind, and he begins to be able to differentiate between the urgings of the spirit and the ego with greater accuracy. Not with selfishness, but with great intent of purpose, he begins listening to and hearing the inner voice of his spirit. Although there may be, for a time, a battle between the ego and the spirit, he soon begins following the voice of guidance from his spirit with greater frequency. For the starseed moving forth upon the path, this will mean a better use of time and energy. Right use of one's time and energy assists the starseed in the performance of his individual mission, which is, of course, an integral part of the collective starseed mission.

For the starseed, on a real personal level, this means a willful clearing away of barriers, blocks and obstacles to growth. This is not an easy process and is sometimes painful, but for the starseed who is deeply committed to his journey and to both his personal and collective mission, it is necessary. The torchbearer must take the light into his own darkness so that he can see his own path clearly before he can become the guide for others and shine light upon their paths. He must feel the blade of his own sword as he cuts away those things which threaten to strangle his own growth before he can clear a path for others. The Warrior must shed the blood of his own dark force of ignorance before he can stand before the dark forces of others. In the advent of any great transition or transformation, the initiates must be purged and cleansed and prepared for what they have entered to achieve. They must be clear in their purpose, committed and unwavering, intent on fulfillment of the mission, and prepared for the challenges.

What many starseed are presently experiencing is the purging and the preparation which is part of the Passage. It might cause some confusion as one's awareness shifts and his actions are altered. The initiates must change during the cleansing and clearing process which is but the preparation needed to integrate them into the collective mission. The mental, psychological, emotional, and physical changes which may occur will be less confusing and less painful if one flows with the changes rather than resisting them. It is also helpful if the starseed support each other in their collective understanding of what is occurring to individuals.

What basically is happening, as you have been told, is that changes have to occur, and a clearing is critical for the memory cells to open. It is the opening of the memory cells which causes individual enlightenment; it is individual enlightenment which will give birth to collective enlightenment.

So I say to you, do not be fearful of your own process of cleansing and purging and preparation. Do not fear the shifts in your thoughts and actions. Do not fear to trust your inner guidance. You are changing; your own consciousness is being altered and transformed, and this must be allowed if you are to carry the torch.

My blessings to the starseed initiates and to all who will ultimately be touched by the light from the Dawn of a New Age. Remember that as the sun rises, it touches a small area at first and spreads outward as it rises higher in the heavens. The starseed initiates represent the sun preparing to dawn on a New Age.

ESOTERIC GROUPS:
THE HOPE OF RE-CREATION

Esoteric knowledge is knowledge which surpasses human knowledge and human logic. Although it is available to all who would seek to enter its realms, few entities are really willing to seek beyond human knowledge.

There have been esoteric groups since the beginning of mankind, but they seem to spring up in greater abundance when the destruction of a civilization or of an age seems to be looming on the horizon of human history. The purpose of such groups is to preserve cosmic knowledge for future ages and future civilizations. Since you cannot preserve what you do not have, some entities have been selected and have been assigned the arduous task of seeking knowledge both within your world and beyond it. Many entities will join these esoteric groups, but when the search becomes too strenuous or too confusing, some will retreat. Only the true initiates will remain to sift through the illusions in search of true knowledge and essence which results in the finding of the Holy Grail, the wisdom of the Cosmos. The journey into the depths of knowledge requires one to be tireless and fearless in his seeking, but the reward is that of being able to soar to the heights of Cosmic Wisdom.

It is the individual who evolves, and not the masses. The process of moving into higher consciousness is the only true evolution for the individual entity. As a whole, the masses will not achieve this. Certain individual entities shall, and they are the ones who will silently impact on civilizations and ages to come, just as they have done throughout your Earth's history. As more and more entities evolve individually, it will create an evolution of mass consciousness.

Esoteric groups resemble an inner circle within the greater circle of humanity. Without this inner circle composed of true seekers, civilizations and ages would be destroyed, never to be reborn. The New Age cannot manifest into form without entities of higher consciousness to bring it into being. Esoteric groups evolve from the cells of humanity into a specialized cell through the process of moving into higher consciousness. The necessary ingredient for this evolution is that of seeking.

Much study and preparation for the true seekers is required, and all is for a purpose. The true seeker is asked to delve into the knowledge available on your plane of life. He is asked to go within and find his answers. He is asked to connect with the Universal Mind. He is asked to go beyond his five physical senses and to see with new vision and hear with new ears. He is asked to transcend human limitations and enter realms seemingly beyond human comprehension. He is asked to seek Essence and Truth. The sincere and true seeker who is willing to journey beyond himself will never be disappointed; he will always find.

Those who continue this journey are special. They are the initiates of a new and better age to come; they are the preservers of the knowledge and wisdom necessary for continuing creation. Collectively, esoteric groups have a divine and cosmic purpose. Without seekers into the realms

172

of higher knowledge, higher wisdom, and higher consciousness, destruction would have already occurred with no hope of re-creation. Collective high consciousness is the mother which will give birth to the New Age. You are the hope of re-creation.

My blessing and love to you who seek.

CREATE YOUR OWN REALITY
ONE DAY AT A TIME

Creating your own reality one day at a time implies two things: (1) that you have the power to create; and (2) that this should be done in the present.

I take this further within the consideration of time: to the now moment. I stress being aware of each now moment. When you think of a day, your mind tends to consider a longer period within your concept of time. The now moment is all that you are assured of in your space-time dimension. You are not assured of the next moment or day. Now is where you are, and now is where you will experience and learn. Entities who are so bound to the past or caught up in the future do not fully enjoy or learn the lessons contained within the now. How you experience the now oftentimes has a great bearing on future now moments.

With respect to your creating your own reality, you do, to a degree, have power: more power than you think. That which you term reality is perceptual and is based on how you, as an individual entity, see the world. Cosmically, none of your physically manifested illusions represent reality since the true reality is spiritual. In your dimension how you think and what you think are the determining factors in the creation of your individual worlds. Thought energy, when instilled with power, will manifest into a physical illusion. If you create and empower negative thought energy, this is what will be manifested in your individual world. If your perception of reality is negative, you will continue to create and empower negative thoughts which, in turn, will continue to feed your negative perception of reality. It becomes, then, a seemingly endless cycle.

Become more aware of and sensitized to your now moments and send forth positive thoughts. Empower them so that physical manifestations within your world will be of a positive nature. As more positive manifestations enter your individual world, an old cycle is broken and a new one is born.

Human entities tend to look outside themselves and perceive according to the externals. What is created and one's perception of it come from within. The easiest way to live your life is to learn to accept each now moment as it comes to you as a gift given for your learning. Learn from it and accept the next now moment in the same way. This is what is called flow: the acceptance of what is, without wanting it to be anything other than what it is. If you approach each now moment as a fresh and unique experience from a point of neutrality and then create and empower positive thought energy, your personal reality will be positive, and the world you create will be perceived as beautiful and filled with learning and love. Remember that you always choose the reality you create and your perception of it. Therein lies your real power—*your choice.*

A DREAM WITHIN A DREAM

One of your poets wrote, "All that we see or seem is but a dream within a dream." In one sense this is true, but again it depends on how one defines that which is termed a dream. Most human entities think of a dream as being a state of unreality. What is reality, however, but that which you perceive it to be? One's sense of what is real or unreal is perceptual and completely unique to the perceiver. It's rather like truth. What may be true for one entity may be completely opposite for another. Truth and reality are always relative to the individual.

That which you term dreaming has to do with consciousness. You have seven levels of consciousness in your individual mind. These levels are as follows: preconsciousness, subconsciousness, present consciousness, metaconsciousness, supraconsciousness, magnaconsciousness, and omniconsciousness. These levels compose that which is termed as individual mind. The organic brain computer is both a transmitter to and a receiver from mind.

Most of the time the human entity operates within the state of present consciousness. This does not mean that he is not influenced by or acted upon by the other levels of consciousness composing his individual mind which is, in truth, a fragment of the One Mind. With respect to dreams, most input comes from the preconscious, the subconscious, and the metaconscious levels. The preconscious level contains data from past physical lives, the subconscious level contains only data from one's current incarnation, and in the meta consciousness, that which is termed *you* is actually experiencing in another dimension.

Because one's levels of consciousness are layered and because consciousness itself is energy and therefore moving, the various levels flow and move into each other like waves upon an ocean. This wave-like motion is continually occurring. You would not know that you were

174

having the experience of dreaming unless another level of your consciousness touched your present conscious level. If the other levels did not touch your present consciousness, you would have no remembrance or recall of a dream.

In your world most recalled dreams come from your present consciousness being touched by the levels which are closest. When you sleep or experience your down time, which is necessary for the human vehicle to recharge and re-energize itself, it is rather like a part of present consciousness being unplugged for a time. Sleep is similar to flying on automatic pilot. The necessary functions for physical life continue to operate, while present consciousness shuts down.

Recall of a dream occurs when present consciousness is plugged in during that which is designated as an alpha wave. Depending on when you emerge into a totally present conscious state during an alpha wave brain function determines the amount of recall that you will have. For example, you will have greater recall of a dream when your present consciousness is plugged in closer to the end of an alpha wave than you would have at the beginning of one. Oftentimes present consciousness begins to take control of the vehicle at the peak of an alpha wave. By the time you reach the end of the process of complete awakening to full present consciousness, a great portion of so-called dream recall is lost.

Many human entities believe that recall of dreams is important for a better understanding of themselves as they express in the physical world of illusion. I do not believe this to be so. You will dream and will experience other levels of consciousness whether you have recall or not. Many human entities become involved in dream interpretation, and there is some validity in this area simply because dreams are essentially your connection with your other levels of consciousness and therefore are able to present insights into your own wholeness. You in present consciousness are but a fragment of the whole you. No one can interpret another's dreams with complete accuracy for the reason that another's dreams are totally individual and unique to the dreamer. Even though some universal symbols with generalized meanings may appear in a dream, one must always interpret the symbols in their connection with the level of consciousness which happened to have been recalled. Although the symbols themselves may be universal, they can only be applied specifically to the individual who dreams of them. When another interprets a dream you have recalled, please realize that there could be and usually are inaccuracies in the interpretation of it. The interpreter's thoughts are based on his or her own knowledge, wisdom, belief system, and so forth.

Let me discuss the content of dreams. In some dreams you recall something you've seen or done in your present lifetime. Perhaps you've watched a film and portions of it end up in your dream. When this happens, the subconscious level, your data storage area for your present incarnation, is touching your present level of consciousness. If you dream of other times and spaces, your present level of consciousness is either being touched by your preconscious level, the storage area for past incarnations, or by the metaconscious level, which is something another fragment of you is experiencing in either another space, place, and time or in another dimension.

Sometimes in your recall of dreams, the content seems scrambled or disconnected. In other words, the symbols or items within the framework of a dream may appear to have no relevance to one another. Upon awakening the dreamer might have a sense of strangeness about his recall. The truth is that there really is no disconnection present within that which you term as a dream. When the recall of a dream seems scrambled and disconnected to your present consciousness, it is usually because you have not had complete recall or you are attempting to view it from your present level of perception. In a dream analysis you will discover inconsistencies if you attempt to utilize a logical approach in the interpretation. Greater accuracy will be found by utilizing the intuitive approach. You must always remember that what is called logic on Earth is not universal. What you connect up with on another level of consciousness cannot always be understood by your present level of consciousness.

Refining and trusting your intuitive abilities assists you in understanding the meanings your dreams may contain which are relevant to your present consciousness. They are simply a recalling of what other fragments of you are experiencing, or they are data from the storage areas in your brain computer. In some dreams you work out or express feelings which you may have suppressed in your present conscious state.

There are dreams which give you insights into your own life which are relevant to present consciousness, and there are dreams which offer warnings to you which are relevant to your physical life. Remember that your levels of consciousness are multidimensional, and you are able to tap into anywhere—past, present, and future. In your higher levels of consciousness you are able to connect with the higher consciousness levels of any aspect of creation. So dreams can offer warnings of danger and other prophetic messages. If you have recall of being in an alien environment, this is a fragment of an actual experience.

The complete you is multidimensional and is experiencing in a myriad of time warps and dimensions. When present consciousness is unplugged and you enter sleep, other levels of consciousness can be tapped into if you awaken during an alpha wave brain function.

Dreams oftentimes exert a great influence upon your awakened state even if you have no recall of them. When awake, your present consciousness provides somewhat of a barrier from the other levels. When you are asleep you are experiencing those other levels whether you are aware or not, and you still experience them when you are awake. How you awaken from sleep and what you feel like after down time is usually an indicator of what you experienced on other levels. If you awaken bubbly and excited about experiencing in the present, it usually means your dreams have offered you positive experiences. If you awaken feeling depressed, angry, burdened, and so on, it generally means that you have experienced situations which were perceived as negative.

Dreams are fragments of your beingness, and if you learn to be connected to your inner self, you will find these recalls benefit you by offering you greater insight into and greater understanding of the total you. That fragment of you which you recall in your dreams also dreams of you in your present consciousness, as well as other dimensions and times, spaces and places. So you see, all that you see or are is but a dream within a dream within a dream within a dream!

CONTINUE TO SEEK

It is very important for you who are seekers to continue your search for your own truth and your own answers. It is the search and the shedding away of old truths which lifts you higher on your journey toward Absolute Truth. It is this process, this wonderful journey, which continues to ensure the raising of your conscious awareness.

Yes, it is true that your higher levels of consciousness are connected to all of your answers and to Absolute Truth, but for your present conscious state it is like an ascending spiral staircase—a Jacob's Ladder—leading you to the cosmic wonders contained within the magic kingdoms of your mind.

What we sometimes note in our interactions with human entities is that on occasion a seeker will assume that he has all the answers and that his journey is over. He will sometimes claim himself to be a master teacher and draw unto himself students in search of knowledge. What happens is that the teacher will offer his truths over and over again like a broken record, or he will play it until the end of the song, the result being that there is nowhere else to go. The seeking students, desiring to grow further, will leave their teacher and go in search of other teachers.

How does one know if he has stopped his own search? If one says, "I have found all the truth I need," he has stopped. One who has stopped will quit reading books and material by other teachers, he will assume that classes and courses taught by others can no longer benefit him, and he will pride himself into believing that he is beyond all others in his awareness and sense of truth. This is the biggest trap any seeker can fall into, for when he stops seeking, he stops growing. And once he stops growing, he is of little benefit to those who are his students. It's rather like a science teacher or a medical doctor who, after learning a massive amount of data in school, refuses to continue to update this knowledge as new and current data becomes available within the evolutionary processes of science and medicine.

It is important that you keep your minds open and continue to study and learn all the knowledge within your world and beyond it. It is important that you travel in arenas of great diversity and enter expanded areas of learning. Why? Not simply so that you can accumulate more Earth data to fill your brain computers. You are directed to myriad areas so that you can understand that truth exists in all realms and all areas. This causes you to become more expansive in your thinking which enables you to become more cosmic in your approach to all areas contained in your life on Earth. Your vision will be expanded to the point where you will see anew and with greater clarity, and hopefully, with greater wisdom. We want you to continue striving to learn, using all the sources and resources available to you: from books and other written material, from viewed material such as your films and television, from audio material such as music, from experiences within your life, from relationships and interactions with other entities and aspects of Creation, and from those of us who try to assist you not only in seeing beyond surface data, but also into the glories of worlds beyond your physical senses.

Some of you are already masters, but a true master is always the humblest and the most eager of seekers. His mind is like an opening lotus blossom, with petals eternally unfolding. He eats but is never quite filled, and he continues to hunger. He drinks but his thirst is never quenched, and he continues to thirst. He walks on, and though tired at times, he stops only to rest but never to sleep. He shares his knowledge with his students and yet looks into the mirror and sees himself as the student. In the presence of a master greater than himself, he bows and holds out his hands to accept knowledge from a higher master. On Earth, the true master is also the eternal seeker and the eager student. Although he teaches others, his true mission is to continue to learn, for he knows that his learning ensures his growth and unfoldment to the ultimate state of Absolute Truth.

A true master never assumes that he has the truth but realizes that the process of seeking truth is as important as that of finding truth. It is the process which ensures his growth, and not merely the attainment of the goal. To a master, each new truth is like a beautiful pearl. The master knows that one pearl does not a necklace make. His process of seeking is like a string, a string upon which to place his pearls. His seeking, his finding, his seeking again and again and finding again and again creates a necklace which will be Absolute Truth.

Many entities discover a pearl or two and never realize that they should be creating a strand of pearls. Or they find a few pearls and then tire of looking for more. For a master, there is just as much joy to be found in the seeking as in the finding. It is helpful if one remembers that the process and the goal are one and the seeker and the search are one. For you who are students and seekers, continue on in your search. The collecting of pearls is the primary purpose of one's life experience.

TRUE SPIRITUAL GUIDANCE

You have heard statements from others in which they credit their actions to spiritual guidance, using such statements as: "I have received guidance to do this or that" or "My spiritual guidance has directed me to take this action." Listening, you may wonder how one really knows if the guidance is accurate or not or where it's coming from. True spiritual guidance will always direct you into loving actions; it will never direct you into actions of non-love. If your direction guides you into actions which create pain and suffering for others, then the ego-self is in some way involved. This is the only test of the accuracy of guidance.

If you consciously know your actions will cause pain to another, you must assume a degree of responsibility for the suffering caused. Become attuned to the varied and differing levels of awarenesses within others. If you are truly aware, you must know that you are not off the hook if your actions will cause pain for another and you proceed by thinking, "Well, if he is hurt, that's his problem. He is allowing it." This is using metaphysics to rationalize your actions. The one who consciously knows he will cause pain to another is responsible for that. The degree is always based on intent. If you plan and prepare to hurt someone, this is definitely not spiritual guidance, but ego guidance. No Karma is incurred if hurt is created in another in a situation where you had neither intent nor conscious knowing that your action would produce hurt.

Essentially spiritual guidance comes from a point of love and directs the entity into loving actions designed to promote the highest good.

Anything less than this must be analyzed carefully. Spirit always seeks to direct the entity to his greatest unfoldment and lovingly directs that entity into actions promoting the highest growth and unfoldment for all within his individual world.

KARMIC BALANCING AND CAUSE AND EFFECT

The degrees of Karmic reaction are determined by an individual entity's intent or motive. The intent on the part of an individual entity is always the determining factor. You live under the Universal Law of Cause and Effect, which means that all action will result in a reaction. Reaction becomes action with a resulting re-action. If the Law of Cause and Effect were a shape, it would be circular.

When one consciously believes in Karmic balance, he essentially can take control of his own balancing. For example, if you do something to another that you know is wrong, you may go to him and admit you're wrong, being willing to accept whatever reaction they have toward you. If you do not believe in Karmic balancing, you may choose to do nothing. Then the Law of Cause and Effect is in control.

A spirit-led entity generally will accept responsibility, and the more aware he becomes, the more knowledgeable he becomes as to what is in need of balancing within his own life. If you take responsibility to balance your own actions, it does not mean that you are not still under the Law of Cause and Effect, it means that when you consciously take the initiative to balance your actions, the Law of Cause and Effect will be less severe because of your intent. Karma is the balancing you feel led to do in form; Cause and Effect is what the Cosmos feels you must do for your spirit and for the Whole of Creation. You see, the whole Cosmos is always striving to restore balance and harmony when it is not present.

Many humans think of Karmic balancing only when negative actions have occurred, but it also applies to positive actions. When one creates a positive action which will always result in a positive reaction, he lifts up the whole Cosmos. When he creates negative action, this creates imbalance in the Cosmos. You, as individual entities, never realize how very important and vital you are to the All. Once you truly understand this, you will strive even harder to create and maintain harmony and balance within your life experiences. If you truly comprehended that what you do, no matter how big or small, affects the All, you would realize your true value. Most entities travel their paths believing they have little or no real value to the Whole.

Let us return to intent or motive within actions. Karma is primarily a physical law; Cause and Effect is a spiritual law. Cosmic balancing is concerned with intent and motive behind physical actions. An individual entity's intent or motive behind any given action always has its base in either the spirit or the ego. The spirit will always guide the entity into positive action; the ego may frequently guide the entity into negative actions because it is always in the process of protecting itself.

Become aware of individual motives, intent, and reasons behind any action, thought, word, or deed. Being aware of motive and intent will also assist a person in knowing how to maintain positive balance. This gives one great control over his life journey.

ONE'S MISSION IN LIFE

Let us discuss a human entity's individual mission within his life.

Before your spirit enters the form, it is aware of the lessons needed to be learned upon the Full Circle Journey. It selects the space where it believes it can best learn some of these lessons. Although you did choose to enter at a particular time and space, there were other spaces and situations you could have entered into where you could have learned the needed lessons equally well. There were just differences in timing. You had to enter some space at the time you selected. For example, perhaps you needed to enter as an Aquarian so that certain planetary configurations would mark you with certain influences, again necessary for your learning. Timing has much to do with an individual's mission.

Once you entered and began your experience on Earth, your mission began. As you traveled your path, you were met by many external influences which tended to alter and shift your mission. A human entity journeys with many, many entities on his individual path. Each entity exerts an influence on you and causes your mission to shift and alter its course, but only for a time.

Consider all the parents you could have chosen, all the spaces you could have entered, all the possible mates you could have shared your life with. A change in any one of these situations would have altered the course of your life. But would these alterations and modifications have completely changed your mission?

The answer is no. What would have been changed was your approach to the mission. You would have achieved it no matter what the external space and circumstances were, because the mission is inherent in the journey of the spirit. The spirit is always attempting to direct the entity toward the best space to fulfill the mission. This is why you are directed to certain situations and spaces and even other entities, as well as being moved away from certain situations, spaces, and entities.

The spirit always knows the straightest and best course to take to fulfill the mission and learn the needed lessons. But the ego, with its freedom of will, does not like to beeline to the fulfillment of an individual mission, for completion of the mission means exit into the next dimension and the release of the ego. So the ego takes you over mountains and down in valleys; it takes you around curves and detours you off course and even leads you around in circles. Whereas the spirit likes a shortcut, the ego prefers going the long way home.

This is alright because in the ego's wanderings the human entity learns a lot. The spirit is patient because it knows that ultimately it will bring the entity into alignment with the individual mission and will complete it.

WHY TRUTH SEEKERS ABANDON THEIR SEARCH

You are wondering about those people who seek truth and then for some unknown reason seemingly turn away from the search. It's not uncommon for one to make a 180 degree turn. There are many reasons for this.

In some cases the seeking of truth was not real in the first place. In your dimension there are so many new things to do and so many new things to learn. With some entities the novelty of the newness wears off, and they must once again seek something new. But in the area of truth, as in a marriage, the sheer excitement of novelty must grow to something greater and more substantial. If it does not, then it will, like a marriage, be abandoned. There are some entities who move from group to group, marriage to marriage, religion to religion, job to job, and cause to cause.

Another reason that people seemingly turn off from truth seeking is that they become oversaturated. You can become oversaturated in any area of your life, and this is why it is important to have a diversity of interests within your life experience. You've all had periods of oversaturation in your lives, and you know when this condition exists. In this case it's best to back off. By doing this you can return and view it with a fresh approach.

A third reason why truth seekers sometimes turn off happens when they reach a point where they feel they are not growing from their learning. I've told you many times that your vision and perception are too limited to assess your own growth and progress. But some truth seekers, when they receive answers or truth, expect to change overnight and find their lives to be in the flow. It's not an overnight process. It takes a lot of time and effort on your dimension to rid yourself of the conditions which made your life unworkable or unfulfilling—the very conditions which prompted you into truth seeking. You are always saying that some entities seem to want miracles and magic, and these are really very rare results. Your truth comes to you, but you must work very hard to make it work because you are always being challenged by your human ego. And your answers, your truth, must become a part of you. It must transcend your intellectual knowledge. If it does not, it will not work and you will not be in the flow any more than you were before your truth came to you. You all know the truth, you all know Absolute Truth, and you all know how to flow and make your life work. It's within each one of you, hidden perhaps, but there. Truth seeking is journeying inward to your own God essence. You all know who stands at the gate of your essence and challenges you and wages war against you. The war is between ego and essence, between illusion and truth. He is strong, and this is why when you have truth, the path to applying it is difficult. He will put boulders on your path, and he will knock you down. But the truth seeker will labor and climb over the boulders, and he will pick himself up and travel on. He will rest in the valleys of his life, meditate on the plateaus, and sing joyously on the peaks. But he will not allow himself to die in the valley or remain on the plateau or be unwilling to climb to another peak. The truth seeker is not a quitter.

Then, sadly, there is the truth seeker who reaches a point where he believes he has all the answers he needs, and who feels there is no more. He stops seeking, and because the Cosmos is ever changing, he becomes stagnant. He hands down a death sentence to truth, to his own essence. This is not the same as outgrowing a group or religion or job or cause. You can outgrow these things and cease to grow or be fulfilled by them, and then it's best to move on. The one who outgrows does not cease to seek but merely moves on or is led to a new area of learning. It's like making a transition from high school to college.

The saddest of all, though, is when a truth seeker who has grown elects to abandon his truth and return to the materialistic world of illusion because it appears easier and more physically fulfilling; when his eyes become earthbound and he blinds himself to the New Age on the horizon and the myriad of dimensions awaiting him. Aside from merely learning how to live your lives more effectively and abundantly, it is to your advantage to expand your vision to include what you term the future. By learning and preparing on your dimension, you are also preparing for continuance on your magnificent journey into dimensions and worlds beyond your comprehension. There are two ways of packing a suitcase: you can pack meticulously and orderly, making certain you have all the things you might need, or you can throw things together at the last minute and hope that you will have what you need. Or, of course you can pack nothing at all and be without those things you will need on your journey. So it is with preparation, my friends. Truth seeking is preparation. It is packing your bags. How you pack and how much you wish to take is totally up to you, the Cosmic traveler.

POVERTY CONSCIOUSNESS

The Master said that the poor would be with you always. This means that there will always be entities who lack in some way—at least until the advent of the New World. Poor can refer to the mental, emotional, and spiritual senses as well as the physical. One can be physically wealthy and yet poverty-stricken in other ways. There are many well meaning and caring individuals and organizations who work hard to alleviate the suffering and pain caused by physical poorness or poverty, and this is good. But this is not enough, and it only temporarily alleviates the symptoms without touching the cause. Thus the symptoms recur time and again. The cause lies within the consciousness of individuals and groups, and as long as a poverty consciousness exists, poverty will exist, just as fear and hate will continue to perpetuate the war consciousness upon your planet.

Assist those who are in need physically, spiritually, mentally, and emotionally if you have the resources to do so. But it is critical that you go beyond this to try to shift the poverty consciousness to a new awareness. This is done with the power of Love which is the energy needed to remove the cause of poverty.

It's easy to become locked into a poverty consciousness just as it's easy to become locked into a fear consciousness. Sometimes it's easier to stay in a lack condition than to move out in trust and freedom and work to rid yourself of your poverty. Poverty will exist until each realizes that lack is not necessary and not a condition of life. The Universe is for you and not against you, and the Source never intended anyone to suffer. Remember the words, "It is the Father's good pleasure to give you the Kingdom." He wants you to have abundance in all things; not lack, poverty, or suffering. If abundance is within your life, then it is within your belief system and within your consciousness.

THE INSANE ON HIGHER LEVELS

Those whom you consider the insane on your plane of existence are in the flow on higher levels to the same extent as those who are not considered to be insane. Insanity is a malfunctioning of the physical brain computer, and the seeming disorders may manifest within the lower three levels of consciousness of the mind: preconsciousness, subconsciousness, and consciousness. The upper four levels of consciousness (meta, supra, magna, and omni) are unaffected.

Some human entities are assessed to be insane or retarded. This is because man has established a condition which he terms normal. If nineteen out of twenty entities act in a certain way, for example, the condition is termed the normal way of acting. The one entity who does not act in the same manner as the others may be termed abnormal and sometimes even insane or retarded. It is, however, very important not to be too quick to judge one who does not act within the established patterns considered to be normal. Another reason not to lock into definitions of normal and abnormal has to do with creative expression, wherein the unusual and different can be signs of much ability.

Some of those entities whom you term insane or retarded are among you for Karmic reasons; most are there to teach you. Some live in spaces you cannot comprehend, and some are disconnected from the illusions of the Earth plane. Entities tend to pity and feel sorry for those who are not like them, and they sometimes work very hard to pull them back into the established patterns. The normal entity blocks possible communication because of the discomfort he feels, and he resists stretching his mind to connect on another level. The normal entity oftentimes feels fear and sometimes even revulsion. Feel none of these things. God will express in various and unique ways, and at higher levels these entities are the same as you. They are merely spirits contained in a form with a disorder in the physical brain computer. Remember that love is the universal communicator and transformer.

CHAKRAS AND
HIGH LEVEL ENERGY EXPERIENCES

A human entity will oftentimes feel physically tired and drained after the experience of an exposure to and expenditure of high amounts of mental, spiritual, and psychic energy.

As each chakra center opens, the energy level increases and affects all levels of the body: the physical, mental, emotional, spiritual, astral, and etheric. Every particle becomes energized. Many entities open up some or all of their chakra centers and release Love Energy. Energy particles are attracted to and magnetized by other energy particles. An entity not only releases energy from himself, but also attracts energy into himself. During a high energy level exchange an entity will experience vitality and a great sense of physical, mental, emotional, and spiritual well-being. This continues as long as the exchange or the inflow and outflow of energy is occurring.

When an entity is removed from the high energy environment, the chakras begin to close and oftentimes the human entity will feel physically and mentally tired, particularly if he has had a long exposure to a high energy exchange. This is not really abnormal for the human form which has been exposed to increased energy levels. In order to restore balance and equilibrium within the form, rest is required.

Another condition which can occur happens when the higher four chakras are opened fully. These are the heart, the throat, the brow or third eye, and the crown chakras. When these are opened there is a complete connection to the flow from Universal Mind. So when an entity is in an environment where he is pouring out a lot of individual energy and attracting a lot of collective energy from others as well as being filled with the energy from the Universal Mind, his energy intake is greater than his energy release. He will feel vital and energized during the experience, but the intake and the output of energy are not balanced. Thus, the form will insist on restoring balance, and will indicate this by a need to sleep or rest.

A channel who receives from beyond the astral plane will usually channel with at least three of the upper four chakras open. This is why a channel might feel tired after a session and will need to rest, sleep, or meditate until the balance of energy has been restored.

There are ways to maintain a balance during a high energy exchange but it requires work to attain it. The best way is to learn how to shut down the three base chakras during the exchange. To do this one must study and learn what these force centers are and what they control or influence. For a time, and until one can naturally close these centers, it might be necessary for one to meditate quietly for half an hour prior to entering a high energy exchange environment and actually use the powers of the will to close the base chakras. I would also advise half an hour of quiet meditation after an exposure to a high energy exchange. This will allow the upper chakras to quietly close while the entity clears, centers, and balances the energies within the total form. The more one practices this method, the easier the opening and closing of the individual chakra centers will be, and with time the entity will be in complete control of maintaining his own energy balance so that exhaustion and tiredness from high energy experiences will no longer be present.

If all the chakra energy centers were open all of the time, the physical form could not handle the energy. So until an entity understands these energy centers which are not physical and learns to balance and control them himself, the spirit controls the opening and closing of these centers. The more aware and evolved a human entity becomes, the more the upper four chakras will be utilized. The root or base chakra, home of the so-called kundalini energy, is the one which creates the greater sense of physical tiredness when it, and the other six centers, are open. This is the energy which most affects the physical form at its cellular level. If one can, at least, learn to close the base chakra when entering the high energy exchange environment, he will feel less physically drained after the exchange.

There are other advantages to being able to open and close your chakra centers at will. This will also assist you in learning to shield your auric field. High energy exchanges can occur in non-loving environments such as situations of mob violence. You can be just as energized in this atmosphere as in one of love if your chakras are open. Chakras expel energy and they magnetize and attract energy to you. Shielding your auric field prevents these energies from being released and from entering you, and thus keeps you from becoming caught up in something which is not right for you. Many entities who were basically good have become caught up in the energies of others and done things they would not have done if they had known how to close their chakra centers and shield their auric fields.

Your auric field is generally only partially shielded because usually there is at least one upper chakra center open. When all the upper chakra centers are open your auric field is unshielded. This is when you are trusting and open to receiving love energy and sharing it. When your upper chakras are closed, your auric field is completely shielded. When one is aligned to his spirit, his inner guidance will tell him when to shield the auric field for his own protection. The aware entity will know when shielding is best, as well as knowing when it's alright to operate with the four upper chakras open. This knowing comes when one becomes attuned to the vibrations of his external world. As one becomes more attuned and sensitive to the vibrations he encounters, he will know when to partially shield his aura, totally shield it, or allow it to be open and unshielded.

DESTRUCTION AND CREATION
ARE THE SAME PROCESS

The reason that destruction appears to take place more quickly than creation is due to your perception of time. Creation appears to take longer because it is, in your perception, a positive action, and yet your collective mind, of which you are a contributor, is negatively charged. Because of the negative thought patterns inherent within the collective mind, human entities have not yet reached an awareness level whereby they can move a positive thought into instant manifestation. Because of the collective energy required to empower negative thought, a negative thought can quickly be brought into manifested form. For example, overall collective mind considers building a house to be a positive action and burning a house down to be a negative action. Because mass consciousness is so negatively charged, it will naturally work against you in a positive endeavor. In the case of building a house, it works against you in terms of time. And again, in terms of time, it will work for you in burning the house down. This is why, on your material plane, the creation of form seems to require more time than destruction of form. You simply have the high collective negative energy either working for you in negative actions or against you in positive actions.

Actually, on a higher level, creation and destruction are one and are cyclic in nature. One moves into the other which moves again back into the other in a rhythm designed to constantly produce growth and continuing unfoldment. On a higher level, they are neither negative or positive and simply form a necessary process in life. If you can reach the understanding that both creation and destruction are but a process in which energy shifts and moves from one stage or phase to another, you will have less difficulty in dealing with your perceived destruction on the Earth plane. If you think of destruction as a death or as an end, or a creation as a birth or a beginning, this is strictly based on your human perception. Energy is all there is, and it foes not die nor does it end. It simply shifts and moves and changes form. Destruction and creation form one process and are simply doorways to one another, leading always to greater unfoldment and growth, and always are part of the Ascension Process.

The only real counsel I can offer you with respect to that which you term destruction in your material world is to reach the awareness level where you are non-attached to your material illusions so that if they are removed you will not be devastated by your perceived loss. You must always remember that energy will always shift and move on your plane of experience and beyond.

HIGH LEVEL SPIRIT CONNECTIONS

A twin flame, as you will recall, is that other polarity of you: spirit split into two distinct energy polarities and on two separate and distinct journeys to achieve Total Experience. Throughout a Full Circle Journey one will always be bound to his twin flame even though they may not always express together in the same time warps or even on the same dimension.

Soulmate connections are formed when physical energy vibrations are aligned between two human entities. A human entity can have many soulmate connections within the experience of a single incarnation. You will only have one soulmate at a time, and it will always be opposite to whatever gender you are expressing. As you grow in awareness, your vibratory level will shift and alter. If your soulmate does not or cannot align to a new vibratory level, he ceases to be a soulmate to you, although he may become a soulmate to another entity whose vibrations become aligned to his. There can be spaces in your life experience when you will have no soulmate. The primary purpose of soulmate connections is to assist one another in growing and unfolding. If two entities, soulmates, unfold at the same rate and remain vibrationally aligned to each other, it is possible to have but a single soulmate within an incarnation. This is rare, however.

High level spirit connections are likewise rare and bear some of the characteristics of both the twin flame connection and the soulmate connection. High level spirit connections are formed over a period of many life journeys. In other words, entities who are thus connected have worked together many times before, and usually their work involved the raising of collective consciousness or the bringing in of a new age. These entities are masters who have taken on human form and who express in such a way that, unless you are aware, they are not recognized. As they perform their work in the manifested world, they may recognize one another and become connected in their higher levels of consciousness. A master will always recognize another master at some level. The first recognition of another master on the conscious level comes when the entities become aware that their particular missions are aligned and that those missions are involved in the raising of collective consciousness and the creation of a new age. The second recognition on a conscious level comes when the entities communicate their wisdom to one another and they realize that that which they deem to be truth is similar.

With these two realizations the entities, masters in disguise, form a conscious spiritual connection with one another. If their vibrations are evenly matched, they may even become soulmates as well. If there is the existence of a high level spirit connection and a soulmate connection, two things are achieved: (1) they assist in the growth and unfoldment of each other in the physical realm; and (2) together they can work with greater success in their similar missions. Because they have worked together so many times before and because they are masters, there is great compatibility present.

Since soulmate connections are based on physical energy vibrations and similar awareness levels, there seems to be a greater need for the entities to spend more physical time together and to communicate verbally with greater frequency. With high level spirit connections this need is not present, although the entities do enjoy the presence of one another and the verbal communication. The communication level which exists within high level spirit connections is much higher and oftentimes very subtle, even going to the point of being unnoticed by others around them. Overall the communication occurs at their higher levels of consciousness and is between the two spirits. Consciously the two entities have a true knowing of each other at the deeper levels of beingness. Consciously they have a deep sense of trust, love, and caring for one another. They oftentimes communicate more through the physical eye or with a slight touch than they do verbally. Knowing that their missions are similar, they are very supportive of each other's work. If two entities involved in a high level spirit connection work together, the power is increased and harmony is assured.

DRUGS: A DEATH WALK IN LIFE

According to a recent report regarding global use of illegal drugs, America consumes an estimated 60%. On a deeper level this means it has become a part of collective consciousness. Because of this, all entities will be touched or influenced by it whether they are drug users or not.

It is time to attempt to determine why there are so many entities who are suffering so much internal pain and emptiness within their lives. What within your culture has created so much pressure that human entities have such a great need to essentially escape from it? Why has life become so painful that so many entities, in their seeking a balm for their pain, have become addicted to the balm?

Many, especially those who are younger, take drugs out of curiosity or pressure from their peer group. Many younger entities haven't grown to the awareness of their own individuality and uniqueness and don't have the wisdom and knowledge to understand the long term effects of drug use, so they end up addicted. Generally speaking, there seems to be a period within the maturation process of the human entity where individuality and being true to yourself is not the way to fit in. In your particular culture there seems to be a time when it is more important to be a part of the group, no matter what that group may be doing, than to be an individual.

During the earlier part of the maturation process, the entity is oftentimes having his sense of ethics or what he has been taught as right or wrong challenged by the external world. The peer group appears so much wiser than the initial programmers (parents, guardians). Think back, Beloved Ones, to how many times your own belief systems have been challenged and shaken. Most frequently in the early programming of a child entity, the child is not taught the beauty and value of his own individuality and uniqueness, but rather how to fit into the culture he will express himself through. He is being programmed to be like others so that he will fit better in the external world. He learns that in order to be accepted, he must be like others. It does appear that the human entity gets along better if he remains aligned to societal and cultural patterns and rules. Most entities don't want to be considered a misfit, maladjusted, antisocial, or abnormal. These are all terms which denote an individual who is out of alignment with the collective set of standards.

If, then, the peer group is experimenting with drugs, an entity who wishes to fit in has already been programmed to believe that in order to be accepted, he must be like others. Many younger entities begin using drugs not because they really want to or really believe it is right to do so, but simply to be accepted.

Another reason younger entities may see no wrong in consuming drugs is because they have been reared in homes where drug use is present. Many entities who are responsible for the raising and the guiding of the young consume drugs which are considered to be legal, including sleeping pills, tranquilizers, pain pills, anti-anxiety drugs, diet pills, or alcohol. The young entity becomes aware that when the present reality is uncomfortable or painful, all one needs to do is to take the appropriate pill to make it go away. If a drug is considered to be legal, the message is that society says it's "okay" to take it; if it's labeled illegal it means that society says it's not "okay" to take it. As you know, children, the legality or illegality of any drug has nothing to do with the addictive potential. One can be a heavy user of legal drugs just as easily as he can be a heavy user of illegal drugs. It's just that the legal drug user can justify his habit more easily: "I can't sleep. I'm under pressure. I need to lose weight. I have a bad headache. I need to unwind. I'm depressed." The legal drug user does not have to hide his habit, and the risks of being arrested for his usage are for the most part, nonexistent.

There is also a considerably high usage of illegal drugs by those who are termed as unemployed or not working for wages. The question would be: Are these entities not working because they are on drugs, or are they on drugs because they are not working? Generally speaking, most human entities need to feel purposeful; they need to feel that their life has some relevant meaning to the Whole of Life. They need to be able to express outwardly whatever gifts and talents they might have. Overall, most human entities upon your planet are not able to do this, and this leads to greater inner frustration which then leads them into seeking something to fill the inner void and to ease the inner pain. Oftentimes it leads to drugs. Your particular culture is extremely stress filled and makes a lot of demands upon a human entity. Success is frequently measured by one's accumulation of things in the outer world, which increases the entity's need to have more. Competition is intense and causes the entity to work harder to be more in order to have more. The one not working oftentimes feels defeated and like a failure and thus will seek something in order to feel better about himself. And sometimes entities, whether they're working or not, will use drugs or other methods of relief to escape from a reality which has become too overwhelming to cope with in present consciousness. If, according to your own polls, over 90% of the people working are unhappy, that should tell you something about the system you have created. If drug use is skyrocketing, then it is time to examine your culture and the collective consciousness which exists. Removal of all your drugs is not going to solve the problem.

Regardless of the reasons an entity may offer for his ingesting of drugs, the risk is the same: addiction. In the trading of one reality for what an entity might believe to be a better reality, the entity essentially enters into a self destructive mode. Addiction to any drug becomes a death walk in life.

Some have said that drugs are beneficial for consciousness expansion because of their mind altering properties. Some have said they will assist one in having high visions, seeing into other worlds, or connecting with the inner essence. Beloved Ones, you don't need drugs for this. You need a brain computer operating at full capacity to receive information from your mind. Your drugs create chaos in your brain computer, and what you receive becomes distorted. So many of your drugs destroy brain cells and cause distorted commands to rage throughout your form, causing you to do things you would not ever do in a clear state of consciousness.

192

The accelerated usage of drugs in your world and in your culture will touch everyone whether they use drugs or not. There will be more deaths, more destruction, more crime, and more unhappiness worldwide. It will affect your productivity, creativity, and economy. All levels of life will be affected, and all will pay the price no matter how innocent they may be.

On one level it looks like a planet of entities who have given up on third dimensional life because, as I stated, high and continued usage of drugs is a death knell to the human form. It appears that those who use drugs and have become addicted no longer care. And that's what drugs do—they create a temporary release from present reality in which one doesn't care. The caring returns when the drug wears off and the entity needs another fix.

So why, Beloved Ones, are you globally being challenged by this problem, and what can be done? It's not a simple task. You are creating mandatory drug testing in industry, you're having dogs sniffing out drugs in schools, you're creating more laws and greater punishment for offenders and sellers, you're creating groups to support and rehabilitate those who wish to give up their addictions, and you're creating campaigns to program entities into not wanting to use drugs. All of these things will assist and all will have beneficial effects.

Because all individual consciousness feeds directly into collective consciousness and impacts it, be it ever so slightly, you must begin at home within yourself. You must examine your attitudes concerning drug use. If you are a legal drug user, examine why you ingest drugs and the amount you are using. What kind of messages are you programming the young in your home with? How do you feel about yourself, your home, and your job? If you are an illegal drug user, you must examine what in your life is causing you so much pain that you wish to escape from it.

Beloved Ones, in spite of all that I have said, it is important for you to know that I make no judgments with respect to those who use drugs and those who do not. One is not better than the other. All entities, no matter what they are doing, are expressions of God. Drugs, in and of themselves, are neither good nor bad. They just are. They are just another illusion you have created for your learning on the collective level. Everything which has been offered to man was, in its purest form, for the highest good and became tainted in manifested form when man did not understand the original purpose or discovered he could make money from it or have power over others by it. Most of your illegal drugs which are causing so much pain in your world today, in their purest form could have been used

193

in the healing of the human form. They've been used in ignorance rather than in wisdom, and thus you have created a new challenge and a new lesson.

The shift away from illegal drug use will not come by removal of the drugs, but rather by the removal of the problems creating the need for drugs. Most human entities who begin using drugs and become addicted to them are attempting to fill a void, ease inner pain, or escape from what the outer world is showing to them. For the habitual drug user, the journey is always downhill, and it doesn't matter whether it's Librium or Valium or cocaine or heroin.

What must occur is a shift in collective consciousness regarding the usage of drugs. Many human entities live in avoidance of life, and when one lives in avoidance and in resistance to the reality he has created by his own thinking, he is not fully living or fully experiencing. Drugs do not change your reality; they change only your perception of your reality. Human entities must come to realize their value and purpose to the All of Creation. Younger entities must be programmed and older entities must be reprogrammed to understand their own beauty and uniqueness as individual expressions of God. When you understand your own value, you will do nothing to knowingly harm yourself. Human entities need to learn how to handle stress in life, and their perceived pain and discomfort, more creatively and with greater courage. When you come to realize that no life experience, no matter how unpleasant it may appear, is permanent, you will not seek to escape from it but will learn from it and move forward. When you reach the awareness that the importance lies not in what happens in life, but rather in how you handle what happens, you will begin thinking properly and taking charge of your own life.

Entities, you always have the choice as to whether you will be in control of your own life or be controlled by the elements in your life. In closing, let me remind you, Beloved Ones, that you were created out of strong stuff. The river of God runs through you. You are connected to and one with the One Power. There is nothing you cannot change or overcome, collectively or individually. Your minds are powerful enough to create your own illusions, and you always have the choice as to what you will create; you have the choice as to whether you will create angels or demons in your lives. When you truly realize the magnificence of your own creation and its relationship to the Whole, you will allow none of your earthly illusions to hold you in bondage. You were meant to be free to express and experience the fullness of life, and you cannot do this if the colors of your life are dulled by your opiates. Life Itself is a continual high once you learn how to live it!

YOU, THE ENLIGHTENED ONE

Enlightenment is not a condition which occurs suddenly, although one can become enlightened about an area of one's life quite suddenly. Enlightenment comes as the result of an ongoing process through Life. It is a journey, and each entity's path of enlightenment is unique to himself. The journey is always an inner one, and the more one feels he has become enlightened about his outer life, the more he comes to realize that true enlightenment is really concerned with his own beingness.

In an entity's seeking to become enlightened and to know himself, he may walk upon many paths, hoping to find that which he seeks in religion, philosophy, or dogma. He may become involved in esoteric and metaphysical studies. He may search for his answers in the area of crystals, pyramids, numerology, astrology, channeling, and all of those things which have been labelled as occult. He may attend workshops and seminars and read many books. As an entity continues to introduce himself more and more to these things, he does become more aware, but he only becomes more enlightened when that in his outer world touches the inner world, removing a shadow, and teaching him something about the truth of himself.

Many entities in the New Age community think that crystals have the power to heal, to raise one's vibratory level, to assist one in being able to center and focus in meditation, and to assist in the communication with higher dimensions of consciousness. It is true that crystals have energy, but then so does everything else upon your physical planet. Whatever power a crystal might have is whatever an entity chooses to empower it with. It is not the power of the crystal which can produce healing; it is one's belief that it can which produces healing. If you believe that a crystal can assist in raising your vibratory level or help you to focus, it can. It is always as you believe. The crystal does not do anything but become empowered by your belief in its power.

Do not feel that I am saying these things are invalid. What I am trying to make clear is that they are tools which can aid you in your search. I want you to understand that it is your own believing, your own empowered thoughts, which enable certain things in your manifested world to work. In the area of healing, for instance, whether it's medicine or a crystal, it is your mind, The Mind, that is the healer.

In the world of physical objects, collective belief also plays a role in how much power or value an object is assigned. A rhinestone or a dewdrop on a rose shimmers just as brightly as a diamond, yet the diamond has been assigned the higher value by the collective mind.

Whatever value or power the objects and symbols of your world have is whatever the individual and collective mind have agreed on through belief.

Such things as the Tarot, the casting of Runes, the I Ching, and other forms of divination can offer you great insights into yourself. They can offer you insights as to where you are in consciousness and where you may travel if your present consciousness does not shift. In the area of methods of divination, the validity and credibility of them has much to do with how attuned and credible the reader or the interpreter is. Most entities who seek in this area are really desirous of knowing what's going to happen next: the future. You must always remember that your future is not preset. There is a myriad of possible futures, and what happens in one's life walk is directly influenced by where he is in present consciousness and by what thoughts he chooses to generate and empower. The slightest shift in consciousness and thinking can move one toward a different choice of that which you call future. Beloved Ones, you have greater control over that which is called tomorrow than you realize. To be frank, there is no future; there is only your now moment, and it's the now moment which determines your next moment. The more enlightened you become, the less need you will have of forms of divination, psychic readers, and channels. As you grow, you will be able to know where you are and where you are heading just by being attuned to your own present consciousness. You will know when your own empowered thoughts are carrying you where you may not wish to go, and you will know how to shift them. You will learn to take control of your own life and take responsibility for what it may or may not contain.

Astrology is a little different in that entities are influenced to some degree by objects within your sun system and beyond it. As with divination, the accuracy of an astrological reading has to do with the wisdom, knowledge, intuitiveness, and integrity of the interpreter. An astrological reading can provide insights about oneself and the planetary patterns and movements which may have an effect on individual and planetary life. An entity enters the material plane at a preestablished time, and this is the only thing which has been set prior to entering. Before entering you have chosen when you will enter in order to learn what you must learn and teach what you must teach.

With respect to the Ouija board, again you must look at this with discernment. The Ouija board is a tool and has no power in or of itself. The power or influence lies within the entity who is using it. One who uses it seriously is doing no more than channeling, using the board as a tool or focal point. Information still moves through the human channel. Many entities call it the tool of the Devil and see it as something dangerous or evil. It is only as good or as evil as the human entity who uses it. When you decide to use your telephone, you have the choice of whether you will make a threatening, obscene call to someone or a kind and loving one. The phone is simply the vehicle, the instrument. What is received via the Ouija board is directly related to the awareness level, the credibility, and the integrity of the user, the human channel.

The serious seeker who yearns to become enlightened may travel upon many paths, and he may involve himself in many studies in many areas. He may look out upon a great banquet table filled to overflowing with inviting delicacies, promising fulfillment and the answers to Life. He may sample them all, and in those experiences he learns and grows and becomes wiser. In the end he will discover what he really already knows: that he is already that which he seeks to be. Beloved Ones, you do not have to seek enlightenment. The Life Journey itself is enlightenment. Life is a process of growth, change, and unfoldment, and this is enlightenment. Life is always a movement toward Light. The term enlightenment is nebulous, and the Holy Grail you seek so diligently upon the Banquet Table of Life, or the Excalibur you wish to pull from the stone, is really the knowing of yourself in totality. Enjoy your journey, but remember that the real journey is within. All that lies outside yourself on the material plane is but an instrument to guide you back to the inner plane of your own being and help you discover the truth and beauty of You, the Enlightened One.

A TIME FOR WINGS

Many human entities experience their life journeys feeling a sense of loss. One entity at the New Year's passing stated: "I feel I've lost a year. I'll never have it again." With a greater sense of loss, others have recently said: "I've lost the love of my life." "I've lost my job." "I've lost my husband." "I've lost my home". These are sad statements coupled with a deep longing for what has been perceived as being lost.

But, I ask you, Beloved Ones, can you ever really lose what is no longer right for you to have in your process of growing and unfolding? Does springtime's butterfly cry in her winged flight, "I've lost the security of my cocoon?" Does the chirping baby robin bemoan breaking free from his tiny blue egg? Does the autumn apple tree weep when the winds come and strip her branches bare of their crisp leaves? You have heard that within the process of Life there is a time and a season for all things, and when things change within your lives it is not loss, but only

Life preparing you for new adventure, new experiences. You will always have what is right for you to have within the process of growing and unfolding, but oftentimes you do not see this because your consciousness is focused upon loss. Whatever your consciousness is focused upon is what you shall empower and draw to you, and it becomes what is right for you in that moment.

Whenever you say you've lost something or someone, it indicates that at some level you felt you possessed that something or someone. If you did not, you would not experience a sense of loss. It also indicates that at some level that someone or something had value, for you do not experience a sense of loss over that which you do not value.

The truth is, Beloved Ones, you cannot possess others, and everything which you have in your lives is really on loan to you to make your lives happier, easier, and more comfortable. You own nothing, as you will understand in your own passing. So, when changes come, as they must do for you to grow, then you must release and move forward, making way for the new to enter. As long as you hold onto loss consciousness, you will block the path of the new. As long as you hold onto a lost relationship, a new one cannot begin. As long as you hold onto the sadness of a job or a home lost, doors cannot open. In truth, nothing is ever lost except in your own perception, and likewise nothing is ever found except through your perception. That is why I say, perceive anew and you will no longer see loss, but merely growth and change.

You will never lose what is right for you to have on your journey, but when you grow beyond your right to have it, it will be removed from your life for the purpose of your unfoldment. And when it is removed, you have the choice as to whether to perceive it as a loss or as an opening to enhance your own growing. One perception imprisons you while the other frees you and opens you up to the gifts of the universe. You can kneel huddled with your arms clasped to your breast, or you can stand up and throw your arms wide open, ready to receive. Nothing can be placed in hands held in the fist position. To receive, they must be open and extended. This, by the way, is also the hand position for giving.

Life is a process of shifting, changing, movement, transformation, transition, regeneration, and renewal. It flows like a timeless river to the sea of your own being. Life is a wondrous and exciting journey, Beloved Ones; a journey filled with newness and adventure and challenges and opportunities. Remember that the cocoon of the butterfly had its purpose and reason for being in its own time and season, but now the time is right for springtime's wings!

LIFE: A GIFT MORE THAN A RIGHT

The process called abortion is the stoppage of the development of a fetus through artificial means. In your culture it has become a political, legal, moral, and religious issue and often an explosive one. It is an issue fraught with diverse opinions, judgments, and perspectives. So, what I will offer to you concerning this issue will not be a judgment on the rightness or the wrongness of abortion. This is something each individual entity must decide for himself based upon his own level of awareness and belief system.

Life, itself, is a gift more than it is a right. Many of your entities speak of "the right to life" and "the right to live." But then you have to determine what life and being alive really mean. Does it simply mean that one's brain is functioning and his heart is beating and blood is circulating throughout the physical organic system? Or does being alive mean something more, such as the quality of life? You have only to look at your world, Beloved Ones, to see that thousands of children perish of starvation and disease before they ever reach adulthood. You have only to look at your own culture to see the increasing numbers of homeless families with children struggling just to survive. Many of your entities concern themselves with the rights of the unborn while seemingly forgetting about those child entities already born. This, children, is not a judgment but merely an observation.

Ideally, of course, no child should be born who is not wanted, but this is not always the case, as your incidents of child abuse, child molestation, and child deaths indicate. Just as there are entities who should not be pet owners, there are those who really should not take on the responsibility of parenthood.There are many human entities who become parents who should not become parents, and the lessons for all concerned become painfully hard on the mundane level. So many do not understand that the role of parent carries with it great responsibility. The parent is guardian, protector, and teacher for part of the child entity's journey. He is the one who prepares this child to enter the adult world, and what a child learns is oftentimes what he takes with him, be it love or hate or pain or joy. And, generally, what he takes with him, unless he is strong enough to overcome adverse programming, he passes on to his children and the cycle remains unbroken.

Remember that physical form is the illusion. It is the vehicle needed for the expression of the spirit during its journey through the mundane world. Spirit is the reality, and although you can seemingly destroy (or change) form, you do not have it within your power to annihilate the spirit.

In that process called abortion where form is seemingly destroyed, is it murder? Is it killing? In truth, nothing ever dies. Energy is changed into new energy; it is shifted, but not really destroyed. Therefore, you cannot really kill anything.

For those considering abortion, examine your intent and motive behind that potential action, and evaluate—from a place void of fear and filled with love and unselfishness—what would serve the highest good. For each individual it will be different, because each individual circumstance will be different. What might be perceived as right action for one may not be so for another. It should be an individual choice as to what will truly serve the highest good.

Life is a gift, Beloved Ones, and the children who come through you represent both a gift and a promise, particularly if they are loved and wanted. Seek your higher guidance for answers, and when those answers come to you, trust them and act on them. As with most issues, there is no one way, one answer, or one truth. Each individual contains his own answers and his own truth.

THE PURPOSE OF TERRORISM
AND HOW IT CAN BE TRANSFORMED

There has been much media and public attention directed at terrorist actions. Within the mass consciousness two things create and generate fear, hatred, want of revenge, and a host of other negative vibrations: (1) the actual overt actions of non-love by those entities labelled as terrorists, and (2) the perceptions and interpretations of these actions by the press, world leaders, and governments. Depending on where one lives (Libya, Israel, the United States), a different interpretation will be offered to the peoples of those nations regarding terrorist attacks. So the facts and truth which will be offered to you will be different from those which are offered in Libya, for example. This is what you must always remember when reading or listening to the news about conflicts between nations: there are many perceptions of the truth. How you, as an individual entity, perceive an external illusion within your world will always be based on your belief system, your current level of awareness, and by how much your thinking is influenced by mass consciousness.

Terrorism is an action designed to create and promote a reaction of intense fear. How one perceives an action will determine his reaction. Those who are aware enough not to yield to, submit to, or be intimidated by another's actions will be able to see beyond the overt external action (illusionary reality) and into the internal causes behind the overt actions.

Yielding to or being intimidated by what has been labelled as terrorist actions will blind you to whatever truth or lessons are contained within those actions. Fear always creates a blinding effect and paralyzes the mind from proper thinking, preventing the appropriate reaction necessary to bring peace and balance into being. One might also consider the following question: If the intent of terrorism is to create intense fear and to intimidate and if this action is thwarted by a lack of fear, then does terrorism really exist? I think you can understand that terrorism works because the mass consciousness allows it to work, and its negative energy is increased by not only fear, but hate and a desire for revenge as well. "An eye for an eye" has never been a workable solution because it keeps the Karmic wheel turning. And sooner or later, all the eyes are gone and all men are blind.

Now, you may wonder if there is any value or purpose in acts of terrorism? In your world of duality, it would appear that these illusions are necessary for the unfoldment of mankind. If they weren't, you wouldn't create them. Your world is filled with entities of varying levels of awareness and myriads of belief systems. From the awareness levels and belief systems of the masses of human entities, thoughts and perceptions and manifestations are born. Until entities grow beyond their own prejudices and assumptions that only they can be right, then conflict will continue. And until entities begin listening and really hearing one another, that which you call terrorism will continue. Realize about terrorist actions, particularly those of revolutionaries, that the destruction of lives or property is not the primary objective. The primary objective is to create an awareness of some kind, to make a statement. If you can only see and react to an overt action, you will never understand the statement being made. Some of you who recall the time warp of the 1960's understand that sometimes revolutionary methods seem to be the only way to create positive shifts within a culture which may be deaf. Until man evolves beyond what he presently is, it appears that positive shifts oftentimes must be born of chaos and violence.

I caution those of higher awareness levels to take care that they do not make judgments. Remember that you are given but a paragraph of the whole story. You see but one scene within the unfolding drama, and you can't see behind the scenes or with accuracy interpret the playwright or know what is in his heart or his totality. You do not have to like what you see, nor do you have to agree with the script, but do not judge when you are not able to see the whole drama.

I realize that you find actions of non-love appalling and you find difficulty in comprehending how some entities can destroy others so easily or even how they can give up their lives to perform missions of terrorism. It's not necessary that you understand this. What you should understand are those things you already know: there are no accidents, there are no victims, there is no death, and all is agreed on by involved entities on a higher level. Most human entities do not believe this, but it is this knowing that will cause you to move beyond the external overt actions and move you into a greater cosmic awareness of the true lesson contained within the action. You move from what happened, how it happened, when it happened, and who did it, to why it happened. When you are ready to seek the "why," you will journey to your own center and know why because you are a part of everything that happens. You are connected to those who die and those who kill.

Acts of terrorism, as with other acts of non-love, can be transformed only by the Love energy. It begins in your own inner being. It begins by releasing yourself from those things which block your own Love energy: such things as hate, fear, prejudice, desire for revenge, and so forth. If you give power to negative thoughts, you increase the negative vibrations within mass consciousness. If you say "we should kill all terrorists," you are adding negative energy to collective mind. Lift your awareness to the level where you are able to understand your connection with all aspects of Creation. Once you can feel this connection, you will hate and fear nothing. Once released from fear and hate, you are free to move out in Love. From Love comes healing, transformation, and positive change—the Birth of the New Age.

WIND, TREE AND ROCK TYPE THINKING

Mass consciousness is very much like a great sea with many depths of moving energies and vibrations. The highest vibrational entities ride atop the waves, much like a master surfer. Others who have not yet learned to master or control their vibrations spend most of their time under the waves. They become trapped within a certain vibrational level. Others lie on the bottom and are either unwilling or lack the knowledge of how to move upward through the depths to the surface. This is, of course, the lowest vibrational level.

Each human entity adds his own individual energy and vibrations to the great sea of mass consciousness. How one thinks and perceives has a critical bearing on the vibrations and energies he pours into the great sea, and his individual energy and vibrations determine his placement or level within the sea.

Thinking and perceiving are critical to what is poured into the sea of mass consciousness. Each human entity, in truth, bears some responsibility for what is contained within it. You cannot separate yourself from it, and if you desire to play a part in shifting mass consciousness to the higher vibrational levels, you must, as I've always told you, begin first with yourself. Once an entity has become a master of his own vibrations and energies, he must be willing to teach others to swim from the lower depths. No one can swim for another, and no one can master another's vibrations, but he can become an example or a teacher.

There are many different kinds of thinkers and perceivers in your world, but I am going to concentrate on three, using as symbols the wind, the tree, and the rock.

An entity who thinks like the wind has a mind which is in continual motion, moving at various and changing velocities, ready to experience everything it comes in contact with. It is a mind which is open and free. It is always seeking and always learning. It cannot stop. It is like a cup never filled and yet never empty.

An entity who thinks like a tree is one who is rooted to the earth, yet allows his branches to be touched. Thus, there is some movement. He will allow his thinking to only go so far because he is truly rooted to his belief system and his programming. He is partially open. If some of his roots are pulled from the earth, he has difficulty coping with what he will perceive as a loss. He wants to know only so much and finds comfort in his roots.

The one who thinks like a rock is firm and set in both his belief system and his perceptions of truth. He feels he has all the answers he needs, and he has no desire to seek or know more. He is immovable and limited. Although he might feel comfortable, he is imprisoned by the earth which is his bed.

There are, of course, many levels of thinking between the rock and the wind. To discern where you might be within the vibrational sea of mass consciousness, it is necessary to study your own process of thinking, the way in which you perceive your illusions, and your attachments to your current belief system. What things, if any, are you rooted to? How firm are you in those things you say you believe in? What have you been programmed by?

A human entity, whether awake or asleep, is always receiving thought energy from the Universal Mind, other human entities, and even mass consciousness itself. Your brain computer is constantly being bombarded with thought energy. A large portion of thought energy filters into the brain computer data storage areas without ever being acknowledged on the conscious level. Thought energy is neutral until it is dealt with on the conscious level, and is acknowledged by individual perception. It is individual perception which charges it with either negative or positive vibrations. Individual perception is influenced greatly by one's prior programming. Most programming, with the exception of basic survival programming, comes from prior experience or from what has been told to you by others. The programming you have accepted for yourself comprises your belief system.

To change your own vibrational level and affect the mass consciousness you must be willing to become more like a wind thinker. You must begin perceiving thought energy with more neutrality. When you charge your perception of a thought with negative or positive vibrations, it should be based on your now moment rather than on prior programming. You must also be willing to shift your belief system when new data is supplied to you.

To charge your now perceptions with positivity, learn and understand that all of your experiences and illusions are neutral in themselves. They stand before you like a painting or the words upon a page. Your response or perception charges them with positivity or negativity. In other words, you make a judgment. Judgments are often made out of fear, prejudice, prior programming, and rock-solid belief systems. The human entity will seldom, if ever, remain neutral in a perception. If you cannot perceive with neutrality, strive to seek the gift within each now perception, because it is there waiting to be perceived. You must move beyond labeling things as right and wrong, truth and falsehood, good and bad. These are perceptual judgments. They are individual distinctions which pour into mass consciousness and become part of its energy. If mass consciousness appears negative, it is because there are more entities upon your planet perceiving negatively and sending this energy and its vibrations into the collective mind.

Each entity does make a difference within collective mind. The more entities who can become masters of their own thinking and perception, the greater their influence will be within collective mind. Entities always have a choice as to what kind of thinkers they will be, and they always have the freedom to move from the rock to the wind.

THE PURPOSE OF MONEY

It has been said that "the love of money is the root of all evil." This is true when entities believe that accumulation of money should be the primary objective of life. When one holds the attitude or the belief that the

204

accumulation of money is the primary goal in life, this goal becomes his god, and other things can enter in: such things as greed, selfishness, want of power, and egocentricity.

In your world a system has been created whereby money is exchanged for things: food, houses, clothing, land, cars, and on and on. This is what money is: what you exchange for something else, one created illusion to exchange for another. There is nothing wrong with your system if you will see it for what it truly is: merely something to exchange for something else.

To receive money a human offers his time, knowledge, talents, and abilities in service to another. The one who works only for money will never truly be happy, for he is offering himself for the wrong reason.

You may say, "Well, I must do work in order to survive, and to survive I need money!" In your system this is partially true, for you do need something to exchange for the elements of your survival, and *all* that you do is the Creator in you expressing, and this is to be blessed. If you learned to see yourself as God expressing in all areas, then you would find joy in all that you do. You would not differentiate between work and play. You would simply be God expressing through you in different ways.

Part of the problem which many entities have in the area of money has to do with mass consciousness. There is an idea that an entity is only successful if he accumulates a lot of wealth, money, and things. In truth, success is what you believe about your own self. It has nothing to do with the standards and definitions set up by mass consciousness, and has nothing to do with wealth or lack of it. It has to do with how you feel about your own being.

Let us talk about the value of money. If you were in the desert and were starving and dying for want of food and water, and a man came along and offered you a choice between a bag filled with gold coins and jewels and a basket filled with food and water, which would you choose? Your sense of value would shift to what you needed, and food and water would have greater value than gold and jewels.

What I truly want you to do is to see money for what it is within your system: a medium of exchange. It is nothing else. So do not make the accumulation of money your god, for it is truly a false and temporary god. When you leave your plane of experience you will take none of your created physical illusions with you, for beyond your plane they will have no relevance. When you work, do so with the joy of offering your time, talents, abilities, and knowledge, and be grateful that you have been gifted with abilities and talents. Do not see your labors as unimportant or without value. Whatever you do is God expressing, so enter into it with joy.

In the New Age, your system of exchange will no longer be based on money. All entities will offer their individual gifts, talents, time, and knowledge to the whole, and humankind will prosper in abundance and love. Perhaps this sounds utopian and idealistic, but it is the primary method used by advanced beings in other sun systems, and it is called the Love System. The time will come upon your planet when money will be obsolete. It is not yet here for there is still much planetary unfolding to take place, but you can prepare a bit by reviewing your own attitudes and perceptions about money and its value to you.

A NEW ORDER LIES WAITING

Perhaps the primary reason that human male entities and female entities have conflict between them is that they do not think or perceive in the same way. Each individual perceives, thinks, and interprets uniquely, but generally speaking, members of the same gender are able to understand each other and have great difficulty with members of the opposite gender.

Each individual entity contains both feminine and masculine energies, and each has the tendency to express either the masculine or the feminine energy to a greater degree. In other words, most human entities are not in balance; males tend to express the masculine energy to a greater degree, and females the feminine energy. A lot of masculine and feminine expression is due to programming, as well as genetic tendencies. Programming is more responsible for conflict between the genders than genetic tendencies.

When an Earth child is born, he or she already has certain genetic tendencies to be either masculine or feminine, and Beloved Ones, one's genetic tendency has nothing to do with outer form. Masculine tendencies can be inherent in the female form, and feminine tendencies can be contained within the male form. As the child grows, masculinity or femininity is taught or programmed by the entities within the culture in which the child is reared. Little boy forms are programmed to be masculine, and little girl forms to be feminine. Stress occurs when the inherent tendency is opposite to the programming the form is receiving from the outer world. For example, a male child may have inherent feminine tendencies, and because he is male in form, he receives masculine programming. This creates stress because of a misalignment.

Fortunately, this has begun to shift, and the early programming is changing a bit. When the shift is complete, what you will have will be entities expressing the greater truth of their beingness. Since the human entity contains both energies, each will discover that it is alright to express both qualities of femininity and masculinity. When male and female entities feel free to express all of their qualities, then there will be understanding between the genders. When there is understanding, there will be no conflict.

At the present time, however, there appears to be great confusion between the genders, and hence, much conflict. An obvious manifestation of the confusion is seen in what are termed your divorce rates in the past 25 or 30 Earth years. Prior to this time, most human entities who entered into that which is termed marriage remained together. Were these entities happier and more fulfilled than you? Not always, but they were less confused about their roles and what was expected of them by the outer world. Earlier, human entities knew their places, and they did not think about masculine and feminine energies, and in the earlier eras, the outer world and collective thought were predominantly masculine in orientation, as you well know.

In the late 1930's and 1940's of your Earth time, there was a great influx of spirits entering forms. These new entities I have called starseed intitiates, lightworkers, or preparers for a New Age, whose mission was to shift the consciousness of your planet. They began their work in the Earth time of your 1960's, and it has been continuing since then. Although that period appeared chaotic and filled with rebellion, great and positive changes resulted. Remember, Beloved Ones, that destruction and creation are part of the same process, and that the seed must break before the flower can come forth and stretch to the sun.

It was that time period which increased the confusion between the genders, particularly for that group of entities born in the 30's and 40's to change collective consciousness. They had been programmed by entities of another age, and they were creating a new order, a new way of thinking, perceiving, and interpreting. The offspring of this group will be less confused about their roles, and be more balanced with respect to their masculine and feminine energies.

Many of the entities who chose to enter in the 1930's and 1940's are in confusion because they have been doubly programmed—by the old order of thought and by the new order they have created. There is something within which feels a certain loyalty to the old ways and something else which stretches forth to the new; hence, the inner confusion. In that which is termed as the marriage relationship, for example, there is a feeling that a couple should remain in the relationship no matter how unhealthy it may be. There is oftentimes the conflicting belief that each individual has an inherent right to be happy and fulfilled

207

on the Life journey, and if the relationship is no longer bringing forth growth, it must be closed. The entity in this particular grouping has possibly had to do more releasing from prior programming than others in past times, and this is simply because he has been the recipient of dual programming. So closures of relationships are quite prevalent in this group of entities.

What has been created within our consciousness over the past 25 or 30 Earth years? There has been greater acceptance among entities and increased understanding. Beloved Ones, you are discovering that you do have the right to be happy and fulfilled in Life. You are discovering that in your god essence you contain both feminine and masculine energies and that it's alright to express both. You are discovering that you are not your form, but rather God expressing beautifully and uniquely through form. You are discovering that you are not just male or female, but are multifaceted, multidimensional beings. You are discovering that you are the creator of your own reality, and the architect of your own life, and that you are responsible for your own actions and reactions. You are discovering that relationships are gardens for your growth, learning, and unfoldment, and that if these are no longer producing flowers, you must move forward. You are discovering that there are many levels of awareness in your world and that they all contain truth for someone. You are discovering that there is no higher or lower, better or worse, or good or bad, but only differences. You are discovering that it does not serve you to blame, judge, or compare. You are discovering that you are just where you are supposed to be in a now moment. You are discovering that you are One with All Creation. You are discovering that you must love and accept the beauty and wonder of your own beingness and find joy and excitement in the process of your own becomingness. And you are discovering that you must allow yourself the freedom to be who and what you are in your now moments. You are your own reality and your own world and your own gift. Beloved Ones, what you do for the beauteous creation called you, you will offer to others. The freedom and acceptance that you offer yourself, you will offer to others.

What I am really talking about is freedom and allowance: freedom to be and to become, and the allowance of others to be and become. With that will come understanding and communication, and from that the honest and loving relationships between the genders. As a planetary people, you're not there yet, but you will be one day. The time will come when you will be aware of only essence, and you will see organic form and all the many judgments and prejudices about form as illusion.

Consciousness is shifting, confusion is lifting, and a new order lies waiting on the horizon.

Essentially the male and female entities of planet Earth are journeying in transitional and transformational times. With transition there is always struggle, the need to release from the old, confusion, reprogramming, and perceived chaos. The gift of transition, children, is transformation, the wondrous emergence of a new creation, a new being. The transition, the process from the cocoon of the old, brings forth the flight and freedom of the butterfly into the new. You live in wondrous times, so bless your struggles and your confusion, for they contain the clear vision of a new order.

THE GRASS IS ALWAYS GREENER

The student pointed and said to his master: "Look, Master, across the valley. The grass is so much greener than it is beneath our feet." The master smiled and replied: "My son, grass is green wherever it is nurtured and cared for. It has little to do with which side of the valley it grows upon."

You've heard the saying, "The grass is always greener on the other side," and sometimes it is, sometimes it isn't. The greenness of grass or anything else is dependent on your own individual perceptions.

So many human entities spend their life walks feeling so dissatisfied and unfulfilled that they are forever looking outward from themselves and wanting what is not present in their own lives. The dissatisfaction and wanting cause the entity to be blind to whatever good is in his own life. Hence, he cannot nurture the gifts he has been blessed with.

Many human entities, because they envision the grass to be greener on the other side, will give up what they have in order to possess something else, only to find that the something else was not what they wanted after all. Greater dissatisfaction is experienced when an entity realizes that that which he gave up was of greater value, and this becomes a great lesson to him. To lose something or to give something up only to discover its value later can be very painful indeed. To realize that the grass in your own life was green all the time and that you were too busy looking over your neighbor's fence to notice creates a deep sense of loss. The saying, "You never knew what you had until you lost it" can become a profound awareness.

There is nothing wrong with desiring more in Life, Beloved Ones, for oftentimes the desiring is an inner urging to stretch more and to grow into greater beingness. The wise entity knows that no matter where he is, the greenness of grass is dependent upon his own willingness to care for and nurture it. Stars glitter and twinkle in the distance, but become hot, fiery suns the closer you come to them. They are not what they appear to be in the night sky. So also the grass across the valley may not be as green as you may think.

The wise entity, even when he is dissatisfied with his life, will look around at what is contained within it before moving on to what he may perceive to be greener pastures. The reason that there are so many broken relationships and missed opportunities is simply because human entities sometimes move too quickly without thinking. In frustration, perhaps, the dissatisfied entity will look at his life and determine that it has little or no value, and he will quickly move to abandon it in order to chase another rainbow. Rainbows are but lights shining through droplets of water producing beautiful colors. In time they dissipate.

As you've been told, you cannot make a mistake, for you will learn from all of your actions and decisions whether they have been well thought out or made with impulsiveness. What I'm trying to tell you, entities, is to learn to see the value present in your lives and the gifts contained therein.

The one who is dissatisfied with his life and who thinks the grass may be greener elsewhere believes he is dissatisfied because of something outside himself. Another person is not doing what he wants, his job is not challenging enough, or he can't have the material possessions he desires. In truth, the dissatisfied entity is dissatisfied with himself. In order to justify the dissatisfaction, he looks outward and blames the world around him. These entities devalue everything in their lives, abandon it all and move on to what they perceive as greener pastures. Once there, the pattern is reestablished. It will continue to be a pattern until the choice is made to break the pattern. If the pattern is not broken, the entity will never really experience satisfaction and fulfillment in his life, nor will he ever have the awareness of his own gifts.

To break the pattern, an entity must stop and see what is really contained within his self-created world. He must look and see those entities who share his world. It is only in the seeing that you can assess value because although you look with your ego and your eyes, you can only see with your mind and your heart. Looking can cause you to perceive greener pastures somewhere else, but seeing knows whether they are or not.

On your life journeys, children, you will experience many changes— in relationships, jobs, places, and belief systems. You will go through many transitions and transformations. You will cross many valleys, climb many mountains, and wander through many deserts. But wherever you are and before you move on, look and see where you are and discover the gifts and value that are present now. When you do move on, do so with higher vision, God vision, and not with ego vision which is oftentimes blind. Then you will move upon your life path, not chasing rainbows or seeking greener pastures, but merely discovering higher and finer beingness, and finding that the grass is always emerald beneath your feet.

WHY WE SOMETIMES FEEL
DETACHED AND DISCONNECTED

Sometimes we experience disconnection and feelings of detachment from our life experience. We sense a feeling of lowered vibrations and energy. This is more apparent to those who are growing in awareness, and it may be upsetting to them for the simple reason that they feel that one who is aware should be able to control and overcome these feelings which seem to permeate and invade the mental form.

This is a space for learning and growth, created by our higher levels of consciousness so that we may stop and become aware of where we've been, where we are, and where we appear to be heading. It's a space created to align us with our inner journey, which is far more important than our external journey.

Yes, it's nice to sit on the mountain peaks of life. Sometimes, however, it's necessary to stand upon a plateau where we can view the peaks and the valleys. We should use this time to become quiet and centered so that we are able to align ourselves with our Selves and with those higher forces that seek to direct us.

Often these periods occur after a time when we've experienced a lot of high activity and have expended a lot of creative energy. Or they can occur when there has been an increased flow of information from our external world. Just as the brain computer tells the artist to lay down his brush and rest or the surgeon to lay down his scalpel, so also do the higher energies tell us to draw back from external activity to rest so that our energy can be replenished. When information is rushing at us in torrents, a dam is put up so that we might have the time to sift through the information and process it in order to find our truth.

These periods of detachment are friends who have come to assist us in becoming more aligned, attuned, and connected. They are friends who have come to give us time to become quiet so that we might be revitalized.

Perhaps they are the ones who make us lie down in green pastures and who lead us beside the still waters and restore our souls.

Use these times to become quiet and revitalized so that you may re-enter life's arena with a renewed sense of enthusiasm, energy, connectedness, and clarity.

BEGINNINGS AND ENDINGS
ARE THE SAME

Due to the acceleration of time brought on by the heightening of the planetary vibrations, many human entities are beginning to experience great changes in their lives and a quickening of movement upon their life paths. For many this is very uncomfortable. The discomfort arises primarily because there is a resistance to releasing from past attachments. There is a fear and an uncertainty present about what the future might hold for them, and there is a confusion about why their life paths seem to be changing so rapidly. Resistance, fear, and confusion will always cause the changes to be more difficult.

If an individual can understand that life is not static, but changing and flowing, and that with each seeming ending a new beginning follows, he will be less resistant to what is occurring within his life experience. Beginnings and endings within one's life walk are but markers along the way to indicate where one has been and where he might be going. They are rather like roadsigns along a highway which denote changes on the road, the rules of the road, and the direction in which you are heading.

Change is occurring all the time on all levels of beingness, and it is change which creates individual growth and unfoldment. Sometimes the changes are so very subtle that human entities are simply not aware that change is always occurring. When change is subtle and goes unnoticed, one's life on the external level oftentimes appears static. So the entity becomes comfortable, complacent, safe, and secure.

When change is such that a major shift occurs, the entity does take notice, and this is where fear and resistance can enter the picture. Humans may not notice slight tremors, but they do wake up when they experience a major earthquake. No human walk is without major shifts, and the reason for this is because it is the major shifts which hold the greatest potential for growth and unfoldment. I say "hold the greatest potential for" because it is the human entity himself who will determine his own growth, as well as how this growth is achieved. Its expanse and magnitude are based on his state of consciousness and his level of awareness.

212

If a major shift occurs as a great change in one's life experience, it means the seeming ending of something. It also means the seeming beginning of something else. What might be ending has already been charged, either negatively or positively. What lies ahead, the new beginning, is neutral, waiting to be charged. If you are resistant to releasing from the old and if you fear the new, you are starting to negatively charge what lies before you. It can be like going through a doorway into a long corridor, and having the door slam behind you. In the distance, you see another closed door and you feel trapped in the corridor. You can't go back but you're afraid to go forward and open a new door for fear of what you may find. You are unwilling to release and go forward, but once you do, the door ahead automatically opens.

You don't have to have corridors in your life if you can understand that beginnings and endings are the same thing. One of awareness can pass through one doorway directly into the next room. Think of your homes. You can easily pass from one room to the next without opening and closing doors if you choose. The kitchen doesn't end because you have chosen to move into the dining room, but it's possible that your work in the kitchen is finished.

In truth, one's life walk is a flow, and it is you who have created the markers of beginnings and endings. There are no beginnings and endings; there is only a flow of your energy moving through that illusion called time, and of your energy flowing through that expression called *you* which is always seeking to better express and unfold to its fullest potential.

The entity who lives his life to the fullest and achieves his greatest potential is the one who is willing to release from those situations which no longer produce growth. He is the one who does not fear what might lie ahead and who views that which is termed the future as holding the gift of greater growth and unfoldment. He is the one who flows from one now moment to the next, who moves from one room of experience to another. He is the one who does not create and become entrapped in the corridors between what was and what might lie ahead.

True flow is accepting the now moment and allowing it to be, having the awareness to know that flow means change. True faith is knowing that you are One with All that Is. When you are in Oneness with the Eternal Flow of Life, you are also moving on the path of your greatest unfoldment and growth.

In closing, I would like to say that when major shifts are occurring on your life path—the earthquakes of the human experience, just know that these are gifts for you if you are not afraid to pull off the ribbons and wrappings and look inside. Those who fear a Pandora's Box will never open their gifts, but will sit out their lives wondering what the box contains. You may wonder what is in the box, what is the gift? It is whatever you think it is or want it to be. You create your own earthquakes so that you might grow. You also have the power to create the most wondrous gifts for yourself. Do not become entrapped like flies in the spiderwebs of illusions. Flow easily with the changes in your life, knowing that there is nothing which you cannot handle. You are strong because of the unlimited God Essence and Energy that flows through and gives Life to that wonderful expression called *you*.

PART VII

QUESTIONS & QUOTES

In the weekly meetings of the Universalia group, we would often channel on a famous quotation or on specific questions posed by one of the members of the group. This section includes some of these assignments. Although they are diverse in subject matter, Kyros continues to offer wisdom and new perspectives.

What is a master?

All human entities contain within them the potential to be masters. A master is one who has knowledge, and more importantly, he has taken his knowledge and converted it into wisdom. A true master is a teacher of wisdom, not merely a giver of knowledge. Knowledge and wisdom are not the same thing. When one takes knowledge and gleans from it those things which will promote the highest planetary good, wisdom is the gift.

Often masters are spiritual beings who attained high degrees of wisdom in other incarnations and other dimensional experiences and who have agreed to enter and undergo physical life for the purpose of ushering in a new age and raising the collective consciousness. With the birth of a new age there is a planetary need for enlightenment. What makes these beings different from earth masters is simply that the wisdom is already present within them and does not have to be attained during the present incarnation.

The wisdom does, however, need to be unlocked; the master does have to be awakened from his slumber. Most of these human entities go through normal life experiences gaining more knowledge and teaching just like everyone else on the planet. But a time will arrive when there is a need for the master to awaken, and the need is a planetary one. The awakened master begins to teach wisdom rather than knowledge, and the whole intent is to assist in the evolutionary shift of collective mind. This is presently occurring all over planet Earth.

An awakened master will always recognize a brother in a slumbering state or one who is struggling through the transitional process from

215

slumbering to awakening. Because the need for masters is so great during planetary and universal transcension, an awakened master will work with his brother to bring him into the full awareness of that which he already knows at deeper levels. He will essentially guide the awakening master to deeper levels, to his inner pool of attained wisdom, and assist him in moving it up to the surface waters of the conscious state. This is where the newly awakened master comes into full power and is able to perform his mission which, collectively, is that of planetary enlightenment. So I say again to all of you, do not be resistant to new energies that enter your lives, although do be discerning. If you should happen to be a sleeping master, these new energies may well be your guides back to what you already know. An awakening master will know, if he is attuned to his inner guidance, who his guides are. The awakened master will journey with his brother until he senses that his brother is fully awake and ready to move outward on his own and become a teacher himself.

So, you may ask, if one is an awakening master, how does he know it? There are frequent transformational shifts in his awareness and in the way he views planetary life. He begins moving away from his ego base and into greater spiritual alignment. He becomes sensitized to all of Creation and begins to become aware of his connection to it. He ceases to question because when one knows, he does not need to question. He does not run around telling others he is a master but simply and quietly does his work which has been assigned him. Although he is connected to all of Life, he is at the same time detached from it, for he knows that to attach to any single thing is to surrender power, and to be attached to any single thing in the illusionary world is to fragment Life. Even though the mission of these masters is to shift collective mind through the process of enlightenment, he does not live in the future but rather works within timelessness, which is the now moment.

Many who do not understand will try to pull him back into the seemingly safe net of traditional programming, but once the master is fully awakened, the change will have been so great that he can never return. The whole point of his life journey on planet Earth was to reach the Earth time warp where he could do his work. Rarely will these masters awaken before the Earth time of thirty years of age, and sometimes the process will be slow, particularly if the Earth entity has been operating from a strong ego base. You will find these entities in all walks of human experience. Do not presume to find them only in the high spiritual centers, for masters reside in the ghettos of human life as well. And do not presume that they will always speak their wisdom, for some of the greatest wisdom is conveyed more through a look or the touch of a hand than from the golden tongues of your finest orators. Wisdom is impersonal and is channeled through its chosen vessels in myriad and diverse ways. If you would seek wisdom, then you must be willing to journey into the very heart of Life and experience the pulsating heartbeat of All of Creation.

Let the dead bury their dead.

Your Christian theologians most often interpret the term dead in this quotation as that of being spiritually dead. Spirit cannot die, but through an entity's choice or free will, it can be inactive on the physical plane. Spirit is always alive in higher levels of consciousness but if it is blocked, usually by the ego, it cannot manifest in one's physical life to any great degree. Some perceive an entity who blocks the spiritual flow as being spiritually dead when he really should be perceived as spiritually inactive.

If one is spiritually inactive, only he can remove the blockages which prevent spirit guidance from flowing into his consciousness. Only he has the free will to remove blockages or maintain them.

Essentially then, this message which states, "Let the dead bury their dead" simply means that a spiritually inactive entity is the only one who can remove and release himself from the blockages to spiritual flow. When it says *let* it means that it is not your mission to try to do it for another, because you can't. You can encourage another through the offering of your love, your support, your wisdom, your knowledge, and your sharing. But in the end it is the person himself who will make the decision to release those obstacles which prevent spiritual flow into the conscious and manifested state. It is he who will bury those things which prevent spiritual flow. In so doing and through free will, he becomes spiritually active on the manifested plane.

What is God?

Very simply, God is everything that is. If you think this to be untrue, it is only because of your limited perception and your inability to recognize One Power. If you are unable to recognize One Power, you will perceive duality, and not oneness. A coin has two sides, but it is one coin, and both sides are molded from the same metal. You may look at one side and say it is heads, but turn it over and it is tails. These are but the illusions etched into its two sides. Once it was simply a metal coin, the same on both sides until the illusionist made each side unique. Your duality is illusion. In truth, everything is in a state of Oneness, and everything is born of that Oneness. I know that when I say *born of* it sounds as though separation is occurring. Not so. The Creator expresses through Creation in unique and diverse ways so that the illusionary perception appears to be one of separation and fragmentation.

Think of the Creator, the One Power, the One Life, as a gigantic lotus flower. The fact that individual petals unfold does not make the petals separate or less than the flower. They are not part of the flower; they compose the flower. Therefore, you are not part of God; you are God. You are the Creator expressing creatively and uniquely through a creation called you. Once you truly connect up with this truth you will have all the love and the power which you like to separate from. The Christ knew this, and He said, "I and the Father are One." Some religionists like to say that God stepped down and incarnated into human form in the man, Jesus. God did not step down from anywhere. He always was. The Master Christ knew this and connected with this knowing, and thus He had the power and the love which is there for anyone who releases from perceptual and illusionary fragmentation and separation.

What is the truth about the following statements contained within the copy of the New York Times article on the New Age Movement? "The New Age Movement is essentially the maturing of the Hippie Movement of the 1960's... It is the most powerful social force in the country today... If you look at it carefully you see it represents a complete rejection of Judeo-Chirstian and bedrock American values... I think the drug of the 1980's is Cosmic Consciousness."

All of the statements you have asked about contain partial truths, which are relative, of course. To say that the present movement is the maturing of the hippie movement is not really accurate; it is the maturing or rather the awakening of higher consciousness in that particular starseed group. That starseed generation, primarily post-Atlantean, entered with the primary mission of shifting mass consciousness. Even though the time warp of the 1960's was filled with extremes, intensity, dissension, and oftentimes revolution, you will note if you study this time period that many shifts were made within collective consciousness. There is generally a relatively quiet period following revolutionary shifts, and so it was with this particular starseed influx. They married, had families, and tried to adapt to more conventional living. Most, after the age of thirty, began preparing for the major thrust to bring forth the collective enlightenment of planet Earth. They are still preparing by studying and by teaching the successive starseed generations.

218

Within the land of the Eagle, the New Age Movement is not yet the most powerful social force but it is accelerating, and the time is approaching when it shall be. Once considered to be a subculture, it is now beginning to permeate all aspects of human and planetary life. It is this fact which is creating such fear among conservative systems and fundamentalist religions. There will be divisions among people, and battles will rage for a time. Remember that when one fears, he will challenge those he perceives as his enemies. As the energy contained within the New Age Movement increases, it will threaten all existing social systems upon the planet. New Age initiates know that what is occurring is a cosmic cycle and another stage of planetary and human evolution. As your philosopher Nietzche so aptly stated, "Man is a bridge, not a goal." The Aquarian Age is a bridge to a higher order of life. Many upon your planet fear the changes to come and thus will fight and challenge what is already in action and moving toward manifestation. They will resist what is, in truth, a natural, cyclic evolutionary flow to a higher plane of life, and so, for a time, there will be conflict and great challenges for the New Age initiates. It is going to require a lot of strength, courage, love, commitment, and unity for the New Age workers to remain aligned to their individual missions which feed into the collective mission of shifting mass consciousness. Most New Age lightbearers are beginning to realize what their individual missions are and their relationship to the collective mission. Many are beginning to move on their individual courses with great determination. If you will look about you with heightened awareness, you will see how this force is beginning to move into all areas of life. What has been set in motion cannot be stopped.

The New Age Movement is not a complete rejection of Judeo-Christian and bedrock American values. True, some values have been rejected because they can no longer be the truth for the New Age. Those relative truths based in fear and mythological illusions are being rejected as they must be for a new order of life. But values which will serve to create a planet of unity, peace, equality, love, and brotherhood will be retained. The purpose of the New Age Movement is to create an upliftment of humankind and of the planet. When man is lifted and begins expressing his true nature, his God essence, then all aspects of creation upon Earth are likewise lifted up. This will not occur until human consciousness has been raised. All manifestation has its seed in the mind. The New Age Movement is a movement of mind or thought, and life on manifested Earth will mirror what is in the collective mind. This is why the shifting of mass consciousness is so critical.

The entity who stated that cosmic consciousness is the drug of the '80's was not being complimentary, as you could probably discern. He was comparing it to the dangerous mind altering drugs used by some in the 1960's. Cosmic consciousness is not an opiate designed to lull entities into a false sense of reality. Its purpose is to bring one closer to Absolute Truth. It is not mind altering, but it is thought altering. It is definitely reprogramming. Opponents see this as dangerous and liken it to brainwashing. But what many opponents fail to realize is that most people are still operating on the survival programming of the ego. This type of programming will not work in the New Age because it means bondage, not freedom. Many in the New Age Movement are working very hard at reprogramming themselves and raising their own individual consciousness levels. They know that in order to reprogram collective mind, of which they are a part, they must begin on the individual level.

I would advise those New Age workers to remain aligned and committed to their individual missions and to stay attuned to higher guidance. You chose your missions prior to entering, and many have awakened to what those missions are. Even though you may tire and wish to give up, you can be re-energized by the fact that you are presently participating in the greatest renaissance yet known to planet Earth. Your walk is more than an individual walk; it is a planetary walk. You are Servants of the Light and are Served by the Light.

Explain how and why one travels through the Zodiac Signs prior to entrance into the physical dimension.

When thinking of the zodiac with regard to this question, you must allow your mind to think beyond the physical zodiac with which you are familiar. We are referring to a soul or spirit journey which has nothing to do with the physical stars or suns within your own physical star system. We are referring to a cosmic non-physical zodiac through which a spirit passes on its journey to entrance into a physical dimension and out of it. You have given your zodiac signs twelve names represented by unique star patterns in the heavens which you see with physical eyes. These are but manifested symbols of something beyond your dimension.

Each of the twelve physical zodiacal signs contain positive and negative qualities. When an entity enters the physical time-space dimension under a particular sun sign, he will embody more of the negative and positive qualities of that particular sun sign than he will the qualities of the other eleven signs. This creates a distinct imbalance in the human entity, so the spirit passes through all the signs in order to take on qualities from the others. This journey also assists the entity in understanding physical entities born under other sun signs.

In the cosmic non-physical zodiac there are no negative qualities associated with the symbols. But in the physical time-space dimension in which you reside, there are both negative and positive qualities associated with the signs because you have chosen to live in a dimension of opposites. Thus, the positive qualities of a sign are to be encouraged and the negative qualities to be overcome.

Twelve is a symbol of completeness, and thus the cosmic non-physical zodiac represents stages a spirit journeys through in order to enter the physical dimension as a complete and whole entity. Each stage strengthens and prepares the spirit for his journey through the physical dimension, assisting it to maintain as much balance as is possible. Because he must journey through a land of duality, some of the wholeness or completeness is lost. So upon exiting the physical dimension, the spirit once again travels the positive Cosmic zodiac so that he can enter the fourth life expression. The spirit does this with each physical life expression he chooses to enter. This journey is only necessary as a preparation process, and the exit journey is a cleansing process. The spirit will enter at a pre-selected point in a time-space dimension where the physical zodiac signs are aligned in such a way as to produce the vibrations most needed for the growth and learning of the entity. All spirits will express themselves at least once within each of the twelve signs.

The cosmic zodiac journey is a spiral one. A singular spirit may choose to express physically in a particular sun sign more than once. It may also choose to express life in other non-physical dimensions on the Full Circle Journey.

Why do I always let others dictate my moods? Why is my mood or feeling based on the moods or feelings of those around me? I must learn to have control of my own feelings and emotions rather than always being a mirror of others.

This is one of the hardest things to learn: not being a mirror for others. In the physical dimension it's very easy to be affected by the vibrations of others, particularly those with whom you are closest. It also seems that it is more difficult to remain unaffected by the negative ones. It's not that negative vibrations are more powerful than positive ones; it's simply that in your world there are more of them, which means they exert the stronger influence upon a human entity.

The best way to stop being a mirror of those around you is to begin affirming that you are a unique and individualized expression of the Source. There is absolutely no one in the entire Cosmos exactly like you. In this sense you walk alone; your journey is yours alone. In a true sense you can never be a mirror to anyone else. However, you can choose or allow yourself to reflect the vibrations emitted by others. You can ride upon the vibrations of others. This is fine if it's your choice, but you must remember that you, not they, are responsible for how you choose to vibrate or to express.

Because of the presence of free will, you have the right to express any mood, feeling, or emotion you wish, whether positive or negative. You have the right to be affected by those around you. The main thing is to assume the responsibility for your feelings and moods. No one makes you feel anything; you allow it. Likewise, if others elect to ride upon your vibrations, whatever they are, you are not responsible. If you are in a bad mood and someone close to you becomes affected and reflects your mood, you are not responsible. They have chosen to ride your vibrations.

What is really needed is to evaluate the choices you make and accept the responsibility for those choices. If someone around you is expressing a negative emotion, you don't have to pull it into yourself. Allow them the emotion, for they have chosen to experience it. You can still be sympathetic, understanding, and loving without having to experience what another is experiencing. Sometimes it's even beneficial to move out of it more quickly.

Also, don't feel guilty about your choices, for with every choice there is a lesson which means growth to you. If you are feeling a negative emotion, take responsibility for it and work through it. If it means being alone, be alone. If it means sharing it with someone, share with someone whom you know won't take it onto himself, for they are the ones who can help you the most.

I've noticed that in your world most entities either want to blame or give credit to others for how they feel. If entities could realize that each individual is responsible for his own joy and happiness as well as for all the negative feelings he experiences, your world would be easier to live in. It doesn't mean that you do nothing to bring joy and happiness into the lives of others; it merely means that you are not responsible for whether they choose to be happy, any more than others are responsible for your happiness.

What is the cause of homosexuality? Is it a cultural, karmic, or deep-rooted historical phenomenon?

Let me emphasize that there is no single cause for homosexuality and that this condition or experience has only to do with third-dimensional or physical planes of life. Spirit is without gender, being a perfect blend or balance of feminine and masculine polarities or energies. This, of course, produces complete neutrality. The issue of homosexuality and heterosexuality is not a spiritual concern.

With regard to physical sexual unions, many of your patriarchal religions have stated that this union should be only for the procreation of the species. While this is necessary, the experience can also be an expression of love between two entities, and can cause the elevation of love. In your earlier religions which are now labeled as pagan, the expression of love through a physical union was accepted. In many respects these earlier cultures were healthier than the one in which you now live.

Because of the tremendous influence of the patriarchal societies, Western society has warped attitudes, beliefs, and fears about sex. The Age of Aquarius will begin with increased feminine energy and will evolve into a harmonious blending of the two energies. The Piscean Age was oppressively masculine and could never achieve balance.

Cosmically, what is of prime importance is whether the essence of love is expressed between two entities. Your particular culture views homosexuality as being abnormal and heterosexuality as normal. These are the limitations and illusions you have created and accepted. In any physical union where the true essence of love is present, there is always a blending of feminine and masculine energies. Sometimes, however, the feminine energy happens to be housed in a male physical form or the masculine energy is contained within a female physical form. Your culture is perhaps too caught up with the illusions of physical shells.

As to why a feminine energy is encased in a male form or a masculine energy is encased in a female form, sometimes it is Karmic and part of the Full Circle Journey. Remember that on the Journey, one must experience all there is to experience in order to learn. Some of you have already experienced this, some in societies where it was condemned, and some where it was accepted. Sometimes an energy becomes entrapped in an opposing form because of a biological malfunctioning during the formation of the physical form. This is why oftentimes a spirit will not enter the form until later in the development of the form or why it sometimes will exit at birth or shortly thereafter. Though the residing spirit is without gender, it brings with it the dominant polarity for the physical form.

Your culture is overly obsessed with the physical union of forms and all its manifestations. The sexual union, no matter who is involved, should be an expression designed to take one to the highest love. If love is being expressed by two energies, the physical forms do not matter from a Cosmic level. All that is noted is the vibration of love.

We are told not to judge, yet every choice we make requires us to make judgments. Explain and reconcile.

The questioner may be referring to the biblical ideas of "Judge not, lest ye be judged" or "Judgment is mine, saith the Lord." The judgment referred to in these quotations is not merely an assessment, opinion, discernment, decision, or choice. For human entities experiencing in an illusionary world of created duality, these are necessary and sometimes even vital to the survival of the human vehicle.

Being told not to judge, from a cosmic standpoint, refers primarily to your relationships with other entities. The reason you are told not to judge yourself or others is simply that you have neither the authority nor the perfect inner vision to do it with complete accuracy. When a human entity takes it upon himself to assume the authority to judge another, he will use as his base his own belief system, which includes how he thinks another should be or behave. He will judge based upon his own standards and ideas of perfection. He will frequently judge another against himself, and individual human entities have a great tendency to always feel they are right. Human entities, especially those with strong egos, will perceive flaws in others while being blind to their own flaws.

Another reason you are told not to judge, aside from the fact that you have no authority to do so, is that when you do this with imperfect and incomplete vision and knowledge, you will always make mistakes. Mistakes incur Karma and place you under the Law of Cause and Effect. Your judging of another brings judgment rushing in upon you.

Still another reason for working very hard to move away from this type of action is that when you judge another aspect of Creation using your own imperfect standards and changing belief system, you are essentially judging the Creator. It is impossible for imperfection to make a judgment against that which is perfect.

Human entities often not only take the authority to judge, but will also assume the power of executioner of imperfect justice. When this happens

Karma and the Law of Cause and Effect come into action. Learning not to judge is really a protection for yourself.

Make decisions and choices, assess and discern, and form opinions because free choice is part of your programming in your world. Judging is quite a different thing. Spirit will discern but will not judge. The Creator has the sole authority to exercise judgment, even though there are many who attempt to do so.

Your great Master could hate the sin and still love the sinner. He could make judgments against external actions without making judgments against those who committed the actions. He had the awareness to know that, as with a revolving crystal, one can only see the facet being shown. The human crystal has many, many facets. On your plane of experience you will never be able to see them all, not even in yourself.

Be gentle with yourself and others, and remember that no matter how well you may think you know another, you are only experiencing a fraction of his total being.

How can I perceive my own mind when the mind is the perceiver as well as that which it perceives?

You can't, in truth, perceive your own mind when what you are is mind. If the mind is both the perceiver and that which it perceives, it is in a state of Oneness. Oneness cannot be perceived and can only be experienced by entering into that Oneness. To try to observe one's mind, one must see the mind as the object or the thing observed, and this creates the illusion of duality.

Human perception involves the use of the physical senses, and because the senses are limited, so also is perception limited on the human level. Whenever you perceive anything on this level using the physical senses, differentiation and separation enter in and you perceive an illusion of duality. Therefore, even if you choose to think of the mind as an object (which you must do if you try to perceive it at your level), you have created duality and can only perceive fragments.

It has been said that "No observing system can observe itself observing. The seer cannot see itself seeing." The mind cannot be perceived as an object because it is, as one writer stated, "Like a sword that cuts, but cannot cut itself; like an eye that sees, but cannot see itself."

Even the question itself creates separation. "How can I perceive my own mind?" indicates that *I* is somehow different from *my own mind*. Yet the questioner is aware of the oneness when she says "When the mind is the perceiver as well as that which it perceives." Essentially the questioner, at that point, answers the question. The *I* is the mind; the mind is the *I*. Oneness is present. The perceiver, that which is perceived, the act of perceiving, are all in oneness. There cannot truly be a separation.

Recall what you've been told about mind. Mind is not brain; mind is the creator of brain. Mind contains the levels of consciousness which connect with your brain computer. Mind is not limited by time and space; it is not contained within your form. It is *you*. How can you perceive with your physical senses that which is beyond space and time?

So the answer is simply that you cannot perceive your own mind unless you fragment it and detach yourself from it and become subject and object. Once you do this, you create illusion, and your perception is inaccurate and limited. You cannot perceive that which you are; you can only experience its oneness. The question and the answer are the same. There is no subject and object. You and the mind are the same. The perceiver cannot perceive itself perceiving, and the eye cannot see itself seeing.

"Who loses his life, shall find it."

This particular quotation can be seen at many levels, even at the very basic physical death experience level which so many people seem to fear. There are so many human entities who are at the awareness level where death of form is the worst thing that could happen to them. This is because they have not evolved to the point of knowing that Life is continuous or that that which they are, in truth, is not illusionary and temporary form. Hence, they will cling to physical life and dread that process called physical death. With this overshadowing dread, they never allow themselves to express themselves within the physical life journey fully and completely. There is always a subtle cloud veiling the sunshine of their complete beingness in form. This, coupled with much confusion and fear about what lies beyond the exiting point of the physical life journey, keeps many bound in chains throughout their life walk. The truth is, as all entities will discover at their appointed times, that they will simply move to a higher frequency and a grander dimension of Life. The ascending journey continues. Losing the physical life, and releasing from form only means finding or discovering truer life. As one moves from illusions, he moves closer to essence.

This process can be started right where one is on his particular life walk. He doesn't have to wait until physical exit to discover it. Once a human entity begins to raise his consciousness by releasing from his attachments to physical illusions, he begins to discover the essence of

Life. Releasing from the material, illusionary attachments within the physical realm does not mean that you cannot enjoy and derive pleasure from your world. It merely means that you are not imprisoned or held captive by anything within your world to the point that if you were removed from it you would be devastated by your loss. What holds an entity captive to something within the material world, be it a person or a thing, is fear of loss. Fear is always the great jailkeeper within the human entity, and it gives birth to all your lack, insecurity and unhappiness. It is fear which keeps you attached to your physical world of things, causes you to try to possess people, and keeps your own beingness in bondage so that you journey through a world of separation and fragmentation.

Therefore, whoever is willing to lose his life or release from all attachments shall find Life. Life is freedom of beingness and freedom to unfold into what you truly are. Each entity knows those things which hold him in bondage and which prevent him from connecting with All Life. They are not just material things of form, but can be emotions as well, including such feelings as jealousy, greed, anger, possessiveness, desires for power and the whole host of negative emotions. All these things can prevent one from experiencing the fullness and beauty of Life, for they are blocks to our freedom of God expression. If you would find Life, you must be willing to lose or release from those things which keep you in bondage. Self-created bondage within one's life experience is the true death experience. Anything which prevents you from experiencing and expressing who you truly are in a now moment is a death experience.

The Book of Runes says, "We do without doing, and everything gets done." What does this mean?

This is a wonderful statement of flow and connection with Universal Mind. When you just allow yourself to be and when you allow others to be, you will do exactly what you are supposed to do at any given moment.

Many of man's problems emerge because he, himself, tries to determine what it is he is supposed to do within his life experience. By doing this, he is not trusting the Creator. For if you trust the Creator you will know that the only thing you're really supposed to do is allow the Creator to express through you, His Creation. By doing this everything gets done. This, of course, requires flow, which is simply accepting what is and moving gently with it, knowing that when you do, it will always be for the highest good.

Universally and from the Creator's point of view, everything will be done that is to be done, whether you flow or resist. Flowing simply makes it easier and less stressful for you. Resistance causes you to spend a lot of energy trying to determine your purpose and causes a lot of grief and dissatisfaction when you always want things to be different than they are.

You are a fragment of the Creator, and as such your purpose is simply to be whatever you are in a now moment and allow yourself to express in the process of becoming. You exercise not your will, but His. This is the true connection and flow, and where your greatest joy is found.

Is darkness truly the absence of light?

Darkness is not the absence of light. Darkness is simply a part of your world of duality, and both darkness and light are aspects of your physical and created illusions. What you perceive as darkness and light are seen by your physical eye. When you have ascended and been purified you will sense with your inner eye, and what you will experience is energy beyond your comprehension. It is a light beyond your human perception and understanding of light; a light which has no opposite. It is the essence of the Cosmos. In your illusionary world of duality, is there any difference between darkness being the absence of light or light being the absence of darkness? No. They dwell together in neutrality and oneness, and it is your perception which divides and separates them. When you see with spiritual vision, you will cease to fragment them into light and darkness. Once you can do this, you will experience the Oneness and neutrality which is the essence, not only of your planet, but of the Cosmos as well.

If God is us and in us, can there exist incompatibility and vulnerability to vibrations outside of us?

Essentially, the answer to this question is no since the God expression is the highest vibration there is, and that vibration is contained within all aspects of Creation.

However, the various aspects of Creation also have individual vibrations, which are usually not aligned to the highest vibration of the God expression. A human entity vibrates lower because he chooses to do so or he allows himself to. Most human entities vibrate lower primarily because they are more ego-connected than spirit-connected. There are times, however, when a human entity will vibrate the God expression, but this is usually not a constant experience. When one is vibrating the highest expression, he is not incompatible with or vulnerable to outside vibrations. During this experience one is able to connect with all higher vibrations (since none is higher than the God expression), and he need not fear problems sometimes connected with lower astral vibrations. The

God vibration recognizes nothing lower or higher, but rather pulls all into Oneness.

Most of the time a human entity operates at a lower vibrational level even though, as I said, he contains the God vibration within. When he is operating beneath the God vibration, higher vibrations are sometimes incompatible. With the exception of the Master and guides, entities of higher vibrations do not lower their vibrations to communicate with you. When you communicate with higher vibrational entities or energies, it is because you have raised your vibrational energy enough to parallel theirs. Likewise, when the level of your vibrations is similar to those of lower astral energies, you are vulnerable to their influences, whatever they may happen to be.

Sometimes a higher entity can communicate with you, even if there are no matched vibrations, by using your guide as a kind of relay. The personal guides experience at a higher vibrational level, and their vibrational levels are sometimes similar to entities whose vibrations are too high to connect with human entities. So they match with your guide who in turn matches with your vibrations.

Quotation: "A religion without mystery must be a religion without God."

To understand the meaning of this quotation, it is important to comprehend the meanings of both religion and mystery. A religion is a set of beliefs which one adheres to. A mystery is something which is seemingly obscure or unexplained.

Please know that when I use the term religion, I am thinking beyond those belief systems which compose such things as Christianity, Judaism, Buddhism, and so forth. Any set of beliefs can become a religion to you. Whatever your beliefs are is your religion. Since there is no set of beliefs or religion which is completely free of the seemingly unexplained or the mysterious, there are no religions without God. There are religions in which God is not acknowledged by those accepting a set of beliefs, but it does not mean that God is not present.

There is but one power in the Cosmos, and this is God. This energy threads and weaves throughout All Creation. When you reach the highest level of awareness there will be no mysteries; nothing will be obscure or unexplained. And there will be no religion, no set of beliefs. There will only be Total Knowingness, which is far different than believing. What you believe is not always true, and it is changing. Total Knowingness is Truth and is Eternal.

What is thought?

Thought is energy flowing outward from Universal Mind. As it flows down through the levels of consciousness, it enters your conscious state in the form of an individual thought. It no longer has its original purity because the brain computer must interpret symbols, and how thought is interpreted is based on one's level of awareness. Distortions of thought also occur when the human ego attempts to direct thought on its own path.

A thought or thought energy can be manifested or empowered. It cannot be energized because it is already an energy. You bring your thought energy into manifestation through the power of your own mind. The more you concentrate on, affirm, center on, focus on, or visualize a particular thought, the greater your chance of bringing the energy into manifested form. This is one of the things which makes you a co-creator. You take a creation of the One Intelligence, which is Universal Thought, and though it is impure by the time it is processed, you accept this thought, empower it, and manifest it into your own physical illusion. In other words, you are able to render the Absolute into a Relative Space and are able to create Illusion from Pure Reality. The type of illusion that you create from the thought energy flowing to you is dependent on the nature of the vibrations you instill it with: negative or positive.

The mind is extremely powerful, and the thought energy flow is rushing within it continuously. You have control by utilizing this energy properly and by empowering it with positive vibrations. Then you will manifest only positive empowered thoughts. Thoughts which come into your conscious present state, but which are not relevant to your life experience, should be sent to the pre- or sub-conscious levels for storage. You will also have better control of your thoughts if you stay spirit-aligned rather than ego-controlled. Remember that the only energy which flows from the Source is Love energy, so the essence of that which you term Thought Energy is really Love Energy.

How does mass consciousness relate to the astral belt of Earth?

The only way in which mass consciousness relates to the astral belt of Earth is that the astral belt is the holding area for all thought which has been generated by Earth's entities since its creation, and all thought passes through mass consciousness first.

The difference is that the astral belt contains the individual thought energy produced by each entity that has ever been upon Earth. Mass consciousness is the holding area of collective thought.

If it had a location, mass consciousness would lie between the physical Earth and the astral belt. Mass consciousness is part of your physical space-time dimension, and it is always part of the now moment. It contains only present thought energy vibrations of entities living upon your planet in the now moment. As now moments flow and collective thought shifts, the collective thought is broken down into its base parts which are individual thoughts, and these individual thoughts are sent into the astral belt. Breaking down collective thought is rather like breaking a molecule down into atoms. Collective thought is like the molecule; individual thoughts are like the atoms which compose the molecule.

The vibrational thought energy contained in the astral belt has less impact and influence on physical Earth entities than does mass consciousness. This is because mass consciousness contains the vibrations and thought energy of everyone on your planet in the now moment. As an example, your own physical form is more impacted by the vibrational thought energy of Kaddafi, which is part of mass consciousness, than it is by a past entity such as Plato, whose vibrational thought energy is contained in the astral belt. Vibrationally you are more impacted by the thought energy vibrations of those who share your now moments.

In each moment, individual thought moves forward, combines with mass consciousness, breaks back down into individual thought, and enters the astral belt.

How does the hundredth monkey concept relate to the disease we call AIDS?

You all know that the hundredth monkey concept is based on the premise that at the onset a certain number of entities have a particular awareness and that at a certain point if only one entity is given a new awareness, it can cause the new awareness to touch almost everyone, no matter where they are located. It's a psychic mind-to-mind connection.

The tendency, of course, is to consider that awareness will always be a positive quantum leap in man's perception. You must remember however, that awareness is awareness, and is neither positive nor negative in itself. It is neutral, so it is your perception which labels the new awareness as positive or negative.

Once an awareness, no matter what it is, reaches a critical point within mass consciousness, this awareness can touch everyone's individual consciousness. You must also remember that if the awareness is accepted, it can then be brought into manifestation.

With this new disease you call AIDS, and with cancer and other diseases, this leap in consciousness to the awareness of these diseases has occurred. Not only has the awareness of these diseases reached the critical point in mass consciousness, but they have been accepted by mass consciousness. As individual consciousness accepts the awareness perceived by mass consciousness, the individual egos perceive the new awareness through the eyes of fear and ignorance. You have accepted the new awareness, and have also perceived it negatively. Mass consciousness is now generating great fear and hysteria, which are causing the physical manifestations of the disease to increase upon your planet. It is a question of fearing that which you do not know or understand. You cannot know and understand until you release yourself from fear. Ignorance is but fear blocking reason and enlightenment.

By comparison, the numbers of those who fear are greater than those who do not fear, and this is why the physical manifestations are increasing rapidly. But there are a few who do not instill the new awareness with fear, and as they increase in number they will trigger another awareness in mass consciousness, and you will call it a cure. For example, are you really sure that the Salk and Sabin vaccines practically wiped out the disease called polio? Or did mass consciousness accept a new awareness that the vaccine would work? In other words, was it the vaccine which worked or was it the belief by mass consciousness that caused it to work? It's really difficult for me to make you understand not only the power of individual mind, but of collective mind as well. Human entities manifest what they give power to. If they render power through fear, they will produce negative manifestations.

So much of what I have tried to teach you is based on the truth that you are responsible for your individual world, and that your individual mind, being part of collective mind, is in part responsible for your total external world. This is why so much emphasis has been placed on learning to think properly and positively, and on taking responsibility for the creation of your own individual world rather than looking outside yourself at the externals. Your life is how you create it to be, and your world is how mass consciousness creates it to be. As an individual mind, you do not have to buy into anything which the collective mind promotes. This does not mean that you will not be touched by the various illusions created by collective mind, but you always have a shield of wisdom, knowledge, and enlightenment available if you do not block them with fear.

Collective mind tends to be fear-oriented, and this is why I have said before that it is the individual that evolves and not the masses. It is an

232

individual monkey who first washes his potatoes to remove the sand from them. Others then release their fear and follow his ways and add their strength of energy to the action, until the hundreth monkey is reached and the breakthrough into a new collective awareness is made.

Remember also that the hundreth monkey would have no value were it not for the first fearless monkey willing to separate himself from collective mind, and for the second, third, fourth, and so on willing to move out and experiment with new thinking.

As for the disease called AIDS, it might be helpful if you would raise your awareness and seek to understand why mass consciousness has created a dis-ease which breaks down the human immune system. Symbolically, try to discern what collective mind is saying and why it is bringing this into manifestation on your planet.

"Each person is born to one possession that outvalues all others." Mark Twain

Like all the words of wisdom channeled to and through higher minds that your world has sought to save and pass down through your ages, this quotation and the truth contained within it have many levels of meaning. What truth you are able to glean from the wisdom is dependent on your own level of awareness.

Samuel Clemens, better known to you as Mark Twain, gave forth the knowledge that each individual entity is born to one possession that outvalues all others. You may wonder what this possession is and if it differs from entity to entity. On the highest level of meaning, the possession referred to is shared and is common to all entities. That possession is the creative Lifeforce, the Living Spirit of the Creator. The creative Lifeforce is the possession which outvalues all others because without it, all others would be non-existent. The creative Lifeforce is a gift bestowed upon each aspect of creation, which once accepted, becomes its possession. This gift which becomes the possession of each entity is given at the point of origination of the spirit. Perhaps in this context the saying would better read: Each spirit is created by and for one possession that outvalues all others.

Another level of truth which can be considered through this particular saying has to do with individual gifts and talents. Each individual entity enters the Earth plane possessing, or inherent in his being, the seed or embryo of a gift or talent unique only to his expression. If this gift or talent is discovered by the entity and is nurtured and allowed to grow, it will unfold, surpass, and outvalue all other gifts and talents that the entity might have. It will be the open line vehicle or channel for the God essence to express through. Regardless of whether an individual entity discovers his unique possession or not or whether, upon discovery, he chooses to let it lie dormant and unexpressed or whether he takes it and brings it into full blossom, the possession unique to him will still outvalue all others he may have. The value of the possession lies not in whether it is recognized and expressed in your external world, or whether it lies dormant and unrecognized in the entity who possesses it. Its value lies in its presence and is not dependent on expression in your external world.

"Why is propaganda so much more successful when it stirs up hatred, than when it tries to stir up friendly feelings?" Bertrand Russell

Propaganda, as you are aware, is the deliberate spreading of information for the purpose of creating a particular climate of thought within mass consciousness. Because of the way it is sometimes used to spread rumors rather than just information, propaganda oftentimes sounds negative and unethical. Regardless of whether one's motivation is to create peace or chaos, the information which is spread should be based on truth. If it is not, one comes under Karmic Law regardless of the outcome. What I'm saying is that if your motivation is to create peace, yet you spread rumors and false information to achieve this condition, then no matter what the outcome, you are under Karmic Law.

Propaganda, because of the negative ways it has been used in your world, tends to sound manufactured and untruthful in itself. Yet the passing of information in order to create a particular climate of thought within mass consciousness is not always negative. Sometimes it produces growth and a positive shift.

Most frequently, however, when propaganda is used to create a certain climate or mass attitude, it is done so negatively, and its purpose is to create negativity and collective unrest. Those who attempt to create a peaceful, loving climate usually do not call their method propaganda. They call it sharing, raising conscious awareness, enlightenment, and so on. The deliberate attempt to create a shift in mass consciousness through the spreading of information is, in one sense, all propaganda by definition.

The question, however, is why propaganda which is designed to stir hatred is so much more successful than propaganda designed to create friendly feelings? One reason negative propaganda is more successful has to do with the obvious imbalance and inequality which is present on your planet. You have masses of entities who are poorly educated or illiterate, who are starving and diseased, who are poor and have nothing. They are very vulnerable to negative propaganda.

The primary reason is simply that you cannot stir up that which is not already there. You can't stir the pudding unless the pudding is in the pot. Propaganda is only the ladle. What I'm saying is that hatred must already be present before it can be stirred up, and by comparison there is far more non-love than love existing on your planet at the present time. It's not too difficult to see why negative propaganda is more successful.

Although there are many, there are two things I feel are particularly necessary to limit the success of negative propaganda: education and equality. Education assists the individual entity in becoming less vulnerable. The more knowledge one has, the more he is able to detect rumors, and perhaps false information designed to create a certain climate of mass thought of which the individual is a part. Equality, particularly in the area of economics, removes some of the pressures of sheer survival. When these are removed, an entity is also less vulnerable because he is less angry and hate-filled.

If you want to use propaganda to stir up friendly feelings, you are going to have to create these conditions in the physical pot. You have to put these ingredients into the pudding before you can stir them up.

Collective thought is a mirror of what you create on physical Earth. It mirrors your own illusions.

Basically, then, the reason that propaganda is so much more success-ful in stirring up hatred than it is in stirring up friendly feelings is because on Earth there is more hatred present within individual entities than there are friendly feelings. Strive to work toward removing conditions which give birth to hatred, and as always, begin first with your own feelings of non-love.

Quotation: "He who loves father or mother more than Me is not worthy of Me; and he who loves son or daughter more than Me is not worthy of Me..." Matthew 10:37

When reading the words of the Master after the Baptism experience, one must remember that the Christ Spirit and the God Spirit were completely aligned and were connected in Perfect Oneness. When the man, Jesus, spoke, He was verbalizing the will of the Creator. When the Christ Spirit or Consciousness expressed through the words of the man, Jesus, it was really the Creator speaking because of the perfect alignment between the Creator and the Christ Spirit.

This lack of awareness has been partially responsible for a lot of the confusion and conflict within the Christian religions. Many would interpret the above saying as meaning that you would not be worthy of Jesus if you loved others more. However, this is not Jesus who is speaking, but rather the Creator expressing through the Christ Spirit. Jesus was the physical vehicle which housed the Christ Spirit during that particular walk on Earth.

This quotation is really the Creator's way of telling you to release yourself from any attachments which block your alignment and connection to Him. When you are more attached to the people and things of Earth, or to your illusions, you are not worthy by your individual choice. Spiritually, all aspects of Creation have value and worth to the Creator. Your spirit is always worthy; your ego is not. The Creator was speaking to man's ego.

When you love or are attached to the illusions of your world and are not connected with the Creator, your love and attachment are born of your ego. Ego-controlled entities will always love the things of the Earth more than the Creator. Spirit-led entities will love the Creator first and foremost, for in truly loving Him and trusting and remaining connected, they will then be able to love all Creation as well, because they will see the Creator in all Creation. Choosing to love and serve the Creator places you in the position of loving and serving all Creation; choosing to love one's illusions places you in bondage to those illusions. Under the spirit, you can love All.

What is the distinction between entity and energy? Between materialization and manifestation?

With respect to the terms entity and energy which seem to be used interchangeably at times, energy is the correct term to describe everything in your world and beyond it. It is not something which is contained in the All; it is the All, the Absolute Reality. It is the Lifeforce of all Creation: the Creator.

When, for example, you speak of communicating with a spiritual energy, you are absolutely correct. When you say that you are energy, you are correct. In your world you speak of different forms of energy: thermal, nuclear, solar, molecular, atomic, kinetic, crystal, pyramid, and so forth. All of these are but manifestations of the base Energy of the Cosmos. There is but one Absolute Energy which manifests differently depending on one's perceptual level of awareness.

236

Entity, on the other hand, is to a degree a more personalized term to denote a certain energy, such as in human entity, spiritual entity, or extraterrestrial entity. All entities are energies; all energies are not entities. You may call us either spiritual energies or spiritual entities. Energy is a bit less personal, perhaps, but both are correct. On one level of interpretation, entity denotes a condition of beingness; energy denotes the absolute connectedness to the All. Another term for energy is vibration, because all energy is in motion. Another term for entity is aspect, because it, too, denotes a more personalized reference to energy.

Now, with respect to the terms materialization and manifestation, both mean movement from one plane of awareness to another plane of awareness. Everything which you are visually aware of in your world originated on another level in thought form before it was brought to your present awareness in its illusionary material form. Materialization is probably a better term to describe the thought forms which are brought into the illusions of the physical world. Manifestation occurs on all levels and in all dimensions of life, whereas materialization does not. Materialization really means bringing an awareness, idea, or thought into the physical world where it can be perceived by the physical senses. It really has more to do with the physical realm. Manifestation covers all realms. If an ET were to make himself known to you, he might use the process of molecular breakup. When he appeared before you, this would be materialization. If I were to appear before you, I would manifest rather than materialize because I am pure conscious energy with nothing to materialize. If I manifested and you saw a form, it would be an illusionary form which you created with your mind. You would see me as you wanted to see me. I realize that this is very complicated for you to understand.

I cannot materialize, but I can manifest because I can shift from one level of awareness to another. If you see me with your physical senses, you have created the form you wish to see. You are more accurate if you perceive my presence and my energy with your higher senses as occurs in channeling. All energies from non-physical dimensions who communicate with Earthlings manifest their presence into your higher levels of awareness, but they do not materialize. You've heard stories of past Earth entities materializing before Earthlings. What occurs is that the individual mind of a human entity has connected with the astral belt and pulled the ego-personality aspects of a past Earth entity back to the Earth plane. The human entity might think it is a materialization, but it, too, is a manifestation.

You cannot materialize that which is not material. Let's go back to what I said about thoughts being brought into illusionary materialization. Before a thought becomes your thought, it is first manifested into a thought by Universal Mind. The manifested thought moves through the levels of your individual mind before it reaches the conscious state. In the conscious state you are able to bring it into physical illusionary materialization. In the physical world this is one of the things which makes you a co-creator. You are able to take a manifested thought and bring it into illusionary material form.

Even with all of this, these terms will be used interchangeably, and we find no problem with this because we know what you mean and you know what you mean, and as long as understanding is present there is no problem with semantics.

What is divine?

Divine is simply a word you use to denote perfection. On your level of experience you may say, "This or that is perfect because you have standards relative to perfection. You also know that when your standards change, so does your definition of perfection.

Perfection means to be without flaw. No illusion is free of flaw, and perfection is something all would be aware of. It would not be relative. Perfection has no degrees. Something could not be more perfect or less perfect. Perfection is perfection. It simply is. It is a quality and a condition, and it exists only within the essence of the Creator and within the essence of that which He created. This is the true Divinity and perfection in Life.

Many strive for perfection or are perfectionists in what they try to do. This is good. It means they are doing the very best they are capable of doing in whatever they are doing. But still the perfection they are striving toward is based on their own standards and definitions. I agree that you should always strive to do your best, go the extra mile, strive to become a better human being, learn your lessons and perform your mission using all the blessings, gifts, capabilities, and abilities which have been given to you. This attitude is important for your growth and unfoldment.

That essential part of your beingness, however, is already in a state of perfection. It is already divine. It is the God Essence, the creative Lifeforce within you. It is not something you must strive to attain. It is already there.

"Courage is the first of human qualities because it is the quality which guarantees all the others." Winston Churchhill

Cosmically speaking, courage is not the first of the human qualities. Love is the first, and it is love which guarantees all the others, even courage.

Love releases you from fear, and when fear is released it allows courage to surface. Enveloped within Love is trust, which is the quality which releases one from fear and gives birth to that quality you call courage.

On the human conscious level of awareness, you may perceive what you call courage within entities who appear not to be loving. But whether you perceive it from your Earthly vantage point or not, somewhere within that entity love has opened up and trust has entered to release the entity from fear and allow courage to surface.

All courage is the release from fear and its replacement with trust, which is born of Love. Courage should not be measured in daring Earthly feats. The most courageous person is the one who lives each moment and experiences each moment with complete love and trust. When an entity moves through his life experience in this way, he is courageous.

You give awards, medals, and commendations for acts of courage and heroism and bold deeds, yet many live obscure lives filled with courage because they have learned to love and trust. These entities may never receive medals or commendations, but their reward is that they have lived their lives fully.

What is reality?

Reality is relative to each human entity and is based on how you perceive your world, both internally and externally. What you consider to be real within your life experience may be different from what others consider to be real. Reality is uniquely perceptual and is based on your particular programming, belief system, and level of awareness. Because all of these things shift and change within you, your sense of reality changes and shifts as well. Therefore, what you perceive as reality is illusionary and could be better termed illusionary reality.

Take a flower in full bloom, for example. Upon experiencing the flower, you will perceive as reality that the flower is in full bloom. When it begins to wither and its petals fall crisply to the ground, your perception of reality shifts, and the reality becomes that of a flower wilting and dying. On one level both experiences within your perception represented reality to you. On another level, neither represented true reality. Both experiences which fed your perception were facets of the true reality.

The two experiences which created your perceptual reality of the flower were but two pieces of a puzzle. If you could perceive all the pieces, from the Divine Thought of the flower to its physical manifestation, and through its physical life process to its ultimate return to Divine Mind, you would perceive true or Absolute Reality, which is Essence. What is true for the flower is also true for your own reality. The you that experiences and expresses in your present form is but one piece of the puzzle of the Absolute Reality of You. You are but one tiny facet of your own Totality or Youness.

The other pieces of You are expressing and experiencing on other levels of consciousness, in other time warps, and on other dimensions and planes of life. The magnitude of expressions by each facet of You is so great that it is beyond your human comprehension. As you express in your present conscious form you may think that you are separated from the other pieces which compose your Totality, but you are not. The Divine Thought which conceived the Totality of You is eternal. You experience a sense of fragmentation because you have created an illusionary world of duality and separation. The Absolute Reality of You is that You are Total and Complete and are not fragmented and separated. Not only are you in Absolute Reality and at Oneness with your own Totality, your own Totality is also at Oneness with the All of Creation. The Absolute Reality is that there is only Totality and only Oneness and only pure Essence.

When you are regressed you may recall past physical incarnations, you may receive information from other time warps, you may receive information from your other aspects, or you may receive information from pure Essence. What does it matter since it is all You? In regression, in your dreams, in your channeling, in your thoughts, and in your meditations, you are given what you need for your own expansion and growth to the awareness of your own Totality and Connectedness.

You, in your present conscious expression, did not experience anywhere but where you are now. In a past life, for example, you had a different form and a different brain computer. But your spirit, which contains your mind with all that You have ever experienced, are presently experiencing, and will experience (its Totality and Oneness), will direct into your conscious and limited brain computer whatever you need to know and to grow toward the awareness of Totality.

Remember also that those terms which we have designated as individual mind, individual spirit, individual consciousness, and individual thought (all of which denote fragmentation) have been designated as such to aid in human comprehension. In Absolute Reality, All is in a state of Oneness. Oneness means no fragmentation, separation, division, or disconnection. You are Totality.

I realize that this is difficult for your present consciousness to comprehend, and that it's easier to consider your present reality as being both separate and whole at the same time. When you exit your dimension, you will comprehend Totality and Oneness, and will realize that it's possible to express uniquely while in Totality and Oneness.

What is free will?

If all thought originates in Universal Mind prior to entering individual mind, do you really have free will? Yes, you do. Original Thought pouring forth from Universal Mind filters through the various levels of consciousness of individual mind. The rush of Universal Thought is continually pouring into your individual mind. The individual mind is also affected by the myriad of thoughts pouring into other individual minds. A great portion of thought is stored within the subconscious and preconscious levels of the individual mind. You are recording and storing data on all levels of consciousness within your individual mind, and nothing occurs at any level which is not recorded. Essentially you are your own Akashic Record.

Free will enters into the matter of what you do with any given thought. It is your choice as to how much power or energy you elect to give every thought you have. The more power you give to a thought, the more energy you instill it with, and the greater its chance of manifestation into form. This is why it is important to be wise in what kind of energy (negative or positive) you use and how much power you are issuing forth into a thought. So free will involves your choice of what to do with an individual thought whose origin was within Universal Mind. A lot of thought enters the individual mind, is quickly assessed, and is sent to the recording levels. Other thoughts are held within the conscious level where you choose to empower them and add energy to them in order to bring it into form. This is free will.

Free will is never really lost, though it can be surrendered. Perhaps the greatest use of free will is the surrendering of your will to Divine Will, for in this choice you allow yourself to become an instrument or a vessel for a higher purpose. When individual will and Divine Will become totally unified, the power flow is incredible and beyond your comprehension, and universal Thought remains pure as it enters individual mind.

You then become a pure expression of the Source. This is what occurred with the Master.

Free will or your opinion to empower thought or not to empower it is always present, but sometimes your power is blocked for various reasons. Sometimes you cannot energize a thought because your energy is blocked by prejudice, societal or cultural restrictions, fear, anger, ignorance, and a multitude of other man-created illusions you have allowed to become part of your belief system. In other words, you may desire to energize a thought and wish to bring it into form, but your power is blocked by another illusion which has either been created by you or for you. So, in this sense, you have allowed yourself to lose free will if you have allowed your power to energize thought to be blocked. The power is always there within each creation. Whether it can be used or not depends entirely on how many blocks you have set up for yourself.

I might add that when Universal will and individual will are unified, there can be no power blockage. That is perhaps the greatest freedom an entity can experience, for in this oneness all prisons of human illusions are gone.

Listening Is Love:
"True listening, total concentration on the other, is always a manifestation of love." M. Scott Peck, M.D.

I very much agree with the quotation. True listening is not love in and by itself, but it is, as the author states, a manifestation of love, a way of showing one's love to another.

Listening, truly listening, takes work, and it requires the conscious will and willingness to do it. The human brain computer is always activated and is being stormed by thoughts from various levels, so listening is not really so easy, as you well know. Most entities listen by the process of scanning. This means they do not listen to everything which might be said. They listen to one thing here, another there, and then back to here again. They might understand what's been said to a point, but their listening is not complete. And if one does not listen, he does not hear.

There are people who try to listen but who are not adept at concentrating, and so their minds wander. To listen one must concentrate, and concentration does take work and practice. It is always an act of love. Hearing has nothing to do with your ears, but rather with your heart. True listening becomes true hearing, and this is the heart to heart connection.

The worst type of listeners are those so busy thinking about what to say next that they hear nothing of what is being said. Sometimes they will interrupt before another is finished speaking, and oftentimes they will not even allow another to speak. They refuse to listen because they want to do all of the talking. To refuse to listen because you wish to talk all the time shows little or no love for those around you. I'm sure that most of you have been around people with whom you have to struggle just to get a word in edgewise. This is not communication; this is being talked at.

The entities who truly listen, or at least make an effort to concentrate on what another is saying, are loving people. The one who truly listens to another truly loves. Most people know when another is not listening, and it's not necessary to throw out test questions to discern whether you are being listened to or not. Likewise, you know when you are listening.

Much has been said about reaching the state of unconditional love, and aware entities want to reach the point of loving everyone around them. Part of reaching this is learning to listen to others, to concentrate on them, to hear them with your heart. If you master this in your own dimension, it assists you in listening to the information flowing to you from higher dimensions. If you wish to show your love to another, learn to truly listen.

What is rational mind?

Rationality is a brain function rather than a mind function. Symbols enter the brain receiver and are then translated and interpreted into thoughts you can comprehend on your particular awareness level. Man has devised a set of standards by which he determines or judges what is rational or irrational thought, and this judgment is always connected to his individual perception. Seldom will an individual admit to irrational thinking, but he is wonderful at judging the thoughts of others as being such. When an entity acts according to his individual thoughts in such a way that his behavior is not aligned to the standards set by collective mind, you term it irrational behavior. Basically the terms rational and irrational mean that one is aligned or misaligned to the collective standard set by humankind. Always this is perceptual, and as you've been told so often, human perception is so very limited.

The symbols which are received from Universal Mind, and which are processed, translated, and interpreted by the human brain computer, have nothing to do with rationality. They are just symbols. Pure thought energy is neither rational nor irrational. It is what it is without judgment.

It is very important to be careful when judging the rationality of another. You must realize that when you do this you are not only using the definition formed by the collective mind, but are also doing it based on your own comprehension of the definition. And both may be filled with inaccuracies.

When someone makes a statement which is not aligned to your own individual process of intellectual logic and reasoning (brain functions), you may quickly judge the statement to be irrational. On a higher level the statement is neither, yet it is perceived as irrational because you do not agree with it on your particular individual level of awareness and perception. Many of your greatest and most advanced Earthlings have been perceived as irrational or crazy when they shared their thoughts. Some of Earth's greatest progress has been born out of what collective mind perceived as irrational thought.

Therefore, in conclusion then, regarding the question "What is rational mind?"—I say that mind is without judgment. Mind itself is neither rational nor irrational. It is beyond your system of duality. Only thought filtering down from Universal Mind being interpreted by the individual brain computers is judged as rational or irrational. And it is judged based on human perception which has been programmed by standards set by the collective mind. All duality is illusionary and is there for you to unfold beyond.

"All our knowledge merely helps us to die a more painful death than the animals who know nothing." Maeterlinck

In the past Earth time warps I would have agreed with this statement, but little by little mass consciousness is shifting to the point where attained knowledge will assist men to make their transition with less pain. When the statement was made this appeared to be the truth. When man realized that he would die, it was not this knowledge which created the fear. It was a lack of knowledge of what was beyond. He began to imagine all sorts of things, and he allowed himself to be intimidated by others who wished to hold him in bondage. He was caught between a desire for heaven and a dread of hell. So death was feared because he had little or no knowledge of what was beyond the physical plane. Collectively he had an inner knowledge that there was something; he just didn't know what. His fear was based not on too much knowledge but too little, and this fear manifested itself in emotional, physical, and mental pain throughout his journey, and especially at the point of the dreaded transition. Knowledge is expanding, and little by little mass consciousness is becoming more enlightened with respect to the process of transition. This will continue as more and more individuals, growing in their understanding born out of more knowledge, add it to the mass consciousness. Soon all men will know what's beyond and will not fear transition. Without fear, there will be no pain.

With respect to animals, it is an assumption that animals know nothing. The truth is that animals, plants, and all creation do have an awareness of the movement to a higher plane, but they flow with life naturally. What they do not have is ego, which is what gives birth to fear. They do have knowledge of the process of transition, but since they do not have fear, they simply flow through their changing journey naturally and peacefully.

What is the distinction between thoughts, feelings and awarenesses?

Of the three—thought, feeling, and awareness, thought and feeling are closer in nature, although all three seem to be used interchangeably. A feeling comes from within, a thought from without, and an awareness envelops your being. Feeling is of the emotion, thought is of the intellect, and awareness is of the spirit. They are all connected with each other and work together in a process. Let me explain.

Feelings are primarily born of the emotions which are part of the ego. They emerge from your sensitivities to both internal and external life. This is what I mean when I say they come from within.

Thoughts enter the human brain computer from Universal Mind. A thought from Universal Mind journeys down through the higher levels of consciousness until it reaches your present conscious state. The universal symbols are then translated and interpreted by the individual brain computer. How pure the Universal Thought remains during its transition to individual thought has much to do with one's level of awareness. Therefore, thought comes from without, and because of the processing it is part of the intellect.

Awareness is of the spirit. The best way I can explain this to you is by saying that it is like entering a dark room and having the lights turned on. The light surrounds you and envelops you. An awareness is like a sudden knowing or understanding or comprehension. Perhaps this is the key element contained in awareness: comprehension. You are able to have both thoughts and feelings without comprehension. Another difference is that within the physical realm, thoughts and feelings keep changing as more internal and external data pour in. Awareness changes only in that it unfolds into greater or higher awareness. Thoughts and feelings are like the petals on a flower. As feelings and thoughts change,

245

petals fall off and are replaced by new petals. Awareness is the essence of light of the entire flower.

But all three dynamics work together in your own unfoldment process. A feeling is quickly sent to the brain computer where it is processed by the intellect, and the feeling connects with thought and becomes thought. When comprehension and understanding enter, the thought becomes awareness. Without the connection of thought and feeling, there would be no individual awareness.

Awareness is the end product in the process. The process is so fast in terms of time that you are usually not aware of it. A now moment feeling is automatically sent to the brain computer for analysis and interpretation. You actually no longer have the feeling, but rather a thought about the feeling. When you have comprehension about the thought, you also have comprehension about the feeling as well; you have awareness.

Essentially, then, when you are asked to put your daily feelings in writing, you are actually recording thoughts about feelings which have passed out of the now moments of your experience, or you are describing your awareness of the experience. You can only experience a feeling in a now moment; once you begin processing the feeling, it becomes thought about a feeling which has passed from a now moment. Once you comprehend, you have awareness. Feelings are always processed into thought, but thought is not always processed into awareness. Many thoughts are sent to your data storage areas without ever becoming awarenesses. The spirit dictates those things you will have awareness of, and the greater your alignment with spirit is, the greater your awareness level will be.

Is Global Peace Possible?

For most of Earth's history, war has been one of the conditions of its unfoldment. War becomes a condition where entities feel they must either defend their particular ideology or belief system, or when they try to impose their ideology or belief system on others. These are the primary reasons for the condition called war. If you think about all the wars upon your planet, you must agree that most have involved ideology as the root cause.

So, if war emerges as the result of differing ideologies, is there any way to establish a planet of peace when there are so many different belief systems and levels of awareness? Must all entities adopt a common belief system in order for there to be true global peace, and if that were done, would it interfere with the individual's free will and his own unique creative expression?

246

To assure and insure total global peace, it would be necessary for all entities to reach a place in awareness where they could agree to accept a common belief system with respect to the planet itself and their relationship with one another. The key element in this belief system would, of course, have to be love: love of the planet, love of self, and love of others. There would also have to be present a deep realization of the interconnection which exists among all elements of Creation.

Collectively Man has not reached this awareness level, and this is why that which is called war exists. There are many individual entities who are of this awareness level and desire peace. Some of them see all others as God expressing, they honor the belief systems of others, and they allow the other to be the other without judgment. This could possibly bring peace to the planet if all entities believed the same way. However, the majority of entities do not believe in this way. So you have those who are termed political activists who see injustices and inequalities and attempt to actively create change, not only in collective consciousness, but on the manifested Earth level as well. A political activist can be just as spiritually led as one who is more passive and allowing. In your Earth's history you have noticed that there have been many insurrections and revolutions designed to create collective change. Sometimes the manifestations of these actions have been death, bloodshed, and chaos. I am not saying that revolution is the only way or even the preferred way to create change. It is only a way. Sometimes it appears that the only way to bring about a new order is to destroy the old. You must always remember that creation and destruction are two elements within the same process. The analogy of the phoenix is a good one: the mythological bird, the phoenix, had to be consumed by fire and reduced to ashes before something finer could rise out of those ashes. Positive change can be the gift of seemingly negative actions. Sometimes one has to fight to bring forth a positive result. Sometimes one has to die to bring forth change. A peaceful man is not necessarily a passive one. True leaders of peace are actively willing to do what needs to be done. They have purpose, vision, love and tenacity.

In order to create global peace, there must be a common agreement as to what peace is. You could all offer me your individual definitions of peace, and those definitions would be based on what personally gives you peace in your manifested life. Yet what might create a peaceful state of mind for you may not have the same effect on another. Some entities can feel peaceful in situations which produce the opposite in others. One entity may be peaceful with little material abundance, while another won't be peaceful until he has it all. Usually when one defines his individual ideas of peace, he is really describing peace based on the external conditions and the outer environment.

Peace and its seeming opposite, war, are states of consciousness. One who is of a peaceful consciousness will be not affected by his outer world. Likewise one who is at war in consciousness will not experience peace, no matter how calm and blissful the outer world may appear.

All outer conditions and all change begin first in the individual consciousness. Everything which happens on the manifested level of life has its seed in individual thought or consciousness. The individual entity who is desirous of peace on a global scale must first establish peace in his own consciousness. It is individual consciousness which feeds directly into collective mind. And, Beloved Ones, what is true of peace is true of war and its manifestations. An individual must do more than want peace. He must actively pursue it in his own being so that he becomes it. He must not look to his outer world and its illusions to define it.

You must become in your own being that which you seek in the world. You must plant the seed in your own consciousness if it is to flower in the collective mind. It is hypocrisy to pray and meditate for the bringing about of global peace if you are fighting with your spouse, neighbors, or friends, for this is but war on a smaller scale. To create global peace, each individual must start at home within himself. There will be no real peace upon your planet until each entity has journeyed within and established peace within himself and in his individual life. As long as war exists in the consciousness of one entity, total global peace will not be achieved. As long as there is one soul in conflict, no one will experience the completeness of peace.

So, Beloved Ones who desire a planet of peace, look first into yourselves, seek to discover what peace really is, and do not base its definition on what gives you pleasure or on the illusions of peace in the manifested world. Look into the mirror of your own self and determine what and who you war against, for you will not experience peace as long as war is in your consciousness. As long as there is conflict, lack of loving of self and others, and dislike and unhappiness with yourself and others, war is part of your consciousness. If war were not part of your consciousness you would not recognize it, for one does not acknowledge that which he does not know at some level of his being.

If you want global peace, first begin with yourself. Rid yourself of your own wars, lay down your own inner weapons, and become that which you seek in your own consciousness, for in doing so, you plant a seed of peace which can flower into the collective mind. One seed of peace planted at the right time in the collective mind has the potential of manifesting in your outer world on a larger scale. You are so very important, entities, and what you think and how aware you become in consciousness is of tremendous value to the entire manifested world.